LOST IN MOSCOW

LOST IN MOSCOW

A Brat in the USSR

by

Kirsten Koza

TURNSTONE PRESS

Turnstone Press
Artspace Building
607-100 Arthur Street
Winnipeg, MB
R3B 1H3 Canada
www.TurnstonePress.com

Turnstone Press gratefully acknowledges the assistance of The Canada Council for
the Arts, the Manitoba Arts Council, the Government of Canada through the
Book Publishing Industry Development Program and the Government of
Manitoba through the Department of Culture, Heritage and Tourism, Arts Branch,
for our publishing activities.

Cover design: Doowah Design
Interior design: Sharon Caseburg
Illustrations and photos copyright © Kirsten Koza unless otherwise stated.
Printed and bound in Canada by Friesens for Turnstone Press.

Library and Archives Canada Cataloguing in Publication

Koza, Kirsten, 1965-
    Lost in Moscow : a brat in the U.S.S.R. / Kirsten Koza.

ISBN 0-88801-282-9

    1. Koza, Kirsten, 1965- —Travel. 2. Moscow (Russia)—Description and travel. 3.
Camp Orlyonok. 4. Uzbekistan—Description and travel. 5. Camps—Uzbekistan.
I. Title.

DK29.K69 2005   914.7'3104853   C2003-905315-6

For Grandma (and her travel gene)
Irene Lucy Field
née Larsen, 1918

LOST IN MOSCOW

THERE IS NO MILK.
YOU MAY HAVE VODKA.

Toronto's airport was busy and it was hard to find parking. Dad gave the finger to a man in a wood-panelled station wagon.

"Do you have her passport?"

"Yes." Mom had told Grandma that ten times now.

"Are you suuuure?" I could see Dad elbowing Mom. A tease was going to happen.

"Maybe I did forget it." Mom was awful at these games. She didn't like doing it. You could tell she was faking. "Ooops, there it is!" She also could only keep it up for three seconds.

"Rosemary!" Dad was shaking his head. "Jesus."

Grandma had been fooled, though. "Are you sure you have it?"

"YES!!!" We all yelled at Gram. Man oh man.

Dad was moving fast now. He had the bags out of the trunk. I wanted to carry my own bags.

"Just come on!" He looked angry. He almost always looked angry. He had just one big long eyebrow. My friends were all scared of him. He was huge too. The tallest man I had ever seen. Mom was carrying my little sister, Fiona. I had won many public-speaking contests because of Fiona and could still say my

speech off by heart, *Little sisters are a nuisance and I should know.*
Grandma held my hand as we ran through the traffic and into
the airport terminal. You could really smell the planes now. I was
really going to the Soviet Union, without my family, for the
whole summer and it was thanks to Grandma. She'd given my
name to the Canada–USSR Association.

"There's Chip!" It was so crowded, I could not see at first
where Grandma was pointing. The last time I had been in a
crowded airport like this a woman burned me below my eye
with her cigarette. It even made a sizzling noise. I pulled my
hand away from Grandma's. If anyone saw me holding hands
they'd think I was some kind of baby.

Chip waved and pushed her way towards us. She was Grandma's
best friends' daughter. Dad said that Gram and her friends were all
card-carrying Communists. Chip was a little younger than my
mom. I had never met her before.

"Hi, Ki-ersten." Chip looked really nice but she didn't say my
name quite right. She said it with a hard "r" and made it sound
like it rhymed with fear. That was better though than people
who said it like Curse-ten. My name's Kiassten, said with the
Danish pronunciation. I'd even accept Kissten. I didn't correct
Chip. I didn't know why. I always corrected people when they
got it wrong.

"Not all the group is here. Just those of us from Toronto. We
are meeting everyone else in Montreal," Chip panted. She led
me over to a couple of teenagers. "This is Ki-ersten."

"Kiassten," I corrected Chip this time. Before it got out of
hand.

"This is Dee Dee." Dee Dee was tall and skinny, with brown
hair and big teeth. She was wearing super cool flared jeans.

"And this is Karl."

"Hi." He wore mirrored sunglasses. His arms were crossed.
We had studied body language in grade five with Miss Dilly.
Crossed arms meant something. Karl was really tall and brown.
I was not sure but thought he was Indian like Dr. Zhagi, my
dentist. Dr. Zhagi's wife gave my mom a beautiful sari. Dr. Zhagi
gave me fillings I didn't need.

"Where's Little Karl?" Chip looked panicked.

"Talking to our dad." Karl gestured with his head and kept his arms crossed. It confirmed my suspicions. He wasn't closed. He was nervous, but he was trying to act cool. Dee Dee was cool, though. She didn't need to act.

"Little Karl is eleven too, Ki-ersten." Chip said it as if I would be comforted by it. I didn't care about age. She left to get our passports from our parents.

"Wow, do you ever have a huge suitcase," I said to Dee Dee. I bet it was filled with amazing clothes. You could just tell by look-ing at her. I secretly tried to move it with my toe to judge the weight. Yup, it was filled, all right.

"Not huge enough. I couldn't fit half the things I wanted to take in it. The matching blue one over there is mine too." I liked the way she tossed her hair. I would have tried to copy her but I had a head scarf on.

"Where's Adrian?" Adrian was our other leader, Chip's boyfriend.

"I was told he went to Montreal yesterday," Dee Dee replied. "He went ahead to be there for the others or something."

"Oh." I turned to see where my parents were. When I turned back Chip was there with a boy my age. He was inches from me, staring at me.

"Ki-ersten, this is Karl." Chip ran off again.

"Capitalist!" Little Karl sneered in my face, turned and walked away. Dee Dee and I just looked at each other and shrugged. I had no idea what Karl had meant but it was definitely an insult. What a jerk-off. I wanted to ask Dee Dee why the two brothers had the same name, but Big Karl was still standing there. It was the weird-est thing I'd ever heard. They looked alike too. Little Karl was an exact mini-version of Big Karl. Their parents couldn't have known that the boys would end up looking the same. Babies looked like aliens. Fiona's cheeks were bigger than the rest of her body when she was a baby. She had permanent licorice drool on her face too.

My parents came over to me. Mom handed me my carry-on. "There is a boy here your age. Let's take a photo, Herman."

Dad took my picture. "Put this in your bag." He was handing me the camera.

"I can take it with me?"

"Don't lose it," Mom warned.

"Cool." It was a *Time* magazine camera. We got it when we subscribed. Now I'd look like a reporter. I looked through the lens.

"Put it away." Mom was unzipping my carry-on.

"Oh, you'll need this too." Dad handed me one roll of film. This was excellent.

"Take lots of pictures."

"I will, Mom."

"But not as many as your dad takes."

Dad made an exasperated noise and walked away. He and Mom always had arguments on trips about pictures. His pictures sucked because he always wanted to take natural pictures. You were never ready, so you always looked awful. He didn't let you pose or anything. He always had to take hundreds and he still never got a good one.

"We can walk you to the gate, but we can't go through with you. They will want to x-ray your bag, so have it ready." Mom took my hand.

"I know." Gee whiz, I'd flown lots of times.

Chip came over to the group. "Okay, everybody? We will all stay together going through the gate. I am sorry but you won't be sitting together on this part of the flight. It's only an hour, though. You will definitely be sitting together on the flight to Moscow, so don't worry. Okay, let's move." She looked at the parents. "We can say our final goodbyes down at the entrance to the gates." Chip was pixie cute and when she smiled she meant it.

Chip was leaving me at my seat, which was on the aisle, right by the door.

"When we get off the flight, just walk up the ramp and then wait for the rest of us at the top of the ramp. Don't go any further. I don't want to lose you yet." Chip laughed. She went to find her seat.

"Yeah. Okay." Dad hated it when I said *yeah*. He always made me say *yes*. Dad wasn't here now. Yabadabadoo, it was going to be *yeah* all summer! I looked at the two old people I was sitting with.

"Where are you going, little girl?" The lady's hair was super white.

"Russia," I answered proudly.

Little Karl was just passing me. "It's called the Soviet Union. That just proves you're a capitalist!" I hated him.

"Would you like to sit here so you can see out the window?" The old man offered me his seat. That was so nice. We traded seats.

"Where are you going?" I asked as I tried to get my carry-on bag stuffed under the seat in front of me.

"We're just going to Fredricton. Not near as exciting as your trip." The old lady was holding a Life Saver out towards me. It was lemon. I could see the cherry was the next one so I pretended to be busy with my bag in hopes that she would eat the lemon and then I could have the next one.

"Have you ever been to the Soviet Union?" I asked.

"No," they answered together and shook their heads. Her husband took the lemon.

"Have you ever flown before?" the man asked. Yahoo! The cherry was heading my way.

"Oh, yeah, lots." I wished I hadn't said that in case he wanted his seat back. But he didn't say anything. "Thank you very much," I said to the lady as I popped the cherry-flavoured Life Saver in my mouth.

The plane was starting to move backwards away from the ramp. My heart was pounding. I looked out the porthole. I knew my family would be somewhere waving. The airline stewardess was demonstrating how to do up a seatbelt. Were people really that stupid? I ignored her. If people saw me not watching they'd know I was a pro at flying, just like the businessmen who read their papers during the demonstration and during takeoff too. I hoped someone would notice me. I was not too cool for take-offs, though. I had to watch them. I loved takeoffs and landings the most. Oh, and turbulence was always fun too. I hoped there would be lots of turbulence.

Our plane was on the runway. My stomach did a flip. I looked out the window. I tried not to take up the whole window so the old people could still see if they wanted. The engines were roaring and we were going. Fast, faster. There was a bump. The wheels were off. I could feel my cheeks pulling back. I hoped I wouldn't be sick like I was at the Brampton fall fair. I barfed on this ride that went backwards. I was okay on the Tilt-a-Twirl and I could handle any roller coaster. I wasn't scared of anything. But this backwards whizzing thing made me sicker than our swing at home. I barfed right on the ride. Tons of puke. All the people standing around watching saw me too. At first just a few saw, but by the final loop everyone at the midway was looking and pointing at me. After we got off the ride I felt fine. I asked my dad for more candy floss because I had lost mine. He made a big deal about it. I really did feel fine once I was off the ride, though. He just couldn't handle my pink and blue vomit. He was no good when it came to vomit.

The sick feeling passed by the time the "no smoking" and "seatbelt" signs went off. What a relief. I undid my seatbelt and tried to get my bag out from under the seat.

"Do you need help?"

"No, it's okay," I nodded to the old lady and gave up on my bag. I wanted to read the letter my friend Tara had given me. She told me I wasn't allowed to read it until I was actually on the plane to Russia, so it was probably best that I couldn't get my bag out.

"Would you like something to drink, little girl?" What an occupation! They got to fly everywhere. When I was little I couldn't remember the word stewardess, or hostess. I got mixed up and called them mattresses. My parents thought it was hysterical. I still didn't see what was so funny about it.

"A glass of milk, please."

"You don't want some pop?"

I couldn't drink pop. The bubbles gave me really bad hiccups. I hated pop. "No."

"What about some orange juice?"

I hated orange juice more. "A glass of milk, please."

She looked irritated. "I'll have to come back with that."

"Okay." I took the peanuts she handed me and stared down at

the clouds. They looked like you could jump on them. They looked just like cotton batting. If they were made of cotton candy, you could bite them.

I did what I was told and waited at the top of the ramp. I ESP'd to Chip to hurry up. People stared at me. I tried to look cool so they wouldn't think I was lost. I tapped my foot. My bag hurt my shoulder. I hated my sandals but I liked my denim gauchos. I had liked my sandals when we bought them. They had dark blue denim tops and hemp cord-wrapped soles. But now the way my toes stuck out made me think of my grandma's sandals. I didn't like them any more. My only other shoes I had with me were my North Star running shoes. North Stars. Loser shoes. I wanted Adidas. North Stars had two wide blue stripes down the side and Adidas had three thinner ones. Adidas were more expensive. They looked way better.

"Hi Ki-ersten."

"The people I was sitting with let me sit at the window." Chip wasn't listening to me, she was counting us. I kept as far away from the Karls as possible.

I looked at Dee Dee's feet. "I like your sandals." Dee Dee's sandals matched her bag even.

"Thanks." She tossed her hair again. I wished I hadn't said that to her in case she noticed *my* sandals. But she didn't.

We were walking and now my bag really hurt my shoulder. This had to be the longest airport terminal in the world.

"Mirabel Airport is the longest terminal in the world." Chip sighed. "And we have to go from one end to the other."

Both Karls were wearing the same mirrored sunglasses. Inside! They also were wearing the same grey, flat, cabby caps. Inside! In school the boys always had to take their hats off when they were inside. Girls didn't. None of the boys at my school wore sunglasses. I couldn't help wondering if the Karls' mirrored sunglasses were making it hard for them to see and that was why they weren't offering to help carry Chip's, Dee Dee's or my bags. If Little Karl offered to help me I'd punch him anyway. I was a

women's libber. I thought. Or I would be when I grew up and
was big enough to carry my own things.

The rest of the group was standing by a sign that read "Pioneer
Group." Pioneer was the name for young Soviets who went to
camp. The Young Pioneers went to camp for all their holidays, summer and winter. All the kids, twenty-five million of them, no
choice. There were not even twenty-five million people in Canada.
   "All right, everyone, let's introduce ourselves." Adrian had a
moustache and beard. Enid Blyton said you should never trust a
man with a moustache. Moustaches hid thin lips. Enid Blyton
said people with thin lips were cruel and she was right. Just look
at the tutor who came to instruct the Famous Five. He had a
moustache and he was really mean. I had read every single Enid
Blyton book and series. *The Five, The Four, The Secret Seven,
Mallory Towers* and *St. Claires* and *Noddy* when I was little. Mom
said a few months ago that the *Noddy* books were bad because
they were racist. There weren't even any people in *Noddy*,
though, so I didn't get that. I bet Adrian had thin lips.
   "Say your name, your age and where you are from. We'll start
with you." Adrian tapped a tall boy on the shoulder. "And go
around the circle."
   "My name is Jay Williams." Jay was a hunk. "I'm sixteen." His
hair almost touched his shoulders. "And I'm from Port Alberni,
British Columbia."
   "I'm Oksana but everyone calls me Ana." I couldn't even hear
her. She obviously didn't do well at public speaking. The best
thing in my speech about my sister was the part where she
flushed my friends' hats and mitts down the toilet. What I didn't
say in my speech was that she only did it once and I did it the
rest of the time.
   "I'm eleven." Wow, Oksana looked way older. She was a foot
taller than me. She'd probably hang out with the older girls because
she looked at least fourteen. I couldn't hear where she was from.
   "My name is Alexi Rubinoff. I'm sixteen. I'm Ana's older
brother and we also live in Port Alberni, BC." Everyone laughed

as if what he said was funny. I laughed too even though I'd missed the joke.

"Hi, I'm Ignatius but call me Iggy. I know, I know, the list we were all sent says my name is Paul, but it's not."

"You'd be better off if it was, though, eh!" Jay laughed.

"I'm eleven," Iggy continued. He didn't seem fazed. "And I live on a farm in Saskatchewan." Iggy wasn't quite as fat as Duncan Hanes, a farm boy from my class. Duncan's parents should never have named him that because of Duncan Hines cake mixes. Bad name for a fat kid. Though Duncan's parents didn't know he would be fat when they named him, but then they were huge themselves. I'd have to ask Iggy what his dad did with the bulls' balls. Duncan's dad fed his steers' nuts to the farm dogs after he cut them off. Actually, Duncan Hanes *used* to be in my class, but he had failed. Failing would be awful. I didn't have to worry about that. I was smart, one of the smartest in my class. Squirrel and Tara were smart too. Squirrel also lived on a farm. Her hands were shrivelled and wrinkled like an old lady's. I couldn't wait to read Tara's letter. I missed the Karls introducing themselves. I had wanted to hear that. I told myself to pay attention.

"... Halifax, Nova Scotia." Who was that girl? I'd check my sheet later. There was only one girl from Halifax so it would be pretty easy to figure out. She wasn't very pretty. The next girl had big blue eyes and crazy-long eyelashes.

"I'm Rhonda. I'm thirteen and I'm from Vernon, BC."

"I'm from Calgary, Alberta, I'm Sam—"

"Samantha!" Iggy was laughing.

"There have been several mistakes in our contact information." Adrian was looking at the name list. "I think this is another." Everyone laughed again. Sam was cursed. I knew it. You could tell he knew it too. Because of a typing mistake he was going to be dubbed Samantha for the entire trip. He had long blond hair too. He was doomed, destined to be Samantha. Iggy twitched his nose like in *Bewitched*. It was wonderful. Samantha! Samantha was eleven.

"My name is Dee Dee Leduc." She did the hair toss. It was fantastic. "I'm sixteen and from Toronto. The best place in the country." Nobody booed her for saying it. Nobody dared. Dee Dee Leduc had power.

"My name is Kirsten Koza." I was loud. I ennunciated clearly. "I am eleven years old." I was the best speaker.

"Say where you are from." Chip had interrupted me. I was going to say it. My cheeks started to go red. Damn going red. When I went, I really went!

"Look how red she's turning." I heard that. I didn't know who said it. It made me go redder.

"I am from Cheltenham, Ontario," I finished. My face was roasting.

"I'm Adrian Harper."

"And I'm Chip Cameron."

"And we are your group leaders."

"Now, something we have to do, and this is very important, is find out how much money, traveller's cheques or hard currency, each of you is bringing into the Soviet Union. The Soviet government is very strict about this. You have to get this right because you can't leave the country with more money than you entered with, or more goods than the value you are declaring now, and whatever happens you must not leave the USSR with any of their coinage. If you have fifty dollars or less, you don't need to declare it. If anyone has rubles, you will just have to leave them behind. You are not allowed to bring rubles into the Soviet Union because they should never have left there in the first place. Okay?" Adrian looked very serious. We were going around the circle again.

"Five hundred dollars."

"Three hundred dollars."

"One thousand dollars." That was Dee Dee. Holy cow. Everyone was bringing so much pocket money! I didn't know what to say. I didn't want to say how much I was bringing. It was hundreds less than everyone else. I felt my face going red again. I'd have to lie.

"Eight hundred." Eight hundred dollars! Little Karl was only eleven too and he had eight hundred dollars! I was definitely going to have to lie and deal with it later. Everyone was going to think I was some poor kid and my North Star running shoes were going to confirm it. I'd say a hundred. I didn't even have eighty. If I had eighty I'd be rounding it off when I said a hundred. Man oh man, I was in the "don't need to declare it" category. I had fifty dollars.

"Two hundred dollars." It just came out. It was an out-and-out lie. An automatic, very well done, lie. I was going to be thrown in a Russian prison.

We were sitting on board Aeroflot. It looked like any other airplane. I was not sure what I had been expecting. Kids in the neighbourhood had told me that their parents had said I'd have to bring my own seat. It was probably stupid Clancy Murphy that came up with that one. He could suck dead buffalo farts. He was just jealous. The only difference between normal planes and this one was this plane had no first class. We were sitting right at the front, where first class would have been on a regular plane. A stewardess said something to another one in Russian and they pulled the plane door closed together.

"I hate takeoffs!" Rhonda, the girl from BC with the eyelashes, was sitting beside me, at the window seat.

"They are my favourite part of flying. What about you?" I turned to look at the girl from Halifax, who was sitting on the aisle.

"This is only my second time flying. This morning's flight from Halifax was my first."

"What's your name again?" I had looked through my bag for my name list, but couldn't find it. I figured Mom had hoarded it away already for the scrapbook I would have to make when I got home.

"Mary."

I couldn't believe that at Mary's age this was her first time flying. My head scarf was too tight. It was giving me a headache, so I took it off.

"We should chew gum for our ears, so they don't hurt." Rhonda handed me some forbidden bubble gum.

"We aren't supposed to have gum." Mary was horrified.

"This isn't the Soviet Union yet." Rhonda blew a bubble.

"I guess we'll have to finish it before we land." I was hopeful that Rhonda would have to supply us with gum throughout the flight just so we wouldn't be bringing it into Russia. Imagine a country where Bazooka Joe was prohibited! Actually, I liked Double Bubble better than Bazooka Joe. Imagine a country with no Double Bubble!

"Watch this." I tried to blow a bubble inside a bubble. Now there was gum stuck to my left braid.

"Watch this." Rhonda blew a huge bubble and then cracked it twenty-two times. Amazing.

"Who's got the gum?" Adrian looked furious. I now *knew* he was a thin-lipped man. "Get rid of it now! You are showing huge disrespect. This is a Soviet airplane you are on. You are no longer in Canada."

Rhonda spat out her gum and I pulled mine off my braid. We shoved it into the ashtrays. Adrian put his face in his hands and shook his head.

"That was the last piece." Rhonda was batting her eyelashes. I was going to have to try this technique sometime. It seemed to be working. "My mother told me to chew it so my ears wouldn't hurt." Rhonda made her huge eyes look huger. She was good.

"Okay, ladies. Have a nice flight." It looked like Adrian was doing some sort of deep-breathing exercise. He faked a smile. "We are just four rows behind you. So if you need anything come ask, but only if the 'seatbelt' sign is off."

Seatbelt sign? I couldn't see one anywhere.

"I have tons more gum."

"What if you get caught?" I glanced at Mary to see what she thought but she was staring dead ahead. She had a disapproving look on her face. I knew who I'd be hanging out with.

"I won't get caught." Rhonda grinned. I thought about my lie earlier. At least I was going to have company in my Siberian prison cell. "My mother told me to bring gum to give to the Soviet kids. I figure I can probably sell it. Did you bring jeans to sell?"

"No. I only have one pair with me."

"They don't have jeans in the USSR, either. You can make eighty or a hundred bucks a pair."

"They'll pay that much for jeans?" If I sold my jeans and

maybe some other things, then maybe I would have two hundred dollars. But then I wouldn't have any clothes to wear. I was mad at my mom. I only had fifty dollars and one pair of jeans, two dress shirts, one T-shirt with the Canadian flag on it, one pair of jean shorts, one nice outfit (my red, white and blue striped soccer shirt and my gauchos, which I was wearing), one swimsuit, one pair of jammies, and some socks and underwear, one jacket and one red rain poncho with a beaver on it. Oh yeah, and my North Stars. The fifty dollars had seemed like a fortune when my parents gave it to me. I had never had that much money. Now it was an embarrassment. As was my lack of clothes. My suitcase was the smallest by far.

"We were specifically told not to bring gum, or to sell jeans." Mary was still looking ahead. She was right.

"You can probably buy some gum when we stop over in Paris, France." Rhonda was ignoring Mary.

"Yeah, France has gum. Maybe I'll get some gum in France." I liked the sound of that. Maybe I'd just get some gum in France. The stewardesses were doing their demonstration. It was in Russian. I watched them this time. This was more interesting than the English version. The stewardess near us held up a life jacket.

"Where is the life jacket stored?" Rhonda gripped my left arm.

"On Canadian and British planes, it's under the seats."

"Check and see if you can see it." Rhonda ungripped me.

I put my head between my legs and tried to look. "I can't tell. Try and feel it."

"I can't." Rhonda was reaching under her seat too.

"Stop it, you guys," Mary scowled. We both ignored Mary.

"I feel something, Kirsten."

"Is it your life jacket?"

"I don't know."

"Don't pull it out. We'll get in trouble." Then I farted. We both started laughing. I was laughing so hard that I farted again. Rhonda was crying. We were best friends.

"Sssssssshhh." Who was that? We laughed louder. Explosive spluttering snotty teary laughter.

"I have to pee." Rhonda put her hand between her legs. We couldn't stop laughing.

"You can't get up now!" I looked at the stewardess. She was eyeing us and pointing to the exits. Her face made me laugh more. Even Mary was laughing now. That was good. Mary had scared me with her hoity toity behaviour. My great-grandma said that, "hoity toity."

The plane was moving.

"I am going to learn to speak Russian." Mary was obviously in awe of the stewardess.

"They have a different alphabet. I'll show you my address book after we take off. I bought it at the USSR Friendship Centre in Toronto. It has the Russian letters beside the English ones. They have no letter 'w.' And the letter 'r' is pronounced *reeka*." I chuckled. I wondered if Mary really thought she could learn Russian while we were there. We had been taking French in school for two years now and all I knew was how to play Bingo in French. My dad said my French teacher was crappy because she said *ça va*, instead of *common tally voos*. He spoke French to my French teacher and she didn't even know what he was saying. My dad was right about her. But still, I liked playing Bingo. When you shouted it out when you won, you had to say Bengo. That was the French way.

"You are right. Our life preservers are supposed to be under our seats." Rhonda was listening to the English version. "If this plane goes down I'll never be able to get it out."

"Rhonda, if this plane goes down, we'll want parachutes, not life vests, anyway."

"Will you two stop talking about the plane crashing?" Mary looked pretty pale.

"It's not going to crash." Rhonda was staring at Mary.

"It would be pretty exciting if it did, though. I saw this movie once." Mary's face made me stop. She was pleading without saying anything. "Rhonda's right, it isn't going to crash. You are more likely to die in a car accident than a plane crash. That's what the experts say." I nodded informatively.

"Cars are way more dangerous," Rhonda confirmed.

"Way more." I decided to change the subject because Mary still looked awful. "Is your dad a lobster fisherman?" Mary looked offended. It was the only thing I could think of to say. Oh well, she didn't look white anymore. Actually she was a little red.

"No."

"I love lobster. I'd eat it every day if I lived in Halifax." Rhonda was tugging my arm and pointing out the window. I stopped making small talk. I hated small talk, anyway. We were taking off. Leaving Canada. Goodbye lobster.

And hello caviar. Yuck. I looked down in disgust at the meal that had been served to me. Just one huge mound of massive black fish eggs. That was it! Our dinner was a softball-size womp of caviar on top of one piece of lettuce. Ignorant.

"Taste one," I challenged Rhonda.

"You," she challenged back.

I put one in my mouth. It burst and salty, fishy water came out. I thought I was going to barf. "Mmmmm." I rubbed my stomach. "It is delicious. Try it, Rhon."

She put one in her mouth. "You liar!" She wiped her tongue with her napkin. I nudged Rhonda and motioned towards Mary, who was eating the fish eggs. We made faces at each other.

"I've got something for us to eat. Hold my tray." Rhonda took my tray and I ducked down to retrieve my carry-on. I unzipped the bag and reached in. I felt around for plastic, then pulled. Out came a whole pack of five fabulous Crunchie Bars. My mom was the best mom in the world. "Dinner is served," I announced and proudly handed Rhonda the golden wrapped treasure. "Cadbury's Crunchie Bars! Yummy." I gave one to Mary too. I was generous.

"Do you think all the food is going to be like this?" Rhonda was eating her chocolate bar.

"Hope not." I sucked the chocolate off the outside and then ate the sponge toffee on the inside. It was ritualistic. It was like eating Oreos. Unscrew the biscuit. Eat one half of the biscuit. Then lick off the icing from the other half. I could do without the cookie part actually. The icing was the best. Man, I loved

Crunchie Bars. I loved my mom. I had felt two other five-packs of bars in my bag too.

"Tea?" It was the stewardess who had stared at us earlier. She hated us.

"That's a samovar," I told Rhonda and Mary. The stewardess had wheeled it down the aisle on her trolley, instead of carrying a teapot like they did on Canadian and British planes.

"Yes please." Mary was served tea.

Rhonda shook her head "no."

"May I please have a glass of milk?" I asked very sweetly and clearly so the stewardess would understand. I even said "may" instead of "can."

"There is no milk." Those words were hard to comprehend. I didn't think I could spend twelve hours without milk.

"Then what do we put in the tea?" Mary wasn't being rude. She was doing the "when in Rome" thing. I knew the answer to this one.

"We do not put milk in tea." The stewardess, however, *was* being rude. What did Russians know about tea, anyway? Tea was English and the English put lots of milk and sugar in their tea.

"If you do not want tea, you may have vodka." Was she joking? She wasn't joking. Mary, Rhonda and I looked at each other in shock. "Would you like vot-ka?"

"No, they wouldn't!" Adrian's voice whacked the back of our heads. The stewardess moved on with her cart.

"I like the way they say vodka." Mary had missed the point.

"Rhon?"

"I know."

"For real? Did she mean it?"

"All right." Adrian was standing above us. "Time for a chat." I hated the sound of that. Sounded like something my dad might say, after I had received the spanking. "In the Soviet Union children are permitted to drink alcohol. These children are different from you." I'd say. "They have grown up drinking liquor. It is no different to them than milk is to you."

"They don't have milk on this plane." It was so hard to believe. No milk.

18

"That's right, Kirsten." Adrian didn't seem to see the dilemma of no milk. I practically lived on milk and peanut butter and jam sandwiches. "Now, as you are not used to liquor, you are, under no circumstances, even if an adult offers it to you, to accept. It would make you act strange and feel sick." He meant it would make you get bombed.

I'd been bombed before, when I was eight. My dad and mom were drinking gin and tonics on a camping trip. I had said I wanted some. I kept bugging them until finally Dad poured me a tall glass, full of gin. No tonic. He was not expecting me to chug the whole thing back. He thought I'd take a sip and choke. I was tougher than that. I showed him. I polished it off in a second. I remembered, after that, Dad walking me around the campgrounds. A cop passed us and Dad was terrified that he would be arrested for influencing or delinquenting a minor, or something like that. I couldn't remember anything else, except it was really fun. Really fun!

The stewardesses cleared away our trays. It was time for Tara's letter. I'd been saving it to fill in time on the twelve-hour flight. I figured the letter would give me three minutes of something to do. Twelve hours was longer than a school day, longer than driving to Montreal and back again. There was a card and a letter. Lots of stuff was written on the card. *I'd rather be dead than red. Have a good time in Russia.* Then she asked, *Did you bring the gum? P.S. if the R.'s find this they'll shoot ya.* She drew a picture of my dinner. Tara got that one wrong. It was a *chicken leg* and a *roast nothing sandwich.* Tara's letter started, *Your plane is manned by dedicated and experienced pilots. They will keep the plane within the radar span just like Amelia Earhart did.*

"Rhonda. Who is Amelia Earhart?"

"A writer."

"No, she wasn't." Mary was older. "Amelia Earhart was a famous American pilot from the 1920s. She was the first woman to attempt flying around the world. She vanished on her flight and to this day it's a mystery. No one knows what happened to her."

"Ohhh." That was what Tara had meant about our pilots. How did Tara know these things? Tara cut up our stewardesses. She said *their main goal is to be the sexiest girl on the plane.* I looked at the huge mole on the face of the one handing out blankets. Yuck.

"Thank you." I took the blanket and tried not to stare. This was not a sexy stewardess. Tara knew lots about being sexy. We'd go up to her older brother's room in the loft of her parents' house and read his *Penthouse* magazines. Well, Tara read. I mostly looked at pictures. Tara's mom caught us with the magazines one day. It was awful. She called us "dirty little girls." Tara said we were just reading the articles. I was hot and sweaty. I didn't even hear her mom come up the stairs.

"You want to read my friend's letter? It's really funny." I handed Tara's letter to Rhonda, so Rhonda could fill in some time too. I had to go to the bathroom.

"Excuse me, Mary." Mary's eyes were closed but I needed out. She wasn't sleeping yet. "Excuse me!" Mary groaned and moved her legs. I fumbled over her. Jeesus, she could have stood up. I walked down the aisle towards the middle of the plane. I should have asked Rhonda to come with me. We hit an air pocket and I stumbled right by where Jay was sitting. I flushed.

"Hi." The boys would know I had to go to the bathroom. "Just stretching my legs. Long flight, huh? What did you think of dinner?"

"Our steaks were supreme!" Iggy licked his lips.

"You got steak?" I was angry. Then the boys laughed. Now I was mad at myself. "Yeah, well, we had lobster." I kept walking.

I couldn't tell if the toilets were empty or full so I just stood and waited. Then some woman went into the one I was waiting outside. It had been empty. I tried another door. It was empty too. I looked back to make sure the boys weren't watching. I went in. The bathroom was smelly. There was toilet paper on the floor. I pulled down my pants. I tried to squat because there was pee on the seat. We hit another air pocket. I was sitting in the pee. We hit another air pocket. The door flew open. There was a man standing there. The door flew shut. I had forgotten to lock it. My life was over. A man had seen me sitting on the toilet, with my pants down! I stood up and pulled up my gauchos. I hadn't even peed. I couldn't leave. I couldn't let him see me again. I'd wait til he had gone. Maybe I should just go. Should I try to lock the door? I didn't know how. Someone was trying the door. I grabbed the knob and pulled it shut. They were pulling. I was pulling. I heard a woman's voice.

"Just a second." I'd go out now. No, I'd wait. I had to pee still. I'd have to hold it. I'd wait til France. I'd pee in Paris. I opened the door. The man wasn't there. The woman looked annoyed.

THEY'RE WATCHING US.
WE BETTER BE CAREFUL.

The plane was getting lower. My ears had been popping for half an hour. Rhonda and I had not slept all night. How could anyone sleep on a plane?

"The Eiffel Tower!" Rhonda and I had seen it at the same time. We slapped each other in excitement. The pilot was saying something in Russian. The stewardesses were making sure we were all fastened in. We were landing in Paris.

"What was that?" Mary was white-knuckling her seat arms.

"Just the plane tires being lowered. They always make a bump like that." I couldn't believe Mary was frightened. I turned to Rhonda. "Can you see the flaps?" The gum in my mouth made it hard to speak.

"They are putting out the flaps." Rhonda had to press her face to the window to try to see back to the wings. She was lucky to be at the window.

"Flaps slow the plane down," I told Mary. She didn't care. Mary had pimples. I really noticed them now. I turned back to the window. "How long will it take to refuel the plane?" I had to pee so bad that it actually hurt.

"A while." Rhonda gave me another piece of chewing gum.

I had five pieces in my mouth already. It was heaven except my jaw hurt. I'd swallow the wad if I saw Adrian. It would probably take the whole summer to digest. Clancy Murphy told me that if you swallowed gum it stayed in your stomach for seven years.

"We're coming in!" Rhonda and I slapped each other again. "We're down!" The tires screamed. The engines roared. The passengers applauded. We popped bubbles. No one would hear.

The escalators went all over the place in plastic tubes. It felt like *The Jetsons*. We had two hours to kill. We could go anywhere except through customs and out of the airport. Rhonda came with me to the bathroom. I was scared the washroom might be pay toilets like in England. We didn't have any French money. Luckily they were like Canadian toilets. I had been holding it so long that it was hard to go at first. Then when it finally came out it lasted about half an hour. It was a *Guinness Book of Records* pee.

"Where should we go?" Rhonda was combing her hair. I couldn't use a comb on mine because it was too frizzy. Combs just broke in my hair. Anyway, that was why I had worn braids and a scarf. So my hair wouldn't need fixing. I hated brushing my hair. It hurt.

"Let's go back to the escalators and see where they all go." Maybe Rhonda would rather shop or something. Maybe playing on the escalators was too little kid.

"Cool."

A French lady with huge red hair and lips came into the washroom. She was smoking and wearing tons of perfume. She was talking in French to another French lady with blonde hair and pink lips, who was also smoking. Rhonda and I left.

"It's true."

"What's true?" I had no idea what Rhon was talking about.

"French women wear too much perfume."

"My dad pretends to keep a redhead in the basement." Why was I telling Rhonda this?

"Why?"

"To bug my mom, I guess."

"Do you think your dad's redhead is like that French woman?"

"Yeah, that's what I'm thinking."

"Wow."

"Yeah." We were at the escalators. I had to concentrate to step on.

"There's Dee Dee, Oksana and Chip!" Rhonda pointed to the escalator that crossed over ours.

"There's Adrian, Mary and Sam!" I waved at another escalator. It seemed everybody had the same idea. This was great! We waved. Our group was all over. All of us riding up and down; waving and screaming. I was glad I had peed.

The Moscow airport wasn't like the French one. There were stairs and nothing sparkled. Moscow was spelled *Mockba* in Russian. We were waiting to get our luggage and then to finish going through customs. There was a problem. Chip and Adrian were talking to some people with crossed arms. It was not good. We walked over to where the group's luggage was. I saw the problem right away. Half the bags weren't there. I could tell because Dee Dee's big fancy case was missing. I saw my little blue bag. The group was crossing its arms now too. Adrian was doing his funny breathing. The people walked away.

"They have gone to look for the rest of the bags." Adrian looked furious. "They think the French baggage people may have unloaded some of our bags in Paris."

"Whose bags are not there?" Chip motioned us to look at the pile.

"One of mine is missing." That was Big Karl.

"One of mine is missing too, the big one!" Dee Dee's face was right out of a horror movie. She looked like she might cry any second.

"Samantha's are gone!" Iggy was going to get in trouble. He didn't.

"Just wait. Maybe they'll find them." Chip was trying to be encouraging.

Two different Russians approached us. They shook their heads. Holy moly. Adrian went over to them.

"This is ridiculous!" Dee Dee was steaming. Too bad my suitcase had made it. I was good at being angry. I could make a great angry face. I made it anyway to show support. "What happens now?" For sure she was going to cry. "I mean, the jewellery and stuff I had to declare is in that bag."

"I'll find out." Chip went over to Adrian and the frowning men. The Russians left. Adrian and Chip were having angry words with each other now. I wished I wasn't so tired. This would have been more fun if I hadn't been tired. A different set of Russians had now arrived on the scene. They shook their heads too. This was bad. Chip came over to us again.

"Okay, this is what we're going to do. We are going to finish going through customs and we'll just declare what we have now in case the luggage is never found."

"Never found!?" Uh oh, Dee Dee's eyes were tearing up. "My clothes! Oh no, my toothbrush was in that case."

"I am very sorry." Chip *was* sorry. "Let's just go to the hotel. We'll deal better with this when we have eaten and rested. Where's Alexi?" Chip's eyes darted around.

"My dad says never leave without some sort of guarantee of action." Jay looked like he could pop someone. He was cool.

"The thing is, it's not the fault of the Soviets. They say it's France's fault." Chip was trying.

"Yeah, right, and they say they invented hockey too." People snickered at Jay's comment. Bitter, sarcastic snickers. The Karls weren't laughing, though. I had no idea what hockey had to do with the luggage.

"The Soviets *did* invent hockey," Little Karl piped up and Big Karl stood behind him nodding. What the hell was all this hockey stuff?

"I think hockey was invented in Canada." I was sure of it. I was a figure skater. "The Dutch invented skating and Canadians invented—"

"Stupid capitalist!" Little Karl kept calling me that. It sounded so bad that I was sure that I wasn't one.

"Am not."

"Are too."

"Am not."

"We're going. Our interpreters are waiting for us outside the gate and we are not going to get anything accomplished here without them." Adrian clapped his hands. "Everyone who has bags, grab them and let's move."

"Oh, there he is." Chip took a deep breath. "Alexi, please stay with us."

"I can't believe this." Poor Dee Dee. Chip gave her a squeeze.

"This is great!" Sam ran ahead. "I don't have to carry anything!"

"I'd just die if that had happened to me." Rhonda lugged her suitcase. It had wheels but one of them was broken.

"I am sure the bags will turn up tomorrow." Chip was an optimist. I had a sneaky feeling the bags would not turn up tomorrow or the next day.

It was cloudy, raining and cold. I was sitting beside Rhonda on the minibus, heading to our hotel.

"The buses look weird here." I was giggling. Mom would have called me punch drunk.

"What do you notice about this highway that is different from our highways back home?" Brother! Adrian was doing the school trip routine. We looked around.

"There are no billboards." Someone muttered it quietly.

"Who said that? Say it again."

"There aren't any signs. No advertisements." Alexi was the observant one. We all looked out the windows. He was right. It was strange. What would you read on road trips? I loved the moving signs in Toronto. The ones that changed, that read and showed different things. My favourite was the lady on the swing on Eglinton Avenue. They even changed her clothes with the seasons but they were always too slow doing this and she'd end up with bare legs in winter. I loved our signs for things to do and eat and buy.

"The Soviet highways are better than ours," Adrian declared. "They're not full of the clutter of capitalism. Our roads are spoilt by our decadence, our misplaced values."

"Rhon," I whispered. "What is capitalism? Little Karl keeps calling me a capitalist."

"Capitalists believe in making money." She was staring out at the greyness.

"He makes it sound bad, though."

"His family are socialists probably, or communists. They probably think you are bad."

"Why am I a capitalist? I don't make money. I don't even get an allowance." It was true, I didn't. When I needed money for the movies or candy, I just asked for it.

"Your dad is a capitalist probably. So that means you are too. What does your dad vote?"

"We vote Liberal." I said it proudly even though I didn't know what it meant. Even though I didn't vote. But when I did get to, I'd vote Liberal. Trudeau was Liberal. His favourite book was *The Little Prince,* or, in French, *Le Petit Prince.* I adored that book.

"That's capitalist." Rhonda was still staring out at the grey. It was all very confusing. My stomach rumbled. No one seemed to notice. I wanted another chocolate bar but I didn't want to share with everybody. I'd have to wait.

"Are they communist?" I indicated the two interpreters on our bus with us. They had introduced themselves as our translators, at the airport. Nadia had the brown hair, and Sonya had the blonde. They didn't have Russian accents at all. Nadia sounded Canadian or American and Sonya sounded like she was from London or Australia.

"All Soviet citizens are communists." Rhonda looked tired.

"Why?"

"They have to be."

"They're Reds, right?"

"Yeah, they're all Reds."

"Why don't they have a choice?"

"I'm tired."

"Me too."

"I'm hungry."

"Me too." I figured Rhonda didn't know any more than that. She didn't know either why the Soviet people had no choice about being communists. I hated being told what to do. I stared out the window. It was raining. There was a grass median separating the traffic, and trees and flowers were planted there too. There were no billboards and the buses looked weird.

"There's a sign!" I shouted.

"That's different. It's a party sign." Adrian looked proud. The sign didn't look like a party sign to me. It was a big man with big fists. He wasn't very fun-looking and he wasn't at a party.

We had missed lunch so we were given bagged lunches to take up to our rooms. The hotel lobby was glamorous but the hotel itself looked more like a high-rise apartment building than a hotel. Chip and Adrian returned with our keys. Chip, Rhonda and I were sharing one room. Oksana, Mary and Dee Dee had their own room without a group leader. Dee Dee was happy we got Chip. I liked Chip so I didn't care that she was in our room. Adrian was with Iggy, Little Karl and Sam. Big Karl, Jay and Alexi had their own room. If you asked me, the group leaders should probably have been in the rooms with the big kids. Big kids usually did worse things than little kids. Usually.

We headed to the elevators. We fought about pushing the buttons. We were all staying on the nineteenth floor. Really high up!

"What stinks!?!" Jay coughed. He was right. It was obnoxious. We all looked around. It was Iggy. He was eating an egg from our bag lunch. It reeked!

"Iggy!" Sam yelled. It was good Sam was getting some of his own back for all the "Samanthas."

Our floor didn't arrive soon enough. We finally burst out of the elevator. The boys tried to keep Iggy from getting off. Adrian put an end to that, though.

"Here, girls." Chip handed us our own keys. Excellent. We could come and go as we pleased.

"Ta da!" Chip bugled as she unlocked the door. The room was very orange. I had never seen a hotel room with bunk beds in it before. The beds were all single-wides.

"What's this?" Rhonda was holding up a bottle that had been in an ice bucket.

Chip went over to her. "Mineral water."

"Can we have some?" Rhonda sounded doubtful. The bottle looked pretty fancy.

"Of course. Would you pour me a glass too?" Chip was going through her bagged lunch. "Shall we eat?"

"Here." Rhonda handed me the water.

"This water has bubbles in it!" It was kind of salty too. I didn't like it at all. "I think I'll just get some from the tap."

"I don't think the tap water is good to drink." Chip was unwrapping a triangle of cheese. I had never heard of tap water you couldn't drink. And why did they have to make the bottled water like pop? I hated pop.

"I want the top bunk." Rhonda threw her bag up. Chip was sitting on the lower bunk. I got the bed in the corner. It was the only one that wasn't a bunk bed. Brother!

I sat in an orange chair by the window. "Are we ever high up!" I looked through my lunch bag. I took a nibble of bread. It was brown and sour. Gross. The eggs stank. I unwrapped the foil from one of the cheese triangles. I had a nibble. Yuck! I looked out the window. I knew what I was going to do with my lunch. There was a parking lot below us.

"I'll be back in a few minutes." Chip got up with her lunch bag and left the room. Good. I went to the window and opened it. The windows were the sideways sliding kind and didn't have screens.

"What are you doing?" Rhonda was inspecting her lunch with the same enthusiasm as I did.

"Watch." I took the unwrapped soft cheese and dropped it. We watched. It hit the windshield of a car and spread out like bird shit.

"Cool!" Rhonda pushed me out of the way so she could drop hers. It hit the sidewalk. Near a person. We ducked back in the window.

"I'm doing an egg." I had my egg ready. I looked around and tossed. It made a huge cracking noise when it hit the pavement. We could see it spray. People on the street stopped walking. We ducked our heads back in the window. This was brilliant!

"Bread," Rhonda announced and tossed. It went like a Frisbee, then dropped like a stone. "People are looking!" Rhonda yanked me back in. We didn't get to see where it hit.

"Save some for later." I closed the window.

"Why?" Rhonda opened the window and hurled her egg out. We stuck our heads out. Smack! "Holy, shit, that's loud!"

A man on the street was shouting. We ducked back in and closed the window.

The room door banged open. "What the hell is going on in here?" Adrian's face was purple. "There have been complaints from the front desk that you have been throwing things out the window!" Adrian strode over to the closed window.

"Throwing things?" Rhonda looked really innocent.

"Why would we do that?" I actually sat there eating my second egg.

"Were you?" Like we'd tell him. His beard was practically standing on end.

"NO!" We both looked innocent.

"Maybe there has been a mistake." Adrian looked around the room and went back to the door.

"It must have been from another room," I helped. I nodded. I looked concerned.

"Someone could have been killed!" Adrian marched out. A man was standing in the hall. Adrian slammed our door. We went over to listen.

"It must have been from another room." That was Adrian.

"No mistake." That was the Russian man. "It is this room. People see. They say this room. This is very bad."

"These little girls would not have done that." Adrian was really fooled. Rhon and I shook hands. "What do the witnesses say hit the car?"

"They think it may be cheese."

Rhonda and I ran and sat back down. We watched the door. The door did not open. It was okay to start breathing again. We stared at the door. We looked at each other. We looked at the door.

"Shit," Rhonda whispered.

"Fuck," I whispered back.

"That was way too fast!" Rhonda took a sip of mineral water.

"How'd they find out so fast?" I took a sip of my water too. I still hated it.

"How'd they get here so fast?" Rhonda scrunched up her lunch bag and chucked it in the wastepaper basket.

"How'd they know for sure it was this room?" I chucked my bag but it missed. I got up and put it in.

"What should we do?"

"Haven't the foggiest, Rhon."

The door opened. We jumped. Chip waltzed in. "We're all going downstairs. There are people here from all over the world. Bring your pins and pens and postcards and whatever you brought for trading. There are delegates from 139 other countries staying here right now." Chip was riffling through her luggage for Canadian souvenirs. "We are meeting later with a group of Mozambicans but right now is free time.

"Mozam-who-ans?" Rhonda asked.

"Bicans." I knew where Mozambique was because of my grandma. "It's in Africa." When Grandad died, Grandma started travelling all over the world. She brought me a wooden carving from Africa, a native holding a spear. One day it fell in half. There was sawdust all around it. Mom was terrified that Grandma had accidentally brought back African termites hidden inside my Zulu warrior. We lived in a wood house. At night I heard the termites eating the walls. Dad said it was mice. He put poison down and a couple of weeks later the house started to stink. Mom said it was dead mice rotting behind the walls.

I grabbed my blue Adidas jacket with the pins on it. This was going to be neat. We were going to be meeting people from all over the world. I ran into the bathroom. "Hey, you guys!"

"What?" Rhonda stuck her head in the door of the john.

"There's no seat on the toilet."

"Maybe it was broken and someone removed it." Rhonda shook her head. "Maybe we should tell the front desk."

"I think these toilets are just like this." Chip was there, smiling. "I don't think we'll see toilet seats in the Soviet Union."

"What do you sit on?" Rhonda touched the rim with her running shoe.

"I guess you have to squat." I had to go. I wished they'd leave now.

"Or you could sit on the rim. Brrrr." Chip thought it was funny.

"I might fall in."

"Don't drown," Chip said and left.

"Good luck." Rhonda left too.

I looked at the toilet. I couldn't poo squatting. It was hard enough pooing on a toilet that wasn't my toilet at home. I never pooed unless I was at home. I squatted above the rim. It was not going to work. I sat on the rim. Chip was right. It was cold. I squatted again. This was useless. I pulled up my unders and gauchos. I'd try again later.

Hand-gesturing was fun. It was like playing charades. We were actually communicating with a couple of Russian boys our age. They didn't speak one word of English and we knew *da* and *nyet* in Russian. I gave them both Canadian flag pins. I had managed to find out that they were not going to the same camp as us. They said Orlyonok, the camp we were going to, was a good one. But now I was having difficulties. Rhonda had wanted me to ask what their parents did. So far they either thought Rhonda was pregnant or we were mad at someone fat. It was because of how I got Rhonda to mime Mother while I put on my best frown to be Father.

"Does someone need help over here?" It was Nadia, our brown-haired interpreter.

"Nadia, please tell them that Rhonda is not pregnant!"

"Pardon me?" Her face was more than astonished.

"It's my fault." It was my fault. "We wanted to ask them what their parents did for a living and now I think they think *we* are parents."

"Ah." Nadia nodded like this happened all the time. She spoke quickly in Russian to the boys, who started laughing. We laughed too.

"Their parents work for the Soviet government." Nadia took

my hand. She was smiling and pulling. "Would you like to meet some other people?"

"Were those boys Young Pioneers?" I figured they must have been as they were going to a camp too.

"No. They are Komsomols." Nadia had led us far away from them over to another group of people. If they were Komsomols who were young Communist Party members, that meant they were over fourteen. I still didn't know what their parents did. Jay and the Karls were already communicating with this new group. I was glad to note that everyone had been given Canadian pins. I didn't want to run out on my first night. Everyone was miming their ages.

"Why do you think they look so much younger than us, Rhon?"

"I don't know, but that seventeen-year-old girl looks eleven or twelve." Rhonda pointed to a girl wearing braids like mine. She waved at us. We waved back.

"It's because of how they're dressed." Dee Dee's voice behind me made me jump.

"Yeah, look at them," Rhonda agreed with Dee Dee. I didn't quite see what they meant yet.

"Their hair too. They don't have any style." Dee Dee did the swoop with her do just to make her point. She was right. Soviet teenagers looked and dressed like little kids. Their shoes even were little kid shoes, flat with buckles. No one wore buckles like that except five-year-olds. And Dee Dee was right about their hair. They all had pigtails or ponytails or braids. Like mine. They also did not wear makeup and lots of teenagers in Canada wore makeup. Even some of my friends. I didn't. The other thing was they all kept holding hands. Like little kids. The boys did too. You'd get four in a row holding hands. They seemed to touch each other a lot. Girls with girls and boys with boys.

"You're staring." Good thing Rhonda informed me because I was.

Dinner. A long table with a white cloth and dinner; a boiled fish, head on, skin on and I imagined bones in, and a boiled potato.

"Oh man!" Iggy was getting cranky.

"Bet you don't eat like this on the prairies." Jay passed Iggy the loaf of sour brown bread.

"Where's the butter?" Iggy knew there was no butter.

"They don't eat butter with their bread here. The bread is so good it stands on its own," Adrian stated.

"It's so sour it walks over to the sugar bowl on its own." Iggy ate his potato. "Yuck! The potato was boiled with the fish!" Iggy removed the potato from his mouth.

"You should eat something," Chip urged me but there was just no way. At home when people said you should eat something, it was usually over a juicy steak, or broccoli with cheese, or a baked potato smothered in butter and sour cream, or barbecued chicken, or ribs, or lasagna with tons of mozzarella, and it was because I was full. I was always full at home. I was skinny so people tried to get me to eat more. For once I was hungry and I just couldn't eat anything. I normally loved fish. Fish was my favourite dish until now. But I liked fish like in England when it was surrounded by crispy batter or like in Quebec when it was in a creamy wine sauce. I liked my fish with no bones or skin or head. I had also never in my life eaten a boiled fish. Just boiled.

"I can't eat this." Dee Dee pushed her plate away.

"I can't either." Oksana had tried to take the head off her fish.

"Hey Mary. Like your dinner?" Jay had a tone when he said it. It was sarcasm. I didn't know why, though. He was handsome.

"Yes, thank you," Mary nodded and continued to eat.

Jay and Dee Dee laughed. I smiled at Jay.

"People, this is very rude." Adrian was doing a disappointed look. He had finished his food. He ate it like it was Kentucky Fried Chicken. He was sick in the head.

Someone came to clear our plates. They couldn't because the plates were all full. I was glad my dad was not here to make me eat. I hated it when he did that. I had sat at the kitchen table until midnight once. He had told me that I had to stay there until I had finished everything on my plate. It wasn't fair because I wasn't the one who had filled my plate so full. I finally shoved my dinner into the crack between the fridge and stove and went to bed. It was a great hiding place. I used it for a couple of months. It got too full, though, and I had to find other places. I shoved food behind the stove for two years. My parents got a new stove this year and Dad could not believe what a slob Mom was. He actually thought she had dropped all that gunk while cooking. I acted like it was disgraceful. They didn't suspect me at all.

"I don't eat anything that stares at me while I'm eating it." Iggy had a good point.

The confused-looking waiter was back with two other waiters. They just did not understand that they had to take our plates even though they were full. They thought we were slow eaters or something. Sonya, the blonde interpreter, appeared.

"Please tell the waiters that the food is good." Chip looked so concerned. "It is just that the children are not used to food like this."

Sonya translated. They started to clear the plates. "They need to know if you want the ice cream that is scheduled for pudding or if the children are unused to ice cream as well?" Sonya asked Chip but we all answered loudly—

"YES!!! *DA! DA!* YES!!!"

Sonya had a surly look on her face.

I felt my braid being tugged playfully from behind. "You'll like the ice cream." It was Nadia. "Soviet ice cream is some of the best in the world. "

The ice cream arrived. It was in flat-bottomed cones like you got at Dairy Queen, only no ice cream showed over the top. It was just packed into the inside.

"Oh yeah!" Iggy didn't look grumpy any more.

"Why don't they fill the cones?" Sam had almost finished his. I had barely started. It was creamy vanilla. Iggy was right, oh yeah, oh, oh, it was good. Sam was right too, though. Why didn't they fill the cones?

"The cones *are* full." Sonya sounded as indignant as she looked.

I wondered how one would draw a picture of a person eating an ice cream in the Soviet Union without the ball of ice cream on top. It would just look like a square, nothing to tell you it was ice cream.

"It seems silly to put the ice cream on top of the cone rather than in the cone."

"Yes, Sonya, you are right." Adrian nodded firmly to her. "The Soviet way is better. It makes more sense."

I wanted to tell Sonya that our ice cream was not just above the cone, that it was in the cone too. Well, at good ice-cream places. Our way was better because you got more ice cream. Who cared about the stupid cones, anyway. They were just there because you couldn't very well hold ice cream in your hands. Sugar cones weren't bad, though. I liked them. The only problem was they usually had holes in the bottom and then the ice cream leaked all over you. I had to nibble all around my Soviet cone so that I could get ice cream showing above it so that I had something to lick. The cone was soft.

"Why is the cone soft?" I asked Nadia. I had already decided it was best not to talk to Sonya.

"Ice cream is stored in the freezer, in the cone. You buy it already in the cones here."

"And how does it come in Canada?" Sonya asked Nadia. Sonya still had not smiled.

"They usually buy the ice cream in containers and then fill the cones. That way the cones stay fresh and crisp."

"You can buy ice cream in cones from vendors." Mary said this. "But in a restaurant or at home they are separate. And in a restaurant you would have it in a dish. I don't think either way is better. They are just different."

My ice cream was gone. I wished there was more. Even in its soggy cone. Nadia was right. The ice cream was fantastic.

"You have free time for an hour, folks, before we meet with the Mozambicans. Please stay in the hotel." Adrian turned and started growling at Chip. Rhonda and I nudged each other.

"Let's go," Rhonda whispered to me.

"What's that about? Why's he mad at Chip?"

"Who knows. Let's just go back to the room."

First thing we did when we got to the room was run to the window. Rhonda rescued her lunch bag from the garbage and I tried to open the window.

"What's wrong?" Rhonda was shoving me out of the way.

"I can't get it to open."

"Maybe it's the other one."

"No, it was this one." I pushed and pulled. I inspected the other windows. They weren't the opening kind.

"Shit!" Rhonda choked. "Look at this!"

"Wow. Someone has come in and sealed it shut. Look at all these screws. This wasn't like this!" I started trembling. "Rhonda, they know. They know it was us."

"I can't believe this, Kirsten!"

"Someone came in and bolted up this window when we were gone."

Rhonda threw her lunch bag back in the waste basket. "This is spooky."

"Creepy! Who do you think—"

"The Red Army."

"Are we in trouble?" I was scared but excited too. Being scared was the best fun in the world. I always wanted a scary adventure like *The Famous Five* or *The Hardy Boys*. I liked *The Hardy Boys* better than *Nancy Drew*.

"They're watching us. We better be careful." Rhonda was pacing.

"Who's *they*?"

"Them." She mouthed something. I didn't catch it.

"The who?"

"Them." She did it again.

"The 'κ' what?"

"GB!"

"Oh." She could have been right. We were peace delegates from countries all over the world. There were even Americans here. I hadn't seen them yet but I'd heard. Maybe the Soviet government was scared some of us were spies. The window certainly had been sealed shut. That would not have happened in Canada. This was like *The Six Million Dollar Man*. There was a knock on the door. Rhonda and I froze. The knock happened again.

"You guys. Open up." It was Dee Dee.

I ran to the door and opened it. Dee Dee, I had to tell. Oksana and Mary were there too. Oh well. "You will never guess what happened!"

"We were throwing stuff out the window earlier." Rhonda obviously didn't know how to drag things out for suspense.

"Yeah." I backed Rhonda up.

"Since we have been gone from the room, *they* have come and nailed the window shut."

"Yeah." I'd have told it better.

"No way." Dee Dee went over to our windows and tried to open them.

"Why were you throwing things out of the window?" God, Mary was stupid.

"It was that gross lunch they served us." Rhonda was over by Dee Dee, who had given up on the window.

"Why would you throw your lunch out of the window?" Mary was from another planet.

"What else could they do with it?" Dee Dee understood us.

"Did you hit anything?"

"Yeah, Oksana, a car! It was great!" Rhonda pressed her face on the window. "You can't see where unless you can stick your head out."

"You should have heard the eggs hit the pavement!" I could tell that Dee Dee and Oksana were impressed.

"You should have eaten your lunch. That was wasteful and some dangerous." Mary's arms were crossed. I had never heard the word "some" used that way before.

"I cannot believe that people came and screwed this shut. Do you think they went through your things?" Dee Dee indicated our suitcases. We had not thought of that.

Rhonda flew to her bag. She had a lock on it. But she had not locked it before we left the room. "My lock is open!" Maybe she wasn't so bad at storytelling. "If they opened mine they probably opened yours and Chip's too."

Mary made a loud exhaling noise. An impatient, disbelieving noise. She looked at her watch. "We should take this free time and do something constructive with it, like meeting more people from other countries."

"Speaking of other people." Dee Dee's eyes went big as she said this. "Jay and Big Karl were talking to some American girls. They said the Americans got drunk on the plane coming over!"

"Why do Big Karl and Little Karl have the same name?" I had forgotten to ask this until now. Everyone started laughing.

"What do you mean, Kirsten?" Dee Dee was grinning. Her teeth were massive.

"Why are they both named Karl?"

"They're not, you dummy. One of them is Darwin. It's just that they look so much alike that Chip and I started calling them Big Karl and Little Karl."

"Which one is Darwin?" Rhonda had thought they were both Karl too. You could tell she was as surprised as me. I wished she'd said something, so I didn't look like the only retard.

"I don't know. That's why I call them Big Karl and Little Karl." Dee Dee fixed herself in the mirror.

"Little Karl hates me." I fixed myself too.

"He's just a stupid goof. Ignore him." Dee Dee was right.

"Let's go." Mary was a nice girl. She wasn't a gossip. She was fair-minded. She was sensible. My mom would have liked Mary. My parents would have wanted me to be friends with Mary.

"Did you see the Mozambicans earlier?" Dee Dee asked. Her hair was very shiny. "The men wear long dresses."

"They look like fancy housecoats to me." Oksana pulled her hiphuggers down so that you could see her navel when she lifted her arms. Her skin was so pale you could almost see through it. Her hair wasn't red, but more strawberry blonde and it was shiny too. I wished my hair wasn't in braids and was down like theirs.

"I'm leaving." Mary was not concerned with how she looked. It was better to be like that. I continued to play with my hair in front of the mirror. I rebraided a braid. I opened the second button of my shirt.

"Okay, you guys. Enough. Let's go." Mary was still waiting.

"Yeah, I'm ready." Dee Dee did one final hair flip. And we were off.

Chip, Rhonda and I lay in our beds, talking about our first day. We probably were exhausted but we could not sleep. It was 2:00 in the morning. I had never stayed up so late in my life. I had been up til 1:30 once at a sleepover. Two o'clock was a new record.

"Everyone we have met seems to live so differently from us," Rhonda said. She was lucky to be on the top bunk.

"Can you imagine living in a grass hut with a dirt floor? You'd never have to vacuum." I hardly ever had to do housework so I didn't know why I said that. My friend Patty Gluck, from next door, had to do chores every day. She dusted and vacuumed and cleaned and cut grass and did tons of stuff. Once, I told my parents that I thought that I should do chores too. I did for a couple of days. I found I wasn't the chore-doing type. I had thought it would be neat to do chores for an allowance. My way was better, though. Do nothing and ask for money when you need it.

"I hope it stops raining tomorrow for sightseeing." Chip's voice was getting scratchy. Yup, we were tired.

"I didn't write in my travel diary yet!" I leaped out of bed and grabbed it from the top of my carry-on bag. "I'll do it in the bathroom so the light won't bug you." I loved being considerate.

"Thank you." Rhonda was starting to mumble.

I hoped nobody snored. I could not sleep with snoring. My grandma snored. You could hear her two rooms away. I hated sleeping in the same room with her. I bit her arm once when I was in grade three. We were sleeping in the same bed at my Auntie Pie's, in the Queen's gardens, near Windsor Castle, in England. My grandma had dozed off reading. She was snoring and it bugged me. I looked at the meat on her arm and just got the urge to chomp. Her glasses flew right off her face. I left a ring of teeth marks on her arm. The biting part felt good. I'd never forget it, the feeling of the flesh. The shock and pain my grandma went through did not feel so good. She asked me why I did it. I didn't really know. It might not have been the snoring. It might just have been because of the look of the meat on her arm. Like a big chicken drumstick. Human was supposed to taste like pork. It was probably better than the fish we had had at dinner. If I was really starving, I wondered, could I eat it? Could I eat a human?

41

I was sitting on the toilet now with my diary out. I'd try to poo again. I'd poo and write at the same time. Reading always helped so writing might too. At home I read the dictionary on the toilet, so I'd get better at Scrabble and be able to beat Gram. The rim was still cold, maybe colder than before. I could probably eat a person if it was a life and death situation. It would just depend how they were cooked. Boiled was definitely out of the question. I started to write. I wrote, *Russia is a very nice place. When we got off the plane it began to pour with rain. The trip on the bus to the hotel was a very nice one. Right now I am in bed hearing the gentle breathing of my friend and the friendly gossip of two Russian men outside our room.* There, that was enough. That was pretty good. Especially the gentle breathing and the friendly gossip bit. It wasn't all true, but I couldn't very well write that I was sitting on a toilet without a seat. My parents would want to read this when I got home.

A PICTURE WITH THE REDS.

We were on the tour bus singing our "Western" music for the driver. Little Karl knew all the lyrics to every single Jackson Five song, though he said they were called just the Jacksons now, since leaving Motown. Little Karl said he knew more about music because he was black. I didn't say it but the Karls looked way more Punjabi than black. It was raining again. I had on my bright red rain poncho with the beaver on it. They didn't have beavers in the Soviet Union. We were going to the Moscow Zoo. We were going to see Siberian tigers. I didn't care about all the buildings that Sonya was pointing out. Somebody sneezed. Everyone was getting sick. I wasn't, though. The bus stopped.

"We are at the bank," Sonya told Chip and Adrian.

"All right, everyone. We can change some of our traveller's cheques here." Adrian was standing. "You can leave your things on the bus. Nobody steals in the Soviet Union." That was the third time Adrian had talked about there being no crime in the Soviet Union. Nobody stole and nobody killed anybody. My parents had a book by a Russian guy who was kicked out of the Soviet Union. His name was something like Solzen-itchy-chin.

In his Gulag book he said there were lots of prisoners in Siberian prisons. I had pretended to read his book before leaving Canada.

There was a lineup in the bank. "This is going to take hours," I complained. Dad hated it when I whined. But he hated lineups more. Dad never had to wait for anything. I wished he was here to see us to the front. Adrian seemed to enjoy standing in the line. Chip was busy talking to Oksana and Dee Dee.

"You have to make sure you do your signature exactly the same as you did on your traveller's cheques or they won't give you any money." Iggy was behind me, practising writing his name in the lineup. "That was perfect. Maybe if we all sign our cheques now this dumb lineup will move faster."

"DON'T SIGN THE CHEQUE NOW! You have to do it in front of the teller." Adrian didn't need to shout. It was too late anyway.

"He's already done it. It doesn't matter." Rhon wasn't scared of Adrian.

"I was just practising writing my name." Iggy dropped his pen. I thought he was going to wet his pants.

I could never write my name the same twice, either. I didn't have a signature. I had been trying to develop one but I hadn't found one that I liked and when I did do a nice one, I could never do it again. Not only did I have hardly any money to change, they weren't going to give it to me anyway.

"Oh dear." Chip's hand covered her mouth. "How much was the cheque for, Iggy?

"Twenty dollars." Iggy looked really scared. Adrian escorted Iggy over to Sonya. They were obviously going to need help in Russian.

"This is more frightening than going to the principal's office." My stomach was flipping around and my hands were cold.

"You can say that again." Rhonda had her hands on her hips. She did impatient waiting well. "How many rubles is twenty dollars?"

"What's your favourite subject at school, Rhonda? RECESS!" Little Karl jeered. What a little wiener. Chip had said he was really smart. She left the ass off the end of smart.

"Mine's lunch." Iggy was back in line.

"Not if you went to school in Russia." I was proud of that one.

"The Soviet Union, you capitalist pig." Karl was cruising for a bruising. If I punched Little Karl in the bank, would I get in big trouble?

"I am not a capitalist!" I could have done better than that.

"Are too."

Little Karl was pathetic! I wasn't going to do one of those *am not, are too*s. I turned my back on him. Rhonda gave him the bullshit sign.

"What's going to happen, Iggy?" I could see Dee Dee's traveller's cheque. It was for fifty dollars. That would buy a lot in the Soviet Union. Not that we'd seen anything to buy yet.

"If the bank won't cash my cheque, then Adrian is going to have to call American Express when we get back to the hotel. Man, I thought he was going to kill me."

The Russian bank tellers looked very tough. Someone said they might just choose not to give any of us our money. Iggy was in trouble.

Rhonda had the window seat on the bus. I kept taking my Soviet money out of my purse and looking at it. Ten dollars sure got a lot of Soviet money. I was pretty rich in Russia. The bus pulled over.

"You can get out and take pictures if you would like," Sonya informed us. I wasn't sure what we were supposed to be taking pictures of. Probably the big statue of the man in the suit with a beard and big fists. I noticed Adrian tugging on his beard, trying to get it in a point like the statue's beard.

"I'm thirsty. Can we get something to drink from somewhere?" Dee Dee asked Adrian and Chip this question, who, in turn, looked at the interpreters.

"That is a pop machine across the street. We can go there." Nadia was neat. I liked her one thousand times better than Sonya. I wondered if you could get something without fizz from the pop machine. Everyone was pushing and shoving to get off the bus. Everyone was thirsty.

"Watch out!" Chip screamed at Sam.

Man, Soviet drivers were crazy. They drove a hundred miles an hour all the time. Their funny little cars were all over the road, swerving and beeping, brakes screeching, tires squealing. It was a nightmare crossing a road. Looking both ways wasn't enough. Nadia took Rhonda's and my hand and we ran like the Road Runner to get across.

"What's the glass for?" Jay was at the machine, pointing to a small drinking glass on its ledge. "Did someone leave it?"

"The glass is for the pop." Sonya had a kopek in her hand. She put it in the machine. Pop went into the glass.

"You mean everyone has to drink out of that glass?" Dee Dee's nose crinkled.

"How can you take your pop with you? Can't you get a can or bottle?" Alexi inquired while helping Oksana with her change. Oksana didn't feel well. Her throat hurt and she had a headache. I wished I had a big brother.

"No. You drink your pop here out of the glass." Sonya had finished her pop and put the glass back under the dispenser.

"This is very good." Adrian was impressed. "Think of the waste and litter this cuts down on."

"Yeah, but you are sharing a glass with all of Moscow and with no soap to clean it!" Dee Dee was not impressed. Sharing a glass didn't bother me at all.

"This is going to take forever for the whole group to drink a pop." I was eighth in line. I was worried too. I couldn't drink pop fast. But I was so thirsty I didn't want to wait until the end.

"What would you do if someone stole the glass?" Iggy asked.

"No one would steal the glass," Adrian replied. "The citizens here have a great sense of honour. People do not steal here."

"What would happen if someone did, though?" Iggy continued.

"It wouldn't happen." Adrian was solemn and definite.

"Yeah but what if, just say if?" Iggy had his pop now.

"The Soviet people do not steal, Iggy." Adrian was getting irritated. I wanted Iggy to stop.

"Okay, but say one did. What would happen to them? Would they have to go to jail?"

"No!" Adrian was mad now. "No one would steal the glass

here! There are hardly any criminals in Soviet jails." I wondered if Adrian knew what he was talking about. "There is very little crime here."

"Then why are there prisons at all? Who is in the prisons if it isn't criminals?" Iggy had finished his pop.

"We are very proud of how little crime there is here. It is not like Canada or the United States." Sonya smiled for the first time. I didn't think she should have lumped us with the US. Nadia was looking at the ground. Nadia was not smiling.

"But someone is in the prisons. Who?" Iggy was pressing his luck. I didn't know why someone just didn't answer his question, though.

"Give your glass to the next person," Adrian bellowed. Chip said something to Adrian in a hushed voice and Adrian started on Chip again.

"I want two pops." Iggy had more change out. "I'm still thirsty. The glass is too small."

"NO!" Adrian was going all shades again.

"Just wait until the end then, Iggy." Chip was smart. "Wait until everyone has had some and then you can get more."

"NO!" Adrian snapped. "We don't have all day to spend over pop!"

There was one of those uncomfortable silences. No one said anything. We didn't even look at each other. It was crazy having to line up and wait for each person to have drunk their pop before the next could go. My turn finally came. I watched the glass slowly fill. I took the glass and sipped. The pop tasted quite nice for pop. I wasn't sure what the flavour was. It was the colour of ginger ale but it didn't taste like ginger ale. It was nice and sweet. It wasn't quite as bubbly as our pop, which helped me drink it but I still couldn't go fast.

"Hurry up!" Little Karl was behind Rhonda.

"Gee, Karl, you are being as impatient as, um, as a, oh my, as a capitalist." Rhonda dug that one in. It was great.

"No, I'm not." You couldn't see Little Karl's eyes because of his stupid mirror sunglasses. It was cloudy. Good grief, he didn't even need to wear them. "The selfish capitalist is the one hogging the glass!"

"Kirsten, you are going to have to go at the end from now on." Adrian was calmer now. "You take too long to drink."

"Here." I handed Rhonda my half-drunk pop, even though I was still thirsty. "I can't finish it." I already had the hiccups.

"Hold your breath." Like I hadn't heard that one before. I did it to be nice to Jay, because he was cute, but I knew it wouldn't work. It never did. I hicced and exploded.

"Drink upside down, plugging your ears. It makes a vacuum." That was Rhonda. It was drinking that had got me into this dilemma in the first place.

"Boo." Iggy was trying the scaring business. I looked startled to be polite but then hiccupped again. "Brother! You have them bad."

"I can't drink pop," I moaned and hiccupped. Everyone was staring at me. They were violent-sounding hiccups.

"Are you okay?" Chip asked.

"Yes." The problem was, once I started they'd come and go all day. I hated this kind of attention. My grandma gave me sugar cubes to suck when I got the hiccups. It didn't work but I pretended it did. Sometimes I'd just pretend to have the hiccups so she'd give me a sugar cube. For some reason I felt like crying, I wasn't quite sure why. The hiccups were bad but they had never made me cry before. It might have been because Little Karl hated me and was staring at me with a sneer. I wished he'd like me. I hadn't done anything to him. I was also thirsty, really thirsty and hungry too.

The zoo was fun. I always liked zoos but the Moscow Zoo wasn't anything fantastic. It wasn't better than the rest of the zoos in the world, like Adrian and the translators made out, and it wasn't anything compared to the African Lion Safari back at home. The Lion Safari was the best because you got to drive your car through the park and the baboons climbed all over it. A big baboon with an ugly blue and purple butt crapped on the hood of our car last time. It was a huge poo that stood on its end. It stayed there the whole way round the park and I could barely look at anything else. It was humiliating. A giraffe stuck its head in the window too. You were supposed to keep your windows up and not feed the animals. Yeah, right. We always gave bananas to the baboons. The giraffe licked me. Its tongue was black and hairy like a cat's. The lions were great. Driving past lions in your car, wow, now that was better than any zoo that had cages. My friend Trisha from across the road told me that some tourists' car broke down one time at the safari and they got out and walked. They were eaten by the lions. Tourists always did dumb things. You never, never got out of your car at the Lion Safari. It was like the family that went camping in Killarney Provincial Park and they put honey on their five-year-old's face because they thought the bear licking the girl's face would make a good picture. I couldn't remember who told me that one. I figured I knew a million stupid-tourist stories.

"Put up your hood, Kirsten." Chip was right about that. It was pouring. I didn't bother being stubborn or cool. We were at the Moscow Exhibition now. I was so excited when I heard after the zoo and lunch we would be going to the Moscow Exhibition. I wasn't excited any more. There were no roller coasters or rides at this exhibition. It wasn't like the Ex in Toronto. I had only been to the CNE, or Ex, once, with my friend Tara and her parents. It was fun! We went on the Flyer and the Wild Mouse and we played games to try and win prizes. At night we went to a concert with her parents and saw Paul Anka. I'd never heard of him before but I knew one of the songs because Donny Osmond sang it too. I had thought it was Donny Osmond's song but Tara's parents said it was Paul Anka's first. The Moscow Exhibition was some sort of science museum. There were no food tents, games, rides, fortune tellers, weight guessers, concerts, clowns. The bus had let us off below this huge rocket on display in the grounds. We all took pictures, then walked over to this robot that was on display outside a building that looked like an airplane hangar. We took more pictures. Little Karl did "the robot" in front of the robot. He was good at it and soon there were more people watching him dance than there were looking at the Soviet robot, which didn't move at all. Sonya had never heard of Michael Jackson. She said they didn't listen to music from the West. We went inside the airplane hangar. There were no planes in it. There were "innovations" in farming or something that Iggy laughed at. There were robotics things. There was nothing for kids to do. It wasn't like the Science Centre in Toronto. They didn't even have jars with human foetuses in them. I loved looking at the pickled foetuses when my family went to the Science Centre.

"When are we going back to the hotel?"

"Not til dinner, Dee Dee," Chip answered.

"Do you think we will know about the luggage?"

"I hope so."

"Do you think we could do some shopping today? I really need to get a toothbrush at least."

"I'll talk to Adrian," Chip replied. And went to find Adrian.

"God, why can't she just make a decision on her own? And why does she always talk to us like we are in one of her retard classes at school?" Dee Dee threw her hands up in the air.

"Special ed," Mary corrected.

"Chip is really nice," I defended. I liked Chip.

"I know. That is part of the problem." Dee Dee was furious. I did not understand how being nice could be a problem. We were leaving the airplane hangar without planes. It was still raining outside. A group of Soviet soldiers was smoking outside near the entrance. I watched them.

"Chip's pathetically nice," Dee Dee continued. "And Adrian doesn't seem to understand that personal possessions like underwear and toothbrushes are important." Dee Dee did the breath test by blowing into her cupped hand and inhaling quickly. "God! I need a toothbrush. Do you know how much my father spent on these teeth? He'd flip if he knew." I looked at Dee Dee's huge teeth. I couldn't understand why you'd pay money for those.

"Do you think those soldiers would mind if I took their picture?" I couldn't stop looking at them. They were so exciting! They were Reds.

"No way," Rhonda shook her head fast. "You can't take their pictures. You'd probably get arrested or something."

"Yeah," Dee Dee agreed.

I looked at the soldiers again. I wanted their picture so badly.

I took out my camera and walked over to them. I showed them my camera. I pointed to my camera and then to them and smiled. The really handsome blond one stumped out his cigarette. The smaller brown-haired one took my camera, then gestured to my friends. He did the "come here" sign with his finger. Dee Dee came over. He handed her my camera and made a press-the-shutter gesture to her. Then the blond handsome one put his arm around me and the other soldiers stood beside me in a line. Holy cow. I was going to get my picture taken with the Russian army. Dee Dee clicked the shutter. I couldn't stop grinning. I gave the soldiers maple leaf pins.

"Thank you. Thank you." I said it a hundred times. "Goodbye." I backed away from them, smiling.

"*Da svee-da-nya*," they said back. One of them took a cigarette out of his pocket. It wasn't like our cigarettes at home. It didn't have a filter and was really skinny. The soldiers waved and smiled. They were talking in Russian to each other.

"Kirsten, I can't believe you did that." Dee Dee gave me back my *Time* mag camera. Maybe someday I'd work for them.

"Man, you have guts." Rhonda was impressed. I was on top of the world!

"I wish I could have got a picture like that." Oksana was so jealous. She was watching the soldiers move away.

"Look at their uniforms," Dee Dee sighed.

"They looked so serious, so mean, man, I can't imagine what got into you to try that. Man!" Rhonda took some Chapstick out of her purse and put it on her lips. "Want some?"

"No thanks." Dee Dee had her own. I took some. It was cherry-flavoured. Oksana didn't want any. The rest of the group were outside now too.

"Did you see what Kirsten did?" Dee Dee asked.

"She got a picture with the Reds!" Rhonda shrieked.

"So." Little Karl made a face and turned around. Sulky shithead.

"Wow!" Alexi came over to us. "My dad takes me down to the port to talk to Russian merchant sailors. We play chess and sometimes we take them out for a meal. I've not met military personnel ever. Did you talk to the soldiers?"

"They didn't speak any English," I told him.

"Are you ever lucky. I'm not sure if they are supposed to pose for photos." I decided Alexi's hair wasn't red, either, but was strawberry blond like his sister's. I was glad. The only two red-haired boys I had known were both bullies and both beat me up. The first used to chase me and my friends home from kindergarten and grade one. He was awful. He must have been in grade four. He was huge. He had red freckles too. The second, the worst, was Dougie Taggart. The eldest boy of the Taggart family. We called him Doggy Dogdirt, but not ever so he could hear it. A couple of months ago he almost killed Patty and me on our way home from the school bus. The road we lived on was being redone and it was all torn up. There were these massive clods of hard dirt and stone. Dougie heaved them, drilled them, flung them at us all the way home. It was utterly terrifying. We ran as fast as we could but it wasn't fast enough. Dougie was three years older than us and way bigger. He had ugly red freckles too. I hated him. He also did things to his sisters. Sex things. He felt them up and down all the time and more. He cut holes in the wall of his room so that he could watch them change, even. Their house was falling apart. Their mother was dying of a disease and never got out of bed. It was creepy down there. When we first moved to Cheltenham I was five. I had just met the Taggarts. Sherry was in my class at school. We were playing hide and seek. Dougie and I hid in a box in their rabbit barn. Dougie felt me up and down too. It was strange. I thought he liked me. He told me what fucking was. I'd never heard of it before. He showed me his penis. I'd seen a penis before. I still looked though. He hated me now. He never played with the other kids. He never had, as far as I knew. His temper was too bad. He was scary. I wished it was him that was dying of the disease and not his mother. I just didn't like redheads at all. Especially the red-freckled kind.

We were off the bus again and standing in a square. It wasn't the Red Square. We were going there tomorrow. It was another square. It had grey paving stones so maybe it was the Grey Square. This was our last tour of the day. That was good.

"Does anyone need to go to the toilet?" Sonya inquired. "There is a public toilet just over there."

I needed to go. Most of us needed to. We headed over to the john, which was in a brick building.

"Rhon!" I was in utter disbelief.

"Oh my God!" She was too.

"Oh my." Even Chip was shocked.

"I'll see you later." Dee Dee left the bathroom altogether.

The door of one of the toilet cubicles had swung open. There was no toilet at all. There was a hole in the ground with two orange metal foot-pads with a turd on one of them. People were lined up in front of the cubicles. The doors on the cubicles were unbelievable too. They only covered the person's body, not their face. So the lady going to the bathroom was staring right into the eyes of the people in the lineup. We got into line.

"Do you think the men's is like this?"

"Ki-ersten, I think there is a good chance that it's worse." Chip hooked her purse strap over her neck to her opposite shoulder. She was obviously preparing for the worst. It was not like you could put your purse on the floor in this can. Gross. And you sure wouldn't want to drop anything. There was a fat, old woman just finishing up in the one I was lined up in front of. She looked nasty. She swung open the door. Damn! There was a huge lump on the foot place of mine too. The woman next in line went in. Rhonda had entered hers. Rhonda looked at me over the door. I laughed at her.

"Shut up," she laughed back.

I tried not to make eye contact with the woman who was going in front of me. It was too bizarre to look in the eyes of someone who was having a poop. When my cat Muzik went poo his eyes went out of focus. I noticed it was kind of like that for people too. It was my turn. I went in and closed the orange door. I tried to straddle the hole, not using the footpad that Mt. Kilimanjaro was residing on. I pulled down my jeans and looked ahead. I was so short that although I could still see over the top of the door, the bottom didn't cover my bottom half. Everyone would be able to see me below the door with my pants down. What was with these stupid two-foot doors? They weren't doors, they were gates. Why bother? There was no privacy. I wasn't sure I could do this. I had to pee badly, though. I went. Now I knew why there were turds everywhere but the hole. It was so hard to aim this way, standing. My pee splashed on the cement floor, splashed up my jeans. I even felt it spray my hands and arms. There was no toilet paper! It didn't matter. I'd already peed on my jeans. My GWGs were no longer Scrubbies. They were grubbies. An old woman was watching me with angry eyes. I dripped for one more second then pulled up my pants. I barely got out before she was pushing in the door. Her legs were bowed under the weight of her large body. She flattened me against the door frame on her way in. There was nowhere to wash your hands. I ran out into the open air.

"Gomme, gomme?" He was so close to me I could smell him. He was probably Rhonda's age but had a man's voice and whiskers. He did it again. His lips touched my ear. "Chewing gomme?" There was alcohol and cigarettes on his breath. He wore black leather shoes like a grown-up man would wear to work, but they were scuffed and wrinkled and he wore no socks. "I buy gomme?"

"No gum," I whispered or maybe gasped. It was frightening. He made me think of the gypsies I had seen in England. There were more of them now. They all said gum funny, like the way it was spelled on the French side of the package.

"No gum." I repeated it more loudly. "I have no gum."

"You have gomme!" The first one was smiling. Kind of smiling. Maybe not nice smiling. His eyes had a light. They were blue but his hair was very black. "You have gomme," he repeated.

"No, no gum." I shook my head. I patted my pockets and shook my head. Suddenly Nadia was there. She spoke quickly and angrily to the boys. They scattered but stayed close. As our Canadian group moved off, the boys who were like men continued to call out "gomme" and "You sell jeans?" They followed us for a few seconds but then went back to their fountain where they hung out. I saw the first one light a cigarette. He struck the match on the bottom of his shoe. I'd never seen anyone do that before. I could still smell him. I didn't normally like smelly people but for some reason I sort of liked his smell. It was an exciting smell. The smell of adventure. That would have been a good name for an Enid Blyton, *The Smell of Adventure*. *The Ship of Adventure*, *The Mountain of Adventure* and *The Smell of Adventure*. Nadia, Sonya, Chip and Adrian seemed most upset by what had happened.

"Those boys were probably from families who aren't party members," Jay informed me quietly.

"I thought gum was illegal here." I looked back at the fountain. The boys weren't watching us any more. I hicced again, damn.

"It is," Jay said. Again quietly, so Adrian and the grown-up crew would not hear.

"That would be a crime, then, wouldn't it?" Iggy's tummy growled.

"Yeah, man. But *you* would be the one that would be in trouble. I don't know if they'd put you in prison or deport you." Jay was serious. Jay was gorgeous.

"Good thing you didn't have gum, Kirsten," Iggy said. I agreed. What would Rhonda have done? I knew she had some gum left. I hiccupped.

"Excuse me, little girl." Two ladies stopped me in the hotel lobby. "We were hoping that you would like to come have some sweets and tea with us in our room." They looked nice. If this had been anywhere else in the world it would have seemed odd to have two strangers invite you to their room for tea.

"We study language at the Moscow Linguistic Institute. We have been listening to you speak for the last two days and it is very interesting. We were hoping that we could talk to you and listen some more." The woman who said this had long blonde braids exactly like mine.

"I would be delighted," I said. That didn't sound like me. I followed them down the corridor to the elevators. I wondered how or where they could have been listening to me. I liked the idea of people wanting to hear me talk. This was right up my alley.

"Where exactly do you live?" The one without braids asked in the elevator.

"In Ontario, Canada. Just north of Toronto."

They both looked at each other with raised eyebrows. What was that about?

"Are you enjoying your stay in the Soviet Union?" the one with braids asked.

"Yes, very much, thank you." I noticed I was talking differently. Carefully.

"Which camp are you going to stay at, Kirsten?" the one with braids asked.

"Orlyonok." Wait a minute. I hadn't told them my name.

The one without braids opened their hotel room door. "I hope you do not mind that we do not have sugar. We have sweets, though, to eat with your tea." Their room didn't look like a hotel room. It looked like they lived there. There were antiques and oriental rugs.

"Please make yourself comfortable," the one without braids said from the kitchen. "We want to talk to you, rather than the others in your group, because we have noticed that you speak so much better."

I did? I had been concentrating so hard on speaking poorly. I had avoided saying tomato because it was always a dead giveaway. I said "tomato" with the "a" sounding like the "a" in "awe." "That could be because I have spent an awful lot of time in England." I was slipping into my English tea-party accent.

"Well, that would explain some of it." The one with braids laughed. "Not to say that the English necessarily speak the English language better than Canadians." She wrote something in a notebook. "Do you mind if I write certain things down?"

"Not at all."

The other one came back in. "The tea will just take a second. Tell us how you came to spend an awful lot of time in England."

This was difficult to explain. "All my mom's and grandma's family live there."

"What about your father's family?" the one with braids asked and jotted.

"Well, my father isn't my real dad. Mom didn't marry him until I was five or seven. I only found out that Dad has parents, this year. I met them for the first time in the winter. They weren't speaking, my dad and his family. They are now because Dad's mom has cancer. He has a son and daughter from his first marriage too." I hoped the tea would come soon.

"What about your real father, is he English?"

"I've never met him. I don't know what he is."

"When did you move to Canada?"

"I was just born in England. My mom went back there to have me. I spend months in England every year. I go with Grandma. My mother grew up in Egypt. She used to eat mangoes in the bathtub." I just threw that in because it was interesting. It was true. The one with braids stopped writing.

"Do you want to hear something funny?" I was handed my tea and sweets. "Thank you. When I was in grade three, in Canada, the school took me out of regular class for special speech classes because they thought I could not pronounce the letter 'r,' all because of my name being pronounced with a silent 'r.' They thought I couldn't say my own name! My dad was furious. He called the school and yelled at them. He said they'd paid a lot of money for my accent. I think he was talking about all the plane tickets to England. Anyway, the stupid speech therapist … oh … I mean … well, she couldn't even recognize that I had an accent, not a speech impediment."

They both roared with laughter.

I STEPPED OUT OF THE SHUFFLING LINE OF TOURISTS AND INTO RED SQUARE.

We had stayed up really late talking again. There was so much to discuss. I had had trouble waking up earlier this morning, which was unusual for me. I was normally the kid who was up at five in the morning and not just on Christmas morning. I also had the beginnings of a sore throat. Brother! Today was going to be an even more exciting day than yesterday, because today we were using the Soviet subway system, not a tour bus. We were at present walking to the Moscow metro station nearest our hotel.

"In the Soviet Union, they watch for children's talents early," Adrian told us. "If you show an ability in any area the Communist government will fund your efforts. You won't find children here having to quit skating or skiing because they can't afford to do it." What Adrian was talking about sounded wonderful. The Soviet government seemed very generous. "The people of the Soviet Union are its most important resource. That is why it is such a successful nation."

"Rhonda," I whispered. "Some ladies took me to their room yesterday, to listen to me speak, or something. They asked a lot of questions."

Kirsten Koza

"That's weird." Rhonda pulled me closer. "I think they're studying us."

We walked along the tree-lined boulevard. Adrian, of course, commented on the beautiful tree-lined boulevards. We had tree-lined boulevards at home too. He made it sound to Sonya like Canada was a concrete slum. Very irritating. Sonya was getting thoroughly the wrong impression about Canada.

"You are very lucky to live here," Mary said. She was always beside Sonya. Sonya was teaching Mary the complete Russian alphabet. Not just the funny-sounding letters. My name was something like КИРСТЕН and the USSR was СССР. They had all these backward letters and squares instead of o's and stuff. I couldn't even read a street sign.

"Alexi, please stay with us. Don't keep going off on your own," Chip begged.

We entered the subway. "Holy cow, Rhonda," I gasped. "This is more like an art gallery than a subway." My mom had made a coffee table once out of little tiles like this. It was called mosaic. The whole inside of the station was mosaic. Mom's old school friend's husband had made a coffee table too. His was out of old *Penthouse*s and *Playboy*s. He'd made a papier mâché collage of nude women and covered it with glass. Mom's table was better.

"You won't find graffiti on Soviet subway platforms," Adrian said. His beard had breakfast in it. "The Soviet people have great pride and love for the beauty of their subway stations."

I wished they did at home. There was this old train bridge near my house, at Boston Mills. There was always something dumb spray-painted on it about someone going with someone else or someone giving blowjobs. I hated graffiti. You even saw it on giant rocks when driving up north to go camping. I hated it more on the rocks than on the train bridge. It seemed so wrong to spray-paint *Bob loves Jennifer* on a piece of nature. Mom said people had spray-painted graffiti on Stonehenge the last time she was in England. Imagine that. Writing your name on Stonehenge. People bugged me.

Iggy could sing *Disco Duck* just like Donald Duck. He could make that noise out the side of his cheek. I tried to do it again. Adrian scowled at me. People really bugged me.

"Move back, please, everyone." Chip always said please. The subway train was pulling into the station. "Please, let everyone off the subway before you get on." Not many people got off. Everyone was probably at work already.

"Let's sit here." Rhonda plopped down on a backwards-facing seat.

"I can't." I couldn't sit backwards.

"Come on." Rhonda patted the spot next to hers.

"No, Rhonda, I can't sit that way. I have to face forwards. I get sick when I sit facing the wrong way." I found that out when my dad brought home this brand new station wagon. It had a third seat in the back that looked out the back door. That was where I wanted to sit. It was super neato. By the time we got to the top of the street, I knew it was a bad idea. I didn't get the sweet warning spit though, the spit that let me know I was about to puke. I just upchucked all over the new upholstery and carpet of Dad's brand new company car. Dad was really mad, really mad. Maybe if I had known that I was going to be sick I wouldn't have had a glass of Welch's purple grape juice before leaving the house. But you didn't plan vomit. He acted like I did it on purpose.

"Well, I'm sitting this way." She just didn't get it. I didn't fold to peer pressure. Mom was always lecturing me about "peer pressure." I sat across from Rhonda instead of beside her. We got off after just a few stops. I was having fun people-watching and was disappointed that the ride was so short.

"This one is even more impressive!" Rhonda was looking up. I followed her eyes up the gold arches.

"It's not like a subway at all," Dee Dee marvelled.

"I've never been on a subway before," Mary said. I thought she had been a little too excited, and now I knew why. She'd even stopped her Russian lessons. "We don't have subways in Halifax."

Dee Dee was at my ear. "Kirsten," she whispered. "Ask Little Karl if this is an example of communist decadence." I didn't even think. I just did it.

"Hey, Karl. I guess this is what you'd call communist decadence, huh?" I gave a really good smarty-pants look after the comment. Little Karl just ignored me. That was no fun. Adrian scowled at me again, this time a super scowl. The type that said "watch it."

We were in a red brick archway. The Kremlin. We were about to enter the Kremlin Walls! This was more thrilling than going to the Parliament Buildings in Ottawa, which wasn't really thrilling at all.

"More like the Krumblin Walls," Jay said. We all laughed. They were crumbly brick walls, all right.

"Can we talk when we go through?" Iggy asked.

"Of course you may talk." Chip looked surprised. "Whatever made you think you wouldn't be able to talk?"

"Adrian's face," Iggy replied honestly. "He has the church look that my Aunt Stephanie gets."

Inside the Kremlin were beautiful gold-plated onion towers. I lifted my camera.

"No pictures in the Kremlin." Sonya's hand came down on my camera. "You are going to be seeing very old art that was confiscated from the czars many years ago. Cameras destroy the paintings." We weren't even inside yet. I didn't think there were any paintings in the yard.

"That wasn't the real reason you weren't supposed to take the picture," Jay whispered like a conspirator. "Besides, flashes destroy art, not cameras. It's probably so you don't expose any secrets accidentally, or take photos of covert agents or Breshnev."

Inside made me think of King Henry the Eighth's palace in England. King Henry the Eighth's toilet had a red velvet seat. I touched it once. I touched where Henry the Eighth put his bum. There wasn't stuff like that here, though. Some paintings but not very many, and winding stairs. The Soviets didn't seem proud of their history like the British were in England. It was like they didn't want you to know about their old kings and queens or artists or composers. For some reason if you said names from Russia's past, you were treated like you were saying a swear word. It was scary. I didn't know what names were good names and what names were bad names.

I was happy when we left the musty old Krumblin. I snapped a few photos of St. Basil's Cathedral.

"Why can't we go in there?" I asked. The cathedral was exotic, like a Fabergé egg. The onion towers were all sorts of fancy colours and zigzags. I wanted to go up in an onion.

"Because we can't." Adrian gave one of those infuriating grown-up answers. Chip said something to Adrian that I couldn't catch and then boy oh boy he turned on her. He grabbed her arm and hauled her away from the group. It was vicious.

"That is repulsive. What a pig!" Dee Dee was furious.

"Chip might have said something to deserve it." Big Karl liked Adrian.

"Nothing 'said' deserves that." Dee Dee was steaming. "Why does she put up with him? She should dump him."

"It's none of our business." Alexi was looking at St. Basil's and not at our group leaders.

"Adrian just made it our business." Dee Dee's arms were crossed. I crossed mine too. All the girls were mad. It was the girls against the boys.

"Is Chip crying?" Rhonda didn't hide the fact that she was staring.

"No. I don't think so." Jay tilted his head. He did that a lot. "Cut it out," he commanded Sam, Iggy and Little Karl, who were playing bag tag around the ancient warrior statues in front of the cathedral. Iggy latched onto Sam's balls and Sam fell to the ground laughing and groaning. "CUT IT OUT, NOW!"

"Awww man, that hurt." Sam rolled on the pavement.

"Get up!" Dee Dee shouted. "And stop it. Just stop behaving like imbeciles."

Chip and Adrian came back over to us. I hated Adrian. I had a panic feeling. I felt like running. I wouldn't have minded a game of bag tag myself.

Adrian did the speaking. "We are going to continue walking around Red Square so we can get a closer look at Lenin's Mausoleum." Wild. That was where Lenin's dead body was on display. Cool. I hoped we'd get to see his dead body.

"Can we go see Lenin?" Jay asked.

"Not today," Chip answered. Her face was splotchy. "People

start lining up at 4:00 in the morning to see Lenin's body. We'll have to do that when we come back to Moscow after camp. We just don't have time to spend a day standing in line. But we will see him before we leave the country. I promise."

We continued walking round the square. "I wonder why people don't go through the middle," I said to Rhonda as I quickly took another photo of the cathedral, in case the first three had not turned out right.

"Yeah, it's dumb. Everyone is all crowded, walking around the outside of Red Square. Look at all that empty space. Bigger than a football field." Rhonda stopped too.

"We should just go through the middle." I didn't see why not.

"Yeah," Rhonda agreed. "It would be way quicker."

I stepped out of the shuffling line of tourists and Muscovites into the square. "Coming?"

"Yup." Rhonda followed. We were the only two walking through the massive square, which must have been half a mile wide. We got partway when a whistle blew and then another.

"Why are they blowing whistles?" I asked Rhonda.

"I dunno. Oh my God, RUN!"

"THE REDS!" I screamed. From three sides we saw soldiers and police running at us, yelling, blowing whistles. It left only one way for us to go, the long way, across the square. We ran for all we were worth. I was a shitty runner. Absolute, total crapolla, but boy, I was boogying now. The shouting continued behind us. We ran out of the square and across a road. We could hear more whistles now. We were in deep shit. "Keep going," I panted. "We're dead if we're caught." We bolted across a road towards a red brick building and made a right. We fled to the next road, crossed again and made a left. I didn't even have a stitch. I always got cramps from running.

"Keep going!" Rhonda looked back. I didn't dare. It was too scary being chased by the Russian army. We kept running. We turned corners again and again. We crossed a busy road and went down an alleyway. We turned again, again and again. Past the Bolshoi. We had seen that theatre on the tour-bus day but had not been allowed to go into it.

"Rhonda." I was panting. "Look back again. Tell me if you see any of them." I didn't hear whistles any more.

Rhonda looked. "I don't think so."

"Can we stop running yet?" I hoped she'd say yes.

"We better run just a little more."

So we did. We ran down three more streets until finally Rhonda stopped and put her hands on her knees. She was breathing really hard too.

"We lost 'em." I blew out a gust but it didn't help. A man was watching us. "Keep walking, Rhon. That guy is looking at us."

"Just a second." Rhonda clutched her side. "Okay, we'll just keep walking." She looked around quickly. "That way." She pointed down another street. We went. I was glad I was wearing my North Stars and not my sandals.

"I have a wicked cramp." Rhonda was rubbing below her ribs.

"Why'd they come after us like that?" It was terrifying.

Rhonda checked behind us. "We're not being followed." She stopped, took my hand and pulled me flat against a wall beside her. "I don't think we were supposed to go through the middle of Red Square."

"We broke the law, didn't we?" This was really bad. I leaned back on the stone building. "There should have been signs or something. I mean, how should we know?"

"We better move." Rhonda pulled me from our resting place.

"Where should we go?" I couldn't even figure out exactly what direction Red Square was in, any more.

Rhonda put her hands on her hips and thought for a second. "I don't know which way is which."

"Okay," I exhaled. "The Bolshoi Theatre was back over there somewhere, right? And so we should keep going this way for a bit."

We walked for another ten minutes.

"So, what should we do?" I asked. It was super scary. I hoped Rhonda had a good idea.

"We should go back to the hotel."

"Yeah. That's good, Rhonda. Um, how do we get to the hotel?"

"Shit. Shit. I don't know. Do you have any idea where we are?"

"Not really." Well, that was an understatement. "Um, if the

Bolshoi is back that way that means that that Pushkin place was that way." I pointed in the opposite direction. I had got in a stupid argument with Little Karl yesterday in some small park that might have been Pushkin Park, or it might have been the statue that was Pushkin. I didn't know. Little Karl had said that I liked Trotsky. He made it sound awful.

"Maybe we should ask someone." Rhonda looked around. "Someone nice-looking though. There." Rhonda pointed to an old man. We went over to him. "Excuse me." Ronda said it very politely. The man pointed to himself with an enquiring look. "*Da.*" Rhonda said. Rhonda then pointed to us and said, "Hotel, um hotel." She looked at me. "What is the name of our hotel?"

"Uh oh. Rhonda ... I don't know. I have no idea." This was not good. The man was looking very confused.

"It doesn't matter." Rhonda smiled and shook her head "no." "Don't worry about it." She waved at him. "Bye, bye." Rhonda pulled me away. "Holy fuck. We don't even know the name of the place where we're staying. What should we do?"

"The subway," I said. "We try and find the subway and then we just have to go three stops and then for sure we will be able to find the hotel."

"Okay. Good. Let's ask someone."

I looked around. "How do you say subway in Russian?"

"Shit if I know."

"Maybe someone will know English." We continued walking. Every person we passed we smiled at and said "subway?" to. No one spoke English. No one in Moscow spoke English. Some people just kept going. Some people stopped and wanted to help but it was impossible to mime subway. We kept walking. My feet were starting to hurt like they did that time I did the walk-a-thon. "Rhonda?" I had such a bad feeling. "Rhonda, we're lost."

"Absolutely," she agreed.

"What should we do?"

Rhonda stopped. "This may be risky but I think we have to get back to Red Square. It's our only hope."

"Will we be arrested?"

"Maybe, but maybe they won't notice us. If we can find the

Kremlin, then we can find the subway." It seemed to be the only way. We started to retrace our steps.

"I know." I'd come up with a good one now. "We'll ask for directions to the Bolshoi."

"Yes!" Rhonda clapped her hands. "Yes!"

We walked. The buildings were old-looking. We came to a spacious boulevard. "You know what?"

"What?" Rhonda asked

"I think we are going in the wrong direction because the boulevard rings run around the city, right, and we didn't cross one when we were running."

"I wish I'd paid attention on the bus tour. Is our hotel across the river?"

"I think so." I was starting to fear that Rhonda knew less than I did.

"Let's turn around then." Rhonda was looking across the wide boulevard. The cars were moving fast. "We definitely did not cross one of these."

We went back the way we had come.

"I'm incredibly thirsty." Rhonda fished in her purse for kopeks. "Do you want to split a pop with me?" Rhonda went up to the machine and put her coins in.

"Rhonda, stop." I grabbed her arm. "Look!" I was astounded.

"Wow!" Rhonda's pop spilled down onto the ledge that should have held a glass.

"I guess we are not the only criminals in Moscow."

"It might have just got broken." Rhonda looked for signs of crushed glass. "Or maybe stolen."

"Let's keep going." My feet were killing in a big way. I was sure I had a blister and I just wanted to get on that subway train and sit down.

A woman was clucking at Rhonda and shaking her head. She pointed to the fact there was no glass. The woman thought it was dreadful.

"Bolshoi?" I said to her and pointed back and forth to indicate I didn't know the direction. "Bolshoi?" I repeated.

The woman clutched her heart. "Bolshoi," she said and shook her head sadly.

"What does she think I said?" I made a "whoops" face to Rhonda.

"Bolshoi?" Rhonda said it, as if it would make a difference that she said it.

The woman shook her fist at the heavens. "Bolshoi!" She signalled us to follow.

"Oh no." I tugged Rhonda's belt loop and pulled her over to me. "She might not be bringing us to where we want her to bring us to."

"She seems nice, though." Rhonda was right about that.

The woman was really old, probably in her seventies, which was older than my grandma. She was yattering on in Russian to us even though it was obvious we didn't speak a word. Every now and then I caught "Bolshoi." She obviously was not talking about a theatre. That was not how people talked about theatres. At home if someone talked about the Royal Alex it would have been all lovely this and lovely that. This was different, this was like someone talking about a lost or dead friend, or a person who had made them angry. I didn't get it. We were not going to the right place. The way she clutched her heart was odd. We were going to a cemetery. I felt it. I knew it. I was wrong.

"Bolshoi!" She pointed down the street. She said it again with scorn. She wouldn't go any further but I could see it in the distance.

We thanked her. She waved her hands as if to say she had done her duty and she was glad it was over, but it wasn't that she didn't like us.

"Wait," I called to her. She stopped. I fished in my purse. I'd give her something nice. I pulled out my favourite Canadian pin, a beaver, and gave it to her. She kissed me and walked away.

"Now where?" Rhonda was facing the direction of the Bolshoi and I watched the woman vanish in the opposite direction.

"Um, I think we must be really close now. We could just ask someone else for Lenin maybe. Or St. Basil's or even the Kremlin. I don't know." I didn't know. I was so glad that I was not alone. "I think if we walk down to the theatre we'll get a better idea." We jogged. We came around the side of the theatre. "There! The subway is there!" What a relief.

"Let's go." Rhonda was looking side to side. She could have
been in a movie. She made me think of Peggy Lipton from the
Mod Squad. I had mini Barbies that I used to play *Mod Squad* with.
I had a black man Barbie called Van. I had a white man, a black
man and a chick with long blonde hair. They were my *Mod Squad.*
I wasn't playing with them any more, not since I got Big Jim and
his sports camper last Christmas. Rhonda and I headed down the
steps into the subway. Big Jim had a karate-chop arm. My friend
Trisha had big-breasted Barbie and her pink girlie camper. We'd
take Big Jim and Barbie camping down at the creek that ran
through my parents' property. Big Jim would shoot the rapids in
his boat. I'd tie him in so I wouldn't lose him. He had a dirt bike
too. After he was done his sports, he'd return to the campsite and
would have sex with Barbie. I wished Big Jim had a penis. I had to
draw one on for him. We drew pubic hair on Barbie too. I had got
pubic hair now. Quite a bit but not boobs. I would have to say I
was more like a Flatsy doll than a Barbie. The Joey Stivic doll,
which was Meathead's and Gloria's baby, had a penis. I tried to
look in the box to see it when we were shopping for my sister's
birthday. I didn't know anyone who had that doll.

"This is going to be easy now." Rhonda was putting
Chapstick on.

"Yeah." The subway train was approaching down the tunnel. I
felt my ears go. "Do you ever feel like you are always in trouble?"

"No."

"Oh." That ended that. "Are you still scared?"

"I don't know."

"I'm not so scared of the Red Army any more but I'm starting to get scared of Adrian now," I said.

Rhonda was yanking me onto the train. I looked down to
make sure I wouldn't fall in the crack and then hopped on. "He's
going to kill us, Kirsten." Rhonda was pulling me towards a
backwards-facing seat.

"I'll stand." She sat and I stood. "What should we say?" I
always liked to have the story straight when you were dealing
with two or more culprits. If it was just me on my own, I'd wing
it, but you could never trust other people not to make a mistake
when lying.

"I think we should just say that we got so scared that we ran and then we got lost." What was she talking about?

"But that's the truth." The truth was never good enough in situations like this. "He is going to freak about us going through the square in the first place. We have to come up with a reason for going through the square, Rhonda."

"We didn't know that you couldn't." But that was the truth too. Was she stupid or something?

"That's one." I was counting stations. "We missed lunch."

"At least one good thing came out of it." We both laughed.

"Yeah, that was a *good* thing for sure. Maybe if we're really lucky, we'll miss dinner too."

"What do you think we missed?"

I didn't even have to think. "Fish-scale stew and cabbage pudding."

Rhonda was snorting. "There," she spluttered, "are fat people," she could barely get it out, "in Russia. Why?"

"My mom would love this place. She wouldn't have to go on the Masturbation Diet anymore."

"The what?" Rhonda howled.

"Oh, that can't be right. You have to chew a lot. It was invented by The Great Masturbator, in the olden days. No that can't be it ... the word is pretty close. You have to chew every mouthful until everything is like juice in your mouth." My mom was always on a diet. She never ate. She wasn't fat at all, either. My mom was beautiful, the most beautiful mom in my class by far but my mom thought everyone else's moms were better-looking.

"Iggy is losing weight, eh?" Rhonda was sure right about that. It was noticeable already.

"I heard Adrian say to Chip that Iggy has dangerously bad diarrhoea too." I whispered that but then realized it didn't matter because no one spoke English anyway.

"Two." Rhonda had to move over as someone sat down beside her.

"Next one is us!" I was starting to feel a lot better.

Rhonda made the stinky sign to me by quickly pressing her nostrils together with her fingers. She then quickly glanced at the man who had sat beside her.

I'd save her. "Why don't we go stand by the door, now, Rhon, so we can get off first?"

"Good idea!" She was quick to get that. "Oh, my God, Kirsten," she whispered. "I don't think Russians wear antiperspirant."

I remembered the "gomme" guy back at Grey Square. "I think you are right. This has to be the capital of BO. Hey, this is our stop." The doors opened. "This isn't it." I stopped Rhonda from getting off the train.

"How do you know?" She was pulling.

"Because it doesn't look like my mom's coffee table."

"What?"

"The station near our hotel is turquoise mosaic. Maybe it's the fourth stop."

"The doors are going to close!" Rhonda looked scared.

"Stay on and we'll go one more!"

"Are you sure about the coffee table?"

"Yes." I was definite about that.

"Okay." Rhonda sounded uncertain. "But what if the next one doesn't look like your mom's coffee table?"

"It will. It has to." I was more hopeful than certain, really. I tried willing it to look like Mom's coffee table. I tried using all my telekinetic powers. I didn't actually have any yet but someday I would figure out how to use them. I was sure that I had them. We humans only used a tiny percentage of our brains. It was in that other percent that ESP and telekinesis lived.

"What are you doing?"

"Nothing."

"Is your stomach okay?"

"Yeah." This seemed to be a really long ride this time between stations. That was a good sign. I was sure it was a long ride between the first two this morning.

"What do we do if this isn't the one, just say, what if?" Rhonda was bugging me. That kind of thinking might wreck the work I had been doing on willing it to be the one.

"Then, um, I know, maybe we got on going the wrong direction."

"The train is slowing. This is it!" We were pulling into number four. "This isn't it." Rhonda stepped away from the opening door and flung herself down on an empty seat. "Are you sure about the coffee table?"

"Yes! Don't you remember? We said the station looked like an art gallery."

"An art gallery isn't the same as a coffee table."

"I know that. It was mosaic tiles, Rhonda. Just believe me, it was mosaic. We talked about there being no graffiti and stuff. Remember?" She shrugged. "You don't remember? Adrian talked about how proud the Soviet people are about their subways. Remember? Mary had never been on a subway until this morning. Remember?" What was wrong with her? She just wasn't that smart. I liked her but she wasn't that smart.

"We *are* going to miss dinner." She looked at her watch. There was a huge difference in time between Toronto and Russia. We weren't always even on the same day.

"Rhonda, I think we are just going in the wrong direction. If this isn't it we will get out and cross to the other platform and then just count back in the other direction. No problemo."

"We're coming to number five." Rhonda got up again. "Cross your fingers." Rhonda punched her thigh.

"Let's get off anyway." My stomach felt like a toilet flushing. The doors opened. We got off. The doors closed. The train pulled away. We watched.

"So we go five, four, three, two, one and then one, two, three the other way."

"Yup." We crossed over to the other side. The train was already coming.

We were pulling into a station. It was much more crowded again on the train. We had given up our seats so we could see out the windows. We kept near the doors. "Shit." Why hadn't I noticed before? "Shit!"

"What?" Rhonda was squished right into me.

"Station number one is wrong. It's not gold. The station we got out at this morning was gold."

"Maybe we counted wrong."

"No. I don't think we got on at the right station in the first place." This was getting worse. We were entirely lost. No one spoke English. We didn't even know the name of our hotel.

"Let's get off." Rhonda pushed towards the opening door.

"Let's just stay on for one more. I mean, this subway stop is right by the Bolshoi. The one this morning was closer to the Kremlin."

Rhonda put her face in her hands.

"People are staring at us."

"I hate it." Rhonda was looking at the ground.

"Why are they staring so much?" It was creepy.

"Maybe because we're wearing blue jeans."

"I don't like being stared at." Normally I liked being the centre of attention. I liked being on stage except in piano recitals. This past year I had to play "Nicholas & Alexandra's Theme" for an audience. I wasn't ready. I was bad. When I bowed at the end I saw that the audience was feeling sorry for me.

"It's gold! It's gold!" Rhonda was doing the *Locomotion*. I joined in. It was great. We went two stops, then the train started to head deeper down.

"We are going under the river!" Under the river? "We went over the river this morning." There was dripping water and algae on the tunnel walls, just like when going under the Thames. This was wrong. "Let's get off. We have to go back to the gold station."

We returned to the gold station and got off the train. "Rhonda, Rhonda, oh my God, look. There is another set of platforms."

"But which way?" Rhonda slapped her forehead.

"Flip a kopek." That sounded neat. So we let Lenin's head decide which way to go.

The platform was jam-packed with people. "Push," Rhonda commanded. "We have got to get on." We squirmed and wormed our way onto the crammed carriage.

"BO," I said to Rhonda.

"Yeah, man. Russia really needs to Ban the BO with a little

roll-on." I liked Rhonda's giggle. I'd copy it when I got home. Make it my own.

"Rhonda, have you noticed how everyone has gold teeth?"

"I know. That woman over there does and she is probably just twenty. It's so ugly. Why would they get gold teeth?"

"No wonder Dee Dee wants a toothbrush and is terrified that she will have to go to a dentist over here. Could you imagine if Dee Dee was given a gold front tooth?"

"Adrian says it's free to go to the dentist here." Rhonda ran her tongue over her front teeth. "He said we can all go at camp."

"Why would we want to go to a dentist? I'm not going to a Russian dentist, even if it's free. No way." I stumbled as the train went around the bend. I hated not being able to reach the hand holds. I always had this problem. I wished the man beside me couldn't reach the hand holds either. Then his stinky armpit wouldn't have been in my face.

"We're going over the river, Kirsten."

"Yes!" Next stop and we'd know. "Please be turquoise mosaic. Turquoise is my favourite colour. Please be turquoise mosaic. Turquoise is my favourite colour," I chanted. The train was across the river now. Any second we'd know. Any second. It kept going. Soon, soon. It was slowing. Braking hard. Blue. Blue. Blurred blue tiles. Slowing. Mosaic. Yes. Yes. Yes.

"COME ON!" Rhonda pulled my purse right off my shoulder. It fell to the ground, its contents spilling.

"Oh my God! Wait." I bent over. People were filing off around me. "Rhonda, my stuff!" Rhonda was off the train and on the platform. Suddenly the smelly armpit man and the gold-toothed woman were down beside me. Helping me. Grabbing my things and shoving them into my shoulder bag. The doors were closing. A man with a beard like Grizzly Adams put his foot in the door. There was shouting. You could hear the conductor. I didn't understand him but I knew what he was saying. It was "stand clear of the doors, please," but in Russian. The doors opened again. Grizzly Adams blocked them with his boot again. The train made a hissing noise. There was another announcement. I had everything and they were pushing me, escorting me to the door. The two men pulled the doors. It took all their strength but they managed to open the doors just wide enough for me to fit through. I was on the platform beside Rhonda. The train was pulling away. I didn't even get to say thank you. I was shaking.

"My stuff, Rhonda, it was all over."

"Let's get out of here."

"I almost didn't get off the train!" I zipped my purse shut. We headed to the stairs. She didn't say sorry or anything. She had left me on the carriage.

We walked into the lobby of our hotel. Adrian was standing at the front desk. "GO TO YOUR ROOM NOW!" I knew we'd be in trouble.

Rhonda's bottom lip was quivering, blubbering. I wasn't sure if it was real or she was putting it on. She needed to stop ripping at the skin on her lip. "But—"

"NO BUTS! GO!" Adrian was red and purple and violent-looking.

"It wasn't our fault," Rhonda tried to explain. "We were so lost. Please, Adrian, we're hungry. Can we get something to eat?"

"You missed lunch and you missed dinner. Just go to your room." Adrian said something to the person at the front desk. They picked up the phone.

"Let's go," I pleaded with Rhonda. So we went back to the room and had Crunchie Bars for dinner. My throat was getting super duper sore. Rhonda's was too. Chip didn't come back to the room until at least 1:00 in the morning. I could see her sneaking around because there was a moon.

"Chip," I whispered, because Rhonda was sleeping. "Chip, we didn't mean to get lost."

"You weren't the only ones who got lost."

"Oh. Who else did?" It hurt my throat to whisper.

"Adrian and I did too."

"Did you get lost looking for us?"

"No. We didn't even know you were lost. We just thought we were lost."

"But you didn't break the law and weren't chased by soldiers." Chip and Adrian must have been mad at us for that anyway.

"No. The soldiers just chased you but that is because you were further out in the square than we were."

"You went into the square too?"

"Well, we saw you and Rhonda doing it. Some of the time I believe you can go through the middle. I know I have seen pictures with people in the middle of Red Square."

"Wow, Chip."

"We ran in the opposite direction from you two girls."

"Rhonda and I didn't know the name of the hotel. We couldn't ask for help because we didn't even know where we were staying."

"Well, we knew the hotel's called The Little Eagle, but only in English, so that didn't help at all. And you are not quite as bad as Adrian and I because we have been lost twice now. We did it again tonight."

I lay there thinking. What a day. What would I say in my diary? I'd write it in the morning.

SHE WAS SHOVING THE THING DOWN THE BACK OF MY THROAT.

It was the day of the Children's Festival. Children from all over the world were going to be there in celebration of Year of the Child. I looked at my invitation. My name was printed in English and in Russian. I was still lying in bed. So was Rhonda. We were supposed to be getting up for breakfast.

"Rhon?" My voice did not sound like my voice at all.

"Yes," she whispered back.

"I'm sick."

"Me too." And to prove her point, she blew her nose.

"My throat is killing. It's tonsillitis." I'd had it so many times. I knew.

"I can't go today." Rhonda rolled over in bed and faced the wall.

"Get ready, girls." Chip, the morning person, bounced out of the bathroom.

"Chip." My voice was enough.

"Oh, my goodness, sweetheart." She came over and put her hand on my forehead. "You are burning up!"

"I don't feel well, either," Rhonda croaked. Her voice didn't sound as bad as mine. Hers sounded more like a cold. Mine was beyond cold.

"I'll go see what we can do." Chip went to the door and stopped. "We'll bring breakfast back to you." I didn't care about breakfast. I went back to sleep.

It felt like seconds and Chip was back. She had tea and bread. "Girls?" She said quietly, "Girls, you should drink some tea." She put the tea on the table where the mineral water had been. "There is a nurse in the hotel. You are both to go and see her after you have eaten. She's in the basement. I'm so sorry no one can stay with you today. It's sad you are going to miss the Festival but Adrian and I feel you should stay." Like we wanted to go. The thought of walking all day again was not a happy one. Chip left.

"Rhon." I got out of bed and got my tea. Something hot on my throat would feel good. "Rhon, I don't want to go see a nurse in the basement."

"Let's not bother." Rhonda was still lying on her top bunk, facing the wall.

"Okay." I took my tea back to bed. There was a knock at the door.

"You get it." Rhonda didn't move as she said it. So I went.

There was a woman standing there. I'd never seen her before. "You come now to see nurse. You come now." She put her hands on her jumbo hips. She stood in the door.

"We're in our pyjamas." I pointed to my lack of clothes.

"You come now."

"Rhonda?" I needed help.

Rhonda was sitting up. "I don't want to go."

"You come now!" The woman stepped into the room. She looked mean.

I grabbed my jeans and put them on over my night clothes. I wasn't going to mess with this woman. She had the look that said she'd carry you if you refused. I zipped my Adidas jacket over my pyjama top. It made me think of the time I accidentally wore my pyjamas to school. How or why I forgot to take off my pyjamas before putting on my clothes that morning, was a mystery, but when we changed for gym class that afternoon, there I was standing in my pyjamas. I took off my clothes and there were my pyjamas. "Rhonda, hurry up." I put my North Stars on. They killed my heel so I pulled them off and looked for my sandals. The woman made an impatient noise. I put the North Stars back on.

We followed her to the elevator, her bum was huge, and then down, down, to the basement. When we got off, we followed her down a hall. The lighting was dim and everything was cement. We came to a door that led to stairs. We went down the flight of stairs and came out in another dark hall. There was a short queue leading to an office. The woman left us in the line.

"We'll go together." Rhonda wiped snot on her sleeve. She'd left her Kleenex in the room.

I nodded. "Yeah, I'm going with you. I'm not going in there alone."

"I wish a translator was here." She wiped more snot. I hadn't thought of that. We should have asked for Nadia.

"They probably went to the festival with the others." I didn't want to talk any more. It hurt too much. Being up made me feel worse too. I wondered what was wrong with the other people in the line. They were all Russian teenagers and we were the only foreigners.

There were two nurses wearing white. They were nasty-looking like in *One Flew over the Cuckoo's Nest*. It was hard to know what do, what to say to them. They spoke in Russian to us. We spoke in English back. They started to examine us.

My nurse came at me with the most massive Popsicle stick I'd ever seen. "*Otkroitye rot.*" She pushed it against my lips. "*Vysuntye yazyk.*" It was more like a paddle than a tongue depressor. She went over to the metal desk and dipped a big cotton swab on a stick in this brown bottle. The swab came out looking wet and rusty. "*Otkroitye rot,*" she said again. I opened my mouth wide, figuring she wanted to take another look. Next thing she was shoving the thing down the back of my throat. She wiped it all around the back of my throat. I was gagging. I was choking. What the hell was she doing? I had never heard of or seen this in my entire life. I had had a million sore throats and never had my doctor done this. Stupid nurse. Stupid bully nurse. I hated her. Rhonda was drowning. She was coughing. Then they waved us to go. We went back out into the hall.

"What was that?" I was frowning. I was furious.

"Bitches!" Rhonda was angry too.

"Where's big butt?" The lineup in the hall had grown.

"Gone, thank Gawd. Let's go back to the room." Rhonda marched back to the stairs.

"I want to find out what they did." I followed Rhonda. I marched louder. I slammed my feet onto the concrete, trying to make an angry noise. It wasn't too successful in running shoes but I wanted the dumb Russians to know that I was angry and that *that* was not good medicine. All I needed was some antibiotics. Penicillin didn't work too well on me any more. I probably just needed a week's prescription of amoxicillin. My mouth tasted awful.

"Iodine." Nadia was sitting on the end of my bed. "They swabbed your throats with iodine." Nadia had left the festival early to come back and see how we were. She was great. I loved Nadia.

"Isn't it poisonous?" I was sure you couldn't drink antiseptic.

"It will make you better." Nadia stroked my head. "It will kill the bad germs in your throat that are making you sick."

"We've never heard of anyone doing this." Rhonda was still upset.

We'd talked about nothing else for the three hours that we had been back in the room. We were sure we were going to die. We had washed our mouths out and gargled with mineral water as soon as we had got back, to get rid of the rust stuff, which now we knew was iodine. At home no one even used iodine on cuts any more. People used Dettol, Neosporin or hydrogen peroxide for wounds. I fell off my bike last summer and it was really bad. I was going extremely fast down this freshly graded hill to keep up with my mom and Trisha. Their tires were larger than mine so they went faster. My bike hit a pile of new gravel and I went out of control. My monkey-bar handlebars went back and forth and back and forth very fast. The next thing I was sliding along the gravel road. I slid for more than twenty feet. The top came off my thumb and it was just hanging and the inside of my left knee was a bloody mess with stones sticking out of it. You could see fat and maybe even bone through the flesh. We were in the middle of nowhere, just a little country side road. I had to walk home dragging my bike. I wouldn't have been able to ride even if my bike had still worked. Mom wouldn't let me leave it. It was expensive, the coolest bike on my street, a three speed. We had to walk over two miles. I was screaming. When we got back I had to go sit in the neighbour's bathtub. We just had a shower stall in our house. Both my mom and our neighbour Mrs. Bunting were nurses, though Mom wasn't working any more. I sat there in salty water to loosen the stones and dirt from my flesh. Mom poured hydrogen peroxide over my damaged thumb. It bubbled like nuts when it hit my blood and I screamed some more. I still had the scars. The one on my knee was huge.

"Are you girls hungry?" Nadia was nice to have come back.

"Not really," Rhonda answered. It wasn't true. We had just talked about how hungry we were. We just didn't think we could face more Russian food right now. Apparently Chip and Adrian were going to go shopping to get Iggy some vegetables. That was what Dee Dee had said this morning before she left for the festival. Chip and Adrian were really worried about Iggy. We had not been served green vegetables or fruit once since arriving in Moscow.

"What about for good food? Something really good. And you can have ice cream after also. Better ice cream than what you have had here at the hotel." What was Nadia talking about? "It will mean going for a little walk, though. Do you think you are up to it?"

"Yes, please, Nadia." I swung my legs back out of bed. I had to eat. I wanted cold ice cream on my raunchy throat so badly.

Rhonda got down from her bunk. "Is it a far walk?"

"Not far at all." Nadia's smile was beautiful. Her face was wide. Her eyes were wide-spaced and brown like her hair. Brown like milk chocolate. Milk chocolate. I loved milk chocolate, way more than the bitter dark kind.

We stood with Nadia beside a street vendor. The smell was hopeful. The vendor had a cart like the Good Humur man had at home for his Popsicles, but this vendor's cart was an oven instead of a freezer.

"Here you go." Nadia was handing me something. "It's a meat patty. You are going to like this."

"Thank you." It had pastry on the outside like a meat pie. It came wrapped in paper. You needed to keep the paper on it because it was too hot to hold otherwise. I pulled the paper back, blew and then bit. Mmmmm. It was kind of like a knish.

"Thanks." Rhonda had hers. She was watching me, the chicken, to see if I liked it.

"Nadia, this is fantastic!" It was heaven. Pastry had to be one of my favourite things in the world. This was the first meat we had had on our trip too. I liked meat. Nadia was eating one too.

"Shall we go and sit on a bench?" We followed Nadia over to a green park bench.

"Nadia, why is your English so good? You don't have an accent at all." I pulled a piece of paper out of my mouth which I accidentally had eaten with a bite of pie. I couldn't stand chewing on paper.

"Thank you. We train very hard and spend many years learning."

"You speak English like we do, though, like a Canadian."

"Yes. That is what I have been trained to do."

"Have you ever been to Canada?" Rhonda had finished her meat patty already.

"No, but I have been to America. My parents live in Florida."

"Really?" I had another nibble. "Do you go and see them often?"

Nadia looked sad. She sat for a moment looking at her feet. "No. It is not that easy to travel. You have to get permission from the government and that is difficult. I don't think I'll ever be allowed to go back to the United States again."

"Do they come here and visit?" Rhonda was distressed by this too.

"Oh no! My parents cannot come back to the Soviet Union." Nadia clapped her hands. "Look. Here comes the ice cream. I knew he could not be far away." Another vendor was headed our way. Nadia jumped up and started over to him. Now I knew how come Nadia had jeans, not that they were great jeans; they were no-name and too light blue and not light from fading. I now knew why Nadia's clothes were way better than Sonya's. She had probably bought them in the US. She had Florida jeans.

"Rhonda, why don't you think her parents are allowed to come back to the Soviet Union?"

"I doubt that is what she really means. I think she means that if they did, they wouldn't be *allowed* to return to the States. She didn't say they are not allowed to come back here, she said they *cannot* come here."

"That is so sad. I can't imagine not ever being able to see my parents again." I got up. "That stinks!"

"Yeah, really stinks!" Rhonda followed.

"Nadia," she handed me a cone, "how much do we owe you?"

"Oh no, no, no. This is, as you say, my treat or on me."

"Thank you very much." Rhonda smiled at Nadia and took a bite. She didn't wait and watch me this time. Too bad it tasted good.

I wanted to ask Nadia if they only had vanilla in the Soviet Union but I didn't want to sound ungrateful or like I was complaining. I'd have to ask another time. Some time when she hadn't just bought me an ice cream. I was so sorry for Nadia. I just didn't get it. I had never heard of people not being able to travel. You just got a passport and went whenever you wanted. How could a country stop you from going away on a holiday? Why would they? How could they keep you from visiting your family abroad, or keep people prisoner who were returning just to visit? I had never heard of anything like this in my life. It was mysterious. Maybe Rhonda was wrong about Nadia's parents returning. The Soviets couldn't stop them from going back to the States, not if they were now Americans. Could they? Why would they, anyway? No, it was just plain silly.

I loved my ice cream. My mom once made me really mad over ice cream. A pile of my friends were over swimming in my pool. We were having a diving-board competition, diving through my huge tractor-tire inner tube. Sherry Taggart dove through and scraped her belly on the metal thing the air goes through when you fill the tire. She had this eight-inch red scratch right down her stomach. She cried really hard and my mom took her up to the house for an ice-cream cone. Mom didn't give the rest of us ice cream, just Sherry. So we all tried hurting ourselves as well. Mom got mad. Sherry just sat there licking and looking at us. She wasn't that badly hurt. She stopped crying as soon as she had the ice cream in her hand. Sherry had an ugly bikini. Mom could have given the rest of us cones too. The ice-cream tub was full.

When we got back to our hotel room we heard a commotion coming from the common area on our floor. There were animal-like screams and crashing sounds.

"Come on." Rhonda grabbed me and we ran towards the noise.

"Huh." I stopped in my tracks. A chair flew between Rhonda and me. What was Sam doing? He'd gone mental. He picked up a lime green easy chair. He was so little and he picked this huge thing up and hurled it. He swore. He went for another chair. Alexi grabbed my shoulders and pulled me out of the way. The armchair rolled by us.

"What's going on?" Rhonda gasped.

"No one knows. Chip tried to talk to him. She was really good. But Sam's crazy." Alexi pulled Rhonda and me to a safer distance.

Adrian flew into the common space. Sam had just thrown a small table at the television.

"Adrian. I can't calm him." Chip was on the floor. She was near tears. Sam grabbed another end table.

Adrian wrapped his arms and legs around Sam and they tumbled to the floor. "Sssshhhh." Adrian couldn't say anything else as Sam's foot struck his mouth.

Dee Dee was beside Alexi, Rhonda and me. "What's he doing? What happened?"

"Nothing." Iggy was terrified. "Everything was fine. It really was. I don't know. He just lost it. I didn't do anything. I really didn't."

"Everyone get out of here." Adrian was pinning Sam. Sam was wriggling, red in the face, screaming, but he was tiring.

"Please just go to your rooms." Chip was off the floor. "Please, we'll deal with this." Chip turned back to the wrestling match on the floor.

THE KIDS FROM THE USA
ARE SEX MANIACS.

It was our fourth day in the Soviet Union and our last day, for now, in Moscow. Today we would be taking a bus to the airport and then flying to Sochi. Then we would have another bus ride, a long one, to camp. *The Soviet Union*, I wrote in my diary, *is the largest country in the world. It is so big that on one side of the Soviet Union when the people are going to bed, way over on the other side they are just getting up.* I put my pen down.

"We should finish this." I held up the mineral water and pop the hotel supplied. The pop looked like a wine bottle. It had pictures of grapes on it. My throat was killing. Sore throats were always worse in the morning.

"Save some pop for me." Rhonda was packing her suitcase. There was screaming and running feet in the hall. "What now?" Rhonda stopped packing and rushed to the door, opened it and stuck her head out. Water went flying past. "Shit!" Rhonda ducked back in. "It's a water fight between our boys and the American girls."

"Let me see." I peeked out carefully. An American girl with brown hair and big tits was jumping up and down. Her white

T-shirt was soaked. You could see her big tits clearly. Jay had just soaked her. She was giggling.

"That's the Sex Maniac," Rhonda whispered to me. "Dee Dee said that girl has had sex hundreds of times."

"Real sex?"

"Ye-ah, like all the way." Rhonda's head was over mine, peeking out the door.

"She's too young." I was shocked.

"She's thirteen like me." Rhonda's chin kept hitting the top of my head.

"Move!" Dee Dee pushed in our door. "Guess what I heard? The Sex Maniac has been to reform school."

"Why would the Americans send reform-school kids to represent their country?" I'd heard everything now.

"Their trip was paid for by the Boys and Girls Clubs of America. God, it was already cheap to come here because the Soviets have paid for everything except our plane tickets and these people couldn't even afford that! Jay said the Sex Maniac killed a horse on purpose." Dee Dee had stolen our spot at the door.

Killed a horse!?!? Jay knew this and was flirting with her anyway? "Why's Jay hanging out with her, then?"

"You can't be that dumb." Dee Dee made a stunned face at me and then pulled her shirt out at the chest in two points.

"They're ugly. Her tits look deformed." I didn't get why those big bongo bazombas would make Jay want to have a water fight with her. The Sex Maniac reminded me of Paula Hopper in my class. Paula had huge tits by grade four. Huge. She was just nine. It was weird. She was evil too. And a sex fiend. At least this American girl had a pretty face. Paula Hopper was hideous. Paula had declared one recess in grade five that she was going to beat me up. For some reason all the rest of the girls in my class went along with her, like I deserved it. Even my friend Tara. I had never done anything to Paula. I pretty much kept away from her because she had a wicked temper and you never knew when it was going to fly. It was Sherry Taggart who protected me in the end. She stood by me when no one else would. Sherry was a good person. She was also big. I would have to try to be nicer to her. It was not her fault she was a Taggart.

"Yuck. He just wants to feel her up. It's making me sick." Rhonda went back to her packing.

"But she killed a horse and he knows it. She's a murderer!" I had lost something for Jay now. He had lowered himself in my books. He wasn't cute any more.

"The guys think it's cool." Dee Dee was still watching the business in the hall. "Apparently the Sex Maniac got so drunk on the plane coming over that she actually started doing a striptease at the front. She told our guys that she got her shirt off before she was forced to sit down. Oh, oh, and the snobby girl over there is Dr. Spock's granddaughter."

"Spock?" I loved *Star Trek*. I looked at the snobby girl. "My mom loves Vulcans."

"Not that Spock," Dee Dee roared. "The baby doctor guy."

"I'm glad the Americans are going to the other camp." I was.

"Artek," Rhonda said.

"Not even the *Arctic* would be far enough for my liking." Dee Dee opened the door to let Mary and Oksana in.

"Gross." Oksana sat in a chair. "Hurry up and let's go downstairs. I can't listen to this any longer."

"Hopefully Adrian will come back up." Mary was not impressed, either. "You can't even get down the hall."

"They're not going to get us. They probably won't even notice us if we pass," Dee Dee smiled. "Look. Clean teeth. Adrian and Chip bought me a toothbrush yesterday. They said it wasn't easy to find one."

"We think it's second-hand." Oksana curled her lip.

"Shut up," Dee Dee shuddered.

"What? You said it first. The bristles are yellow." Oksana was starting to laugh. "And bent. They look like some kind of animal hair."

"Shut up!" Dee Dee ran her fingers through her hair. "If my luggage doesn't turn up before we leave for camp, I am going to freak!"

"How are you two feeling today?" Mary was nice to ask.

"Much better." Rhonda was speaking for herself. My throat

was still awful. And I didn't feel good in general. Maybe better than yesterday but not much better.

"It's really too bad you missed the festival. You would not have believed all the people in the march. It looked like something you'd only see in a movie. We don't have enough people in Canada to ever make a rally or march look that spectacular. Do you know there are something like 245 million people living in the Soviet Union? Two hundred and forty-five million!"

Dee Dee made faces to Oksana while Mary was talking. It was rude. I'd seen her make faces when Chip talked too.

"Let's go down now." Dee Dee opened the door.

"Do you think it is safe?" Rhonda locked her suitcase. I hadn't bothered folding my stuff, so it had taken me no time at all to pack. I just balled everything in. Mom would have flipped. We had spent so long at home organizing my bags and making everything neat.

"Let's just go for it." Oksana stuck her head out. "We'll go fast."

The water fight was still in progress. Big Karl, Jay and Alexi were running around. The Sex Maniac was standing behind a chair in the common area. The orange and green vinyl chairs had been put back in their places. The TV looked unharmed. There was never anything on it worth watching. The news, which was all I ever noticed playing, was apparently all propaganda too. That's what Jay had said. The Soviets had no freedom of the press. Their government told the news broadcasters what to say.

"See, they didn't even notice us," Dee Dee said as we reached the elevator. Iggy and Sam arrived there too. "I guess we're not interesting enough."

"You mean built enough." Rhonda's boobs were pretty flat too. Actually none of us had big tits.

"Did you get your vegetables?" Mary asked Iggy.

"A cabbage." It was the first time I had seen Iggy embarrassed.

"They bought you a cabbage?" Dee Dee whined.

"You are supposed to just eat a cabbage?" Rhonda wrinkled her nose.

"What are you going to do with it?" Dee Dee pushed the down button.

"I'm supposed to eat it. They said it was all they could get."

"Iggy, you are telling me that in all of Moscow all Chip and Adrian could find was one lousy cabbage? You need to find the Colonel to whip it into a slaw for you." She was talking about Colonel Sanders of Kentucky Fried Chicken. The coleslaw at Kentucky Fried was weird. It was bright green. No cabbage I'd ever seen was that colour. Dad said it was radioactive. He still always ordered it, though.

"I think my cabbage was really hard for them to get. I'm just eating it raw." Iggy was super flushed now. "My stomach doesn't feel too good, though. But they say I have to eat it."

"Your mother would die." Dee Dee was right about that. You could tell Iggy's mom was a good cook. He probably had fresh butter tarts every day. And whole milk, not two percent or homo either, the stuff with the cream. Mmmm. Iggy's stomach made a big noise. It didn't sound healthy. He flushed more.

"My God, what are they doing to you?" Dee Dee stared at poor Iggy, who went redder. I was glad it wasn't me. "You are losing weight too, Iggy."

"I know, but that isn't so bad." He showed us his belt. "Three days. Three notches." He grinned. "I wouldn't mind some pancakes for breakfast, though. What do you think the chances are of sour-dough pancakes, with butter, blueberries and real maple syrup?"

"We are more likely to find that Brezhnev is having breakfast with us." Dee Dee said this and we all laughed. Brezhnev was the Soviet President.

The only part of Russian breakfasts that I was managing to eat was the nasty brown bread. It came in a big round loaf and you had to tear chunks off it. They didn't give you a knife. I put the yucky brown paste they told us was jam on my chunk.

"How did you sleep last night, Jay?" Little Karl was sipping his tea and looking very casual. Way too casual. Something was suspicious.

"Oh, I just lay there listening to the gentle breathing of my friend and to the friendly gossip of two Russian men outside."

I could not believe what I was hearing. Had I heard Jay right? Everyone was laughing, even the girls. Oh, I had heard him. They all knew!

"Ha!" Little Karl slapped his knee and stamped his foot. "Ha, ha ha!" Those bastards had gotten my diary and read it. Why wasn't Adrian saying anything? Adrian just ate. So did Chip.

"She thinks she is some kind of writer." Jay was snickering at me. "The gentle breathing." He said it stupid, with a stupid frilly voice.

"And the friendly gossip." Little Karl imitated Jay's frilly voice to try to be cool. There was nothing cool about Little Karl. The worst part was that I had written that Jay was cute. They'd all know that I thought Jay was cute and now as of this morning I had changed my mind about that, anyway. I didn't like Jay any more, since the Sex Maniac.

My throat hurt worse than ever, as if I had eaten pink fibreglass. I was prickling on the inside, even the inside of my arms. When we moved to Cheltenham when I was five, Patty Gluck and her family came over to welcome us. Patty was just four then. Patty and I went outside to play beside the barn. We played house. We pretended we were squirrels. There was all this fluffy pink stuff. We used it to make our beds for our house. Patty had to pee. She said it would make good toilet paper too. So she peed and wiped her wee wee with the fluffy pink stuff. By the time Patty left to go home I was feeling itchy all over, especially my hands. When Patty's parents got back to their house they called us because Patty was crying. Dad came out with me to the barn to see where we had been playing. He saw the pink stuff and said, "Oh my God. Fibreglass!" Now I figure he was kind of laughing then, but he did a good job of looking upset. I'd never touched fibreglass since.

We had a police escort. More than one. Their sirens blared and they drove like crazies. So did our bus behind them. Important delegates we were. Very important. On our way to the airport and then to camp on the Black Sea. I hoped it wasn't too black. I wasn't sitting with Rhonda. I had the sneaking suspicion that the only way Jay could have got my diary was somehow with her assistance. I hadn't said anything to her. I wasn't sure how to. She hadn't looked at me at breakfast. She was acting guilty. I shouldn't have said "gentle breathing of my friend." I should have said "ignorant snoring." I sat alone.

"Do you think we could speak to someone at the airport about our luggage before our plane leaves for camp?" The others had lost hope but Dee Dee was still pushing for her bags.

"I am afraid we won't have time." Chip made a sad face to Dee Dee. Dee Dee made a pissed-off face and looked out the window. The bus swerved and honked its horn. We were allowed to go through traffic lights without stopping. The police just waved us through. I'd never felt so important.

We left Moscow for farm fields. "No single individual owns land in the Soviet Union. Farms are all Collective or State. The produce from both goes to the State," Adrian said. He always had that tone as if to say the Soviet way was better. These farms didn't look like farms in Canada. Canadian farms were much prettier.

"Is that why there aren't any farmhouses?" I asked. The farmhouses near where I lived were all beautiful. They were mostly brick with gingerbread white trim and long tree-lined drives. My friends who lived on farms were lucky. The farms near me were almost all dairy and horse. The best kind.

"Yes." You could tell Adrian enjoyed my interest. He loved talking about the Soviet system. "We will be briefly stopping at a collective on the way to the airport."

"But then where do the people live?" I didn't know why I was talking to Adrian.

"The people live in communities, in buildings that they call flats. They don't own houses here. They pay rent which is not more than four or five percent of their wages. You will see an example when we stop. It means everyone in the Soviet Union can afford housing. No person here is homeless and there is no unemployment. There is a job for everyone in the Soviet Union!"

"But, Adrian, who are they paying rent to if no one is allowed to own anything? Someone must own the flats."

"Man, she doesn't know anything." Little Karl rolled his eyes at me.

"You know what, Darwin? Just because Dad's a PhD, just because he teaches Karl Marx at university, it doesn't make you an expert. When you get home, you are going to pick up the *Communist Manifesto* and actually read it, rather than pretending to read it," Big Karl scolded. He'd never done that before. It was nice even if it was odd.

"There are no landlords in the Soviet Union," Adrian continued. "Landlords only take advantage of tenants, you see, Kirsten. Soviet citizens pay a very small amount. It's similar to rent but it's paid to the government."

We were pulling into a community now. It looked like a slum. It was exactly like government housing in Canada, only worse. No one in Canada wanted to live in government housing, anyway. And no one wanted government housing built near them, either. Here we were in the middle of the countryside with the worst kind of city apartments possible. There were three sets of "flats." They called them flats in England too. These were not high-rises like Canadian apartment buildings. They were low like British ones, just five storeys. But they didn't have the character of British flats. These flats surrounded a paved parking lot with no cars or lines to mark where cars should park. Adrian called it a courtyard. This was not country life. This was the worst of city life and the worst of country life all put together.

Adrian ordered us off the bus, and kept going on and on about how wonderful the collective system was. Maybe everyone sharing was a nice thing. It meant that no one in the Soviet Union would go hungry. Or if they did, they'd all do it together. But I couldn't imagine living like this, no pool, no yard, no swings.

Adrian. How come, if this is such a great way to farm, how come we haven't had any fresh vegetables yet? Well, I wanted to ask that but I had the feeling that *that* would get me in trouble. Still, here it was the middle of the summer and we had not seen a fresh vegetable or fruit at any of our meals. I liked carrot sticks. I didn't know why we were getting off the bus, either, as there was nothing to see. Flat countryside with flats. I didn't see workers in the fields. I didn't see any sign of farming except for an empty tractor parked in the middle of nowhere. Just flat fields and ugly flats.

"They must get fresh vegetables on the collective." Iggy was dying to ditch his cabbage. "Maybe we could buy something here?"

"Oh no, Iggy. That is the wonderful thing about collectives. They are not allowed to sell anything themselves. It all goes to the State and the State gets first pick and decides where to send everything. The leftover cash, after the village maintenance and improvements, is divided among the members of the collective, the kolkhoz."

"I guess, Iggy, that means not even farmers get fresh vegetables in the Soviet Union." Dee Dee poked Iggy like he was the Pillsbury Dough Boy.

"What it means is that it is equal and fair," Adrian stated.

"If anyone needs to use the toilet, there is one in the central building." Sonya pointed to a hut in the middle of the "courtyard." I still felt it was a parking lot without cars. After all the pop and mineral water we had finished in the rooms that morning, a toilet break sounded like a good idea.

"Last one there is a rotten egg." Sam called it and had started running before he had even said it. We all paused for an uncomfortable second.

"First one there gets to eat it!" Iggy shouted after him. I was glad that Iggy did that. No one ran except Sam. Sam ran into the hut and then right back out. He kept running right back to the bus.

"What a weirdo." Rhonda was beside me. I couldn't decide whether to talk to her or not. Ignoring her, I figured, would be the wise thing to do.

"Oh, gross!" Dee Dee didn't even walk in the door of the hut.

I couldn't imagine anything could be worse than what we had already experienced as far as Soviet toilets went.

"There is only one for boys and girls. It's a 'collective' or 'communal' can, I guess," Dee Dee said as she walked back past us to the bus. "You don't want to go in there, either." She crossed her eyes.

"Stop being so ridiculous. You are all spoilt and rude." Adrian went in. The door to the hut kept swinging open and closed in the breeze. The smell that wafted out was unbearable. Adrian exited. He had the look of Moses parting the seas, just like Charlton Heston. Actually I liked Yul Brynner better so now I always stopped watching *The Ten Commandments* when Ramses died. Besides which, when Moses left Egypt and grew his beard and started wearing long robes, he wasn't worth watching.

Alexi pushed the door open. "Aw man!" He walked away.

"Rhonda, I have to see this." This was getting intriguing. Not even the boys were going in there and Sam had run away.

Rhonda pushed the door open. "I can't see anything." Rhonda was pinching her nose. I put my hand over my nose and mouth and made gas-mask breathing noises. It certainly was dark. There wasn't even a window. The parking lot pavement was all there was for floor. There was a hole in the middle of the paved room. There weren't even foot pads in this one. There were poops on the pavement and far away from the hole, really far. People weren't even trying to hit the hole.

"Rhonda, I can taste it!" I backed out. I was gagging. I made throw-up noises. They were for real. Rhonda was laughing. She was screaming and laughing.

"GET ON THE BUS NOW!" Adrian was furious. He was always furious.

We were on the plane on the runway. This was the first time in my life that I felt fear of flying. This was not like international Aeroflot planes. This was dangerous!

"Rhonda, I don't think my parents would want me to fly on this plane."

"It doesn't have real engines." Rhonda said. She and I were at the wing seats.

"It's prehistoric! It might as well be a Flintstones plane."

"Yeah, Pterodactyl Airways. Flap, flap." Rhonda flapped.

"Have you ever been on a prop plane?"

"No way! Have you?"

"Are you kidding?"

Men outside were inspecting the propellers. Then they stepped back and signalled the pilot. There was spluttering. The propellers were trying to turn on the one side. The other side was still doing nothing. "Oh my God." I sat back. I couldn't watch.

A Russian woman sat on the aisle seat with a bag of groceries. She was probably flying her shopping back from Moscow to the farm it had originally come from. I could see a cabbage crawling out the top of her string bag. Who'd fly a cabbage anywhere? And why? Was Iggy still lugging around his cabbage? I couldn't tighten my seatbelt. And the last person who had used it weighed fifty-seven tonnes.

"These seats hurt." Rhonda was shifting from side to side.

"Yeah, it's like sitting on the toilet."

"How old do you think this plane is?"

"Ancient. You see them get out of planes like this in old movies, like *Casablanca* and stuff." I'd seen millions of movies. I went with my parents to the drive-in. I saw movies that I shouldn't see that way. My folks would hide me under a blanket in the back seat so the ticket sellers in the booth wouldn't see me and stop us from entering because I was too young, not that the ticket sellers would have cared. My parents always let me watch the first feature but then I was supposed to sleep for the second. I could never sleep during a movie or with the TV going. I had to watch. I stayed up the whole time. The only film my parents didn't let me see so far was *Jaws*. I was mad about that. I would sometimes pretend to be Jaws, the shark, in the pool to scare my friends. "Du da ... Du da ... Du da da da du da." We were going down the runway.

"Don't sing that. It's creepy." Rhonda slapped me for doing the *Jaws* theme. It was very noisy and bumpy. I hoped I was going to get to see more movies in my life. Better *that* at this point than having a movie made about me. *A-e-ra-port, The Soviet Disaster Movie.* I wasn't used to takeoffs like this. Rhonda and I held hands. We squeezed.

"My ears!" Rhonda plugged her ears.

"Don't plug them." I had to shout, the noise was deafening. "That is the worst thing you can do. Your eardrums might explode if you don't let them pressurize right." My ears were hurting too. Bad.

"I've never had this going up before."

"Me neither." Having to shout like this was insane. "Yawn!" I yelled and forced a huge yawn. It didn't help so I did it again.

"Look." Rhonda pointed to Little Karl in the row beside us. He was crying. I smiled. It wasn't nice of me. My ear popped. I couldn't hear Rhonda at all now.

The stewardess came by, handing out paper bags. Great. I thought it was for us to puke in until I was handed one myself and found it to contain something already. I looked in the bag. It was lunch.

"This is lunch?" Rhonda hollered.

"Yeah, in a bag! No silverware or anything hot to eat." We shrugged at each other. At least there wasn't any caviar. The sandwich looked pretty okay. It smelled okay too, some sort of salami.

Adrian was talking to Little Karl. Little Karl was still bawling. Big Karl was behind Adrian. He looked worried.

"What's wrong?" Rhonda called out to Big Karl.

"His ears are sensitive because he's sick. I don't think this cabin is fully pressurized, either." Big Karl was definitely upset. He loved his brother.

"He should chew a piece of gum. I have some still." Rhonda went rooting through her purse.

"If you have some, you can give it to me," Adrian called. Wow, I was amazed. Adrian was going to be nice. He held his hand out and took the gum, then scrunched up the package. "Thank you." He put the package in his pocket. "I'll dispose of this later." He didn't give any to Little Karl. Instead, he instructed Little Karl just to keep swallowing. I wondered how much Big Karl still liked Adrian.

"It's just because he has a cold," Adrian shouted at Big Karl. Big Karl nodded.

"God, he can't even admit that this plane sucks." Rhonda was sitting with her arms folded. She was fuming.

We couldn't talk, it was too difficult to hear, so we gave up. Rhonda read her book. I was scared that reading would just make me sick, so I looked out the window. We went over plains first and then brown, rolling hills. I guessed it was badlands and then came the mountains. I'd never seen mountains this way before. My forehead got sore from pressing on the window. It didn't stop me, though. It was kind of like when you got an infected hangnail and squeezed it even though it hurt, or nibbled a canker sore in your mouth. I kept pressing my forehead on the window.

The bus ride had been long and terrifying. It was hard to say if the plane or the bus was worse. The bus made me feel sicker. We had to go on treacherous mountain roads to get to camp from Sochi. There were palm trees in Sochi. Like the tropics. Oh yeah and we had cabbage borscht at this outdoor restaurant. It was the second-best meal so far; the best was the bagged lunch on the flight to Sochi, which was seriously good. The toilets at the restaurant were holes in a *dirt* floor. Anyhow, the bus ride to camp was awful. The buses stuck out over huge drop-offs when going around the corners up the mountains. They went way too fast. I was exhausted by the time we arrived. We were now waiting in a lineup in a big hall. It was probably a gym. There were all these different tables we had to go to. The camp people were inspecting us. I just wanted to be given our room and allowed to go to bed. We were like the cattle at my friend Squirrel's farm being paraded through the corrals at milking time. Being a cow would not be a good life. The medical people had listened to my heartbeat and me breathing. Now they were looking at my throat. My throat was getting better. There was some discussion going on. Now I was being led to a different lineup. My friends were going one way and I was being made to go to another.

"Chip!" I shouted. "Chip! Why can't I go with you!? Why am I over here!?"

Chip pulled out of her line and came over. A translator spoke to Chip halfway. It wasn't one of our translators. Chip came all the way over.

"It is because you are sick, Kirsten. You have to go to the camp hospital with these children."

"Well, Little Karl is sick too. And so is Rhonda!" I wondered why the hell it was just me going to the hospital. I wanted to be with our group. "Why do they get to stay over there? Why just me?"

"They aren't as sick, I guess, as you are." Chip was patting me.

"But Chip, I am feeling so much better." I was feeling better. The worst was over. I didn't have a fever any more or anything. It was just the dregs now. I knew that. Mom would have been ready to send me back to school about now. I wouldn't even be contagious any more. "I am practically back to normal." I tried to look as healthy and energized as possible. "I was sick a couple days ago but I am better now."

"Let me talk to someone." Chip looked lost. I could see it. She felt bad for me. She walked away.

"Chip, don't go! Don't leave me." She disappeared from view. My special line was being moved along. Doctors looked in ears, squeezed under the arms and under the ears and around the throat. I kept searching the crowd for Chip. Shit. Adrian was coming over.

"Kirsten, we are leaving now. You will be fine. We'll come see you. Don't worry." He squished out a comforting smile.

"But Adrian, I am so much better."

"Then you will be out of the sanitorium in no time."

Sanitorium? Did I hear that right? What the hell was going on? That sounded like where you'd send crazies. "Adrian, I don't want to go! I want to stay with you guys."

"You can't. Chip will visit you soon. Maybe tomorrow."

"No one speaks English!"

"You'll be fine." My line was moving away. Adrian put his hands in his pockets and rocked back and forth on his toes. I wished he didn't have that dumb beard and moustache. I couldn't tell what he was thinking.

There were two other girls in my room in the camp hospital. One was Russian and the other I couldn't figure out. It seemed so weird that we didn't say country names the same way people from that country did. Some of them you could figure out, like Italia was Italy. But the French said Angleterre for England and if you didn't know, I didn't think you could figure it out. And Deutschland sounded more like Dutch than Germany. And Holland was Nederland. Well, this girl, I just couldn't figure out. I didn't think she knew where I was from, either. Not even my Canadian flag T-shirt seemed to help. This sucked. It was going to be very lonely. It was nighttime and we were supposed to turn out the lights. A nurse came in with medicine for me. I could have used it a couple of days ago. I hoped it was just antibiotics. I took it even though I didn't know what it was. I pulled out my diary and a red marker. I'd write in red today. I'd make it sound "jolly" like Enid Blyton. I didn't feel jolly, though. I couldn't write what I really felt. I really felt like crying. I had that stupid pre-tears lump in my throat. I wanted to be with the others. I wrote. *Today we first went on a plane then on a bus to the camp. They did a check-up to see if we were healthy. Well, here I am with a couple of girls in the San.* It sounded cheerful. It sounded like maybe some others from Canada were with me, or at least someone I knew. It made me feel better. It was a lie.

No. No. I feel fine.
I am healthy. I am just great.

It was morning. I was sitting on the hospital bed (which I had made, even) in my jeans and one of my nice shirts. It was shiny brown with pictures of city scenes on it. My shoes were on and I was ready to go. I felt fine. The nurse was in a flap and had gone to get another nurse. Now they were both in flaps. They wanted me to put my night clothes back on. I wanted to leave. I was packed. My suitcase was on the end of the bed. Another lady came in. She had obviously been sent for from further away.

"What is your name, little girl?" The lady had Princess Leia fancy-braids.

"Kirsten, and I want to go join my group now!"

"Well, Kirsten, a doctor will have to come and see you before we can let you go." Okay. That made sense. I'd wait for a doctor. I was reasonable. "In the meantime the nurses would like you to return to your pyjamas and go have breakfast with the other children in the meal hall." Hold on a minute. They wanted me to put on my stupid yellow baby dolls and go out in public. Baby dolls were great for the hot weather. They had a sleeveless, frilly, short top, which stopped just around the belly button, and then the bottoms were these big, baggy, frilly panties, like a baby would wear over diapers.

"I can't." I wasn't going to put on my baby dolls and walk around anywhere. Besides which, if the Russians thought I was sick enough to be in hospital, then I was too sick to get up for public meals!

"You must, Kirstyonushka. You have to wear your pyjamas until doctor says otherwise."

The other girls in my room were watching me. The nurses said something to them and they put on their housecoats and left, I guessed for breakfast. They were lucky they had robes with them.

"I want to see a doctor." This was just stupid. I wasn't sick any more. I felt fine.

"The doctor will come and see you after you have breakfast. Now remove clothes and dress in pyjamas."

"No. No, I am not putting on my pyjamas to go and eat. If you want me to go and eat somewhere, I will go like this."

"All the children in hospital eat their meals in meal hall in pyjamas." The interpreter was trying. Her English was not as good as Nadia's or Sonya's but it was good still. I sat on the bed. I wasn't budging. There was just no way. My baby dolls were not designed for co-ed public viewings. They were for sleeping.

"In hospitals in Canada, meals are served to the patients on trays in their rooms."

"Oh, I see. You are confused because we do different here." She smiled and said something to the nurses who smiled and nodded. They thought it was a gap in communication. The real problem was the gap between my stupid frilly panties and my stupid frilly top. "Put your pyjamas back on. It is hospital rules. Come eat your breakfast with the other children."

"I'm not hungry. I'll wait for the doctor."

"Are you not feeling well?" She came over and put her hand on my forehead. This was not going how I wanted it to go at all.

"No. No. I feel fine. I am healthy. I am just great. Look." I leapt off the narrow bed and did a few jumping jacks.

"Well, come eat one meal in your pyjamas with the other children and then if you are well the doctor will send you back to rest of your group after she see you this morning." She tapped my suitcase.

This was a nightmare. A nightmare in reality, in the morning. I opened my bag. I wasn't going to get my own way. I was going to have to do this, but then if I did I'd probably get to leave sooner. I pulled out my baby dolls. Mom had packed them in part because they would take up less space and in part because they would be cool in the tropical weather of the Black Sea and in part because she thought they looked "so adorable" on me. The nurses and the interpreter stayed while I changed. I didn't have slippers so I kept my North Stars on my feet. I was a sight. I followed the nurses and the interpreter down the corridor to the meal hall. The hall was full. There were about twenty long tables filled with children eating their breakfast. I was late. They all watched me enter. Entering in my baby dolls. I had to cross the whole hall. The table I sat at had four boys and five girls, all Russian. Breakfast was put in front of me. It sort of looked like porridge. I liked porridge if you put enough brown sugar on it. I had a spoonful of this and I thought I was going to throw up. It tasted like a mound of topsoil in my mouth. I was eating dirt.

"Kasha," the interpreter said and smiled and pointed at the bowl of porridge.

"I can't eat this." It was literally dirt, like eating black, Holland Marsh topsoil.

"Oh dear. Do you feel that sick?"

"No. I am not sick. I feel fine."

She smiled. "Then eat your breakfast, darling."

I had another mouthful. No way. This was not going to go down. I might as well have been eating out of my grandma's compost. I put my spoon down. The interpreter walked away. She went over to some food-hall woman and pointed at me. Maybe I was going to get something else. Something better. Something I could swallow. The food-hall woman left the room. The other children ate. Some of them even finished and left. I sat there. Finally the interpreter and a nurse came back.

"You may come back to your room now." I followed them back to the room. They directed me to get into bed and wait for the doctor so I did that. They left. The Russian girl was in her bed already. The girl from who knows where was gone. Finally the interpreter came back with the doctor and a nurse.

The doctor said something in Russian and the translator translated. "I am told you did not eat your breakfast. Are you feeling sick to your stomach?"

"No. I feel fine. I feel great. I just don't like kasha."

The doctor came over to me and said, "*Otkroitye rot, vysuntye yazyk.*" I stuck out my tongue to show her how great my throat was now. She made a *hmmm* noise and wrote on her chart. The nurse produced a thermometer. I opened my mouth.

"Roll over," the translator translated.

"No." Oh my God, they weren't going to give me a thermometer in my mouth—they wanted to stick it up my bum like a baby.

"The doctor needs to take your temperature."

"Then she can do it under my tongue." There was a three-way discussion in Russian.

"We do not give children a thermometer to put under their tongue in case they bite glass."

"I won't bite the thermometer." This was outrageous!

"If you want to join rest of your group, the doctor needs to take your temperature this way, otherwise we cannot let you leave the hospital."

They had me trapped. I hated them all. I rolled over. My frilly bloomers were pulled down. The thermometer was freezing. I lay there in full view with a thermometer sticking out of my bum. The Russian girl was looking at me. I heard people in the hall. People came in and out of the room. I hated the girl staring at me. I put my face down in the pillow. Maybe I'd suffocate and die. Normally I did not want to die; right now, though, it would have been better that way, better to die. Several minutes went by. It was quiet now. When was the nurse going to come back and read my temperature, which was going to be normal after all this, anyway? I was fine. I waited. This was going on too long. I waited. They must have forgotten about me. Jeepers creepers! They forgot they were taking my temperature. I peeked at the Russian girl. She was reading now, not looking at me any more. I wondered if I should try to get her to find someone. I didn't want to talk to her, though, not with something sticking out of my bare bum. Maybe I should yell. I'd yell. I couldn't yell. I didn't want all those people to come running in and see me. How could they have forgotten me like this? How could they have left me like this? I heard the sound of a teenage boy. He was saying something to the Russian girl. Why weren't there curtains around these beds? I sunk my face deeper into the pillow. God, was this boy standing there looking at my bum? He said "bye" in Russian. She said "bye" back. I could hear my heart in my ears, the sound of my blood. My bum was burning. Burning with embarrassment. I bet it was red. Hot and red.

"How are you doing, Kirsten?" It was the voice of the translator. How could she ask that?

"Ummmm. I think they could take my temperature now."

"Oh yes. You have been like this for long time!" She left. Good. She was going to get a nurse. I waited. I wondered if I could push the thermometer out with my bum hole muscles; I could say it just fell out finally because they had left me so long. There were footsteps again. I didn't want to look in case it was that teenage boy. The thermometer was yanked out without warning. I pulled up my bloomers. No one even apologized. I must have been like that for fifteen minutes and no one even apologized. The nurse left the room. I rolled over onto my back and pulled up the sheet. Maybe they would let me go now. I'd get dressed. I looked for my suitcase. I looked under the bed. Weird. I looked all over the room. My bags were gone!

The nurse, doctor and translator came back into the room.

"My suitcase and carry-on have been stolen!"

The translator shook her head "no" and grinned. "It hasn't been stolen. It has been put away."

"Well, I'd like it back. I can go now, right?"

The translator spoke to the doctor. The doctor spoke to the translator. The translator translated. "Take these pills." The nurse gave me some pills and a little sip of water. Not even a Dixie cup of water, more like the size of a coffee creamer. "You are not better yet. Maybe you can go tomorrow."

"But I *am* better. I was sick before but I am better now." What did they think was wrong with me? "It was tonsillitis but now it's gone." There was more discussion.

"The doctor says you must stay for treatment."

"Treatment for what?"

"For your illness."

"But I don't have an illness." There was more discussion. The doctor left.

"A nurse will come in afternoon to take you for your treatment. It will make you better. When you are better you will be able to join your group." The translator and the nurse left. Brother! I jumped out of bed and ran after them.

"Excuse me!" I shouted down the hall. "I would like my bags back, please. I would like to be able to at least read, or write in my diary ... please."

The translator and the nurse had words. "You must promise not to get dressed again until a doctor tells you that you may." I didn't like her smile any more.

My suitcases arrived just before lunch, along with a different nurse and different coloured pills. I wondered what they were treating me for. I hoped that Chip or even Adrian would come and see me. I sure felt fine. The Russian girl in the next bed kept trying to talk to me. She was fifteen. I didn't like her. I drew pictographs to try to communicate with her. My drawings were pretty good, but she still didn't understand. She went over to my suitcase and opened it. Holy rudeness, Batman. She pulled out my shiny brown shirt that I had been wearing earlier. She pointed at the shirt and then she pointed at herself.

"No," I said. "*Nyet.*" She wanted my shirt! I hardly had any clothes with me. I was a very generous person normally. "No!"

She was pleading with me. I had to make up a story. I drew a picture of my grandma, an old woman carrying a roast turkey. Not that Gram would make a turkey, she hated turkey. Then I drew a picture of a present wrapped with a bow. Then I drew an arrow to show what was inside the present. I drew a picture of my shirt. Then I drew a picture of a birthday cake with eleven candles. The girl didn't get it. It wasn't the truth, anyway. Mom had bought it and a similar one in pink with bicycles on it for me from Zellers. The shirts didn't mean anything, but I just didn't have enough clothes with me to give anything away. I couldn't explain that. I thought the gift from my grandmother would have been easier to draw. The Russian girl got dressed. I gave her a Canadian pin. She wasn't pleased.

After lunch, which was soup and I ate some of it, and bread and tea, which I liked, I strolled back to my room. I was glad I would be by myself. I wasn't. There was an Oriental girl in the bed that had been occupied by the girl whose country I never knew. There were Oriental and Russian people all around her. She was very, very sick. She was moaning and covered in sweat. I slunk into bed and watched surreptitiously. People ran in and out of the room. The Oriental people rolled the girl over onto her stomach and pulled up her shirt, exposing her back. A woman pounded up and down the girl's back with her fingers. Then a nurse came rushing in with a tray of upside-down glass jars. They put something on the girl's back and then put the glass jar over it. What the hell was this? Was this a "treatment"? The girl was crying and moaning. She was sicker than I had seen anybody be in my life. My doctor ran in and said something and ran back out. This was scary. What were they doing to this girl? Maybe she had some sort of tropical disease. She was lying there now with eight jars upside down over something that they put on her back.

The translator came in. "Kirsten, you are to be moved to a different room."

"Okay." I jumped out of bed. I put everything back into my bags, grabbed my luggage and followed the translator down the hall to another room. This room had ten beds in it and none of them had patients. Yeah! I was alone. "What is wrong with that girl?"

"She is very sick."

"Where is she from?"

"Vietnam."

That was where the war was. It was on the news when I was younger, all the time. We had learned about the war when I was in grade three from Mr. Darlington, my teacher. Mr. Darlington had a handlebar moustache. I gave him moustache wax for Christmas. He told us that the war was over communism. It had meant nothing to me then. I knew nothing about communism back then. It was just a word. Now I knew more. Now I would like to learn more about the Vietnam War.

"What were they doing to her?"

"Making her better." I had never before met people who did not answer your questions like these people from the Soviet Union.

I guessed that girl from Vietnam would not have been from the side of Vietnam that the Americans were helping. She would have been from the North. Wow. For sure. I had been in a room with a Viet Cong girl.

I was following a nurse. I didn't know why. The translator was not there. I wished I had asked the translator her name so that I could have asked for her when I needed to know something. We had gone down three flights of stairs. When we passed people, they stared at me. I figured I was the first model of baby doll pyjamas to appear in the Soviet Union. This would be my last pair. We stopped outside a room with a big metal door. The nurse signalled me to wait. I wasn't alone in the hall. There was a kid in a wheelchair. That would be awful. I tried not to stare but then I felt that I was ignoring him, that I was obviously not looking. How could you act natural around people in wheelchairs? I didn't know what to do. If I looked it would look like I was staring and if I didn't look it would look like I thought him unbearable to look at. I looked at the floor, then the ceiling, then I glanced at him and he saw me so I smiled. Oh, no! I didn't want to do that. I smiled a sympathy smile. Like, I felt sorry for him. I wanted it to be a friendly, hello, everything is normal smile and it came out like kind of a grimace smile, like "ooooo poor you." I looked away. Thank goodness, here came someone from the room. A nurse was leading a little girl away and a nurse with a moustache brought me into the room. I hadn't seen any men working in this hospital yet, except for the guy I saw cleaning the bathrooms upstairs. Nope. Wrong. There was a man in the room. The nurse was leading me to a dentist's chair in the middle of the room. Shit, no! Not a dentist! They both were wearing huge heavy aprons. The man was positioning this thing that kind of looked like the things that doctors used to look into your ears, but this was attached to a machine. He was positioning this thing so the nozzle part was resting on the left side of my neck, well, throat. The nurse was patting my hand. What was going on here? She motioned me to stay, then they both left. I was sitting there all by myself in this big room, in a dentist's chair, with this thing on my throat. Where was Chip? Where was Adrian? Where was Nadia? Why hadn't they been to see me? This must be "the treatment." I didn't feel anything. Nothing. I could hear the machine, though. It was doing something. The nozzle wasn't making a noise. It was just over my skin. I thought there was a light at the end of it. My eyes hurt trying to look down without moving my head. There was nothing in the room to look at. The floor was concrete. The room was grey. Then the machine made a click. It was off. It was over? Yes, the man who must have been a doctor, not a dentist, and the nurse, were coming back into the room. He moved the thing away from my throat and the nurse gave me a slip of paper with a time and tomorrow's date on it. I took it and left. The boy in the wheelchair was being pushed into the room. I didn't know where I was. There was no one in the hall. I waited. Maybe my first nurse, the one who brought me here, would come back and get me. I touched my throat where the machine did its stuff to me. It didn't feel any different. It was all too weird. My doctor at home, Dr. McCurdy, had never done stuff like this to me for a simple sore throat or for anything else. Never. Just antibiotics, vitamin C, lots of liquids and bedrest. Maybe I had got some strange Russian throat infection. But that was a couple of days ago. I was not sick any more. I'd have known if I was sick. No one was coming for me so I wandered back towards where I had come from. I was terrible at remembering where I came from, or the way back to places, more terrible inside than outside. Red Square was nothing. I didn't know what floor my room was on, or where the stairs were. I wandered. People stared.

I didn't eat breakfast again. It was kasha again. I didn't eat kasha. It was right up there with liver. I was sitting in my big empty room by myself, waiting for the doctor to come and say I could join the others, when the translator came in with a boy. He had blond hair, wide-spaced eyes and high cheekbones. I thought he was either Ukrainian or Great Russian. I was starting to be able to tell what part of the Soviet Union people were from. There were over one hundred different ethnic groups in the Soviet Union. Some even looked almost Chinese but not like the girl in my old room.

"Good morning, Kirstyonushka. I have brought you a visitor. His name is Misha."

"Hi Misha." I wanted to ask the translator her name, but now that she was acting like she knew me so well it seemed weird for me not to know her name. Misha was definitely a hunk.

"Misha was hoping that you would tell him about Canada, where you live." Misha sat in a chair at the foot of my bed. He said something in Russian to the translator. His voice was very deep. He was older than I first thought.

"Okay. It is very beautiful where I live. We have a piece of property with a stream running through it." The translator started translating as I spoke. I made my eyes shine. I could do that on purpose. Like Judy Garland or Shirley Temple, whom I played in a school play once. "We have all these wild rabbits on our property. They are so tame that you can feed them with your hands." Now, that wasn't true. I didn't know why I said it. There were no rabbits and for certain no warrens of rabbits where I lived. There was a stream on our property at home. The rest was right out of the Enid Blyton *Famous Five* series. It was a description of George's island in England. Blimey! I was even speaking with an English accent. Sometimes I thought I was possessed.

"Misha says that sounds fantastic." Fantastic was a good word. Fantasy would have been better. I was mad at myself. "He would like to know what you do in Canada for amusement."

"I swim in our pool, play the piano, ride my bike, read, take my dog for walks. My dog is very smart. She can do lots of things. She never chases the rabbits. She loves to eat ice-cream cones." Brother, what was I saying? Yes, I swam, read, biked, and played the piano but Coolit was not a smart dog and she had never had an ice-cream cone. That was Timmy, George's dog in the *Famous Five*. And Coolit would definitely chase rabbits. It was probably why you'd never see a rabbit on our property.

A nurse and my doctor came into the room. They'd better not try to take my temperature in front of Misha. The doctor said something to the translator, who said something to Misha.

"Misha will come back and visit you later, Kirsten." I waved to Misha. He waved back and left. Good. And I won't be here later anyway, I thought loudly.

"The doctor says you missed your treatment this morning."

"What?" I didn't know about a treatment.

"You were supposed to go straight after breakfast. They gave you your time yesterday." That was what that piece of paper must have been for.

"I didn't know what that date and time were for." Gee whiz.

"Well, you should have asked someone, or asked for me."

"I don't know your name."

"I told you, Olga." I didn't think she had ever told me her name. I would have remembered Olga. Just like the other gymnast, not Nadia but Olga Korbut. I could play "Nadia's Theme" on the piano. I would have remembered Olga.

"Can I go back to the rest of my group from Canada now?"

The doctor looked at my throat and then the nurse handed me my blue pill and my white pill with the creamer of water. The doctor said something to Olga.

"Tomorrow, Kirsten. You will be able to join your group tomorrow." Olga moved Misha's chair back against the wall. Tomorrow was not a good enough answer. I wished I knew what they were saying. I wished I knew what was going on.

I had had lunch and my rescheduled "treatment." I had found my way back to my room and was sitting on my bed, doing a word search puzzle, when in walked Chip, Rhonda and Dee Dee. Dee Dee's tan was incredible already!

"Hello, Kirsten. How's our patient?"

"I am fine, Chip. Wholly healthy. I've missed you guys!"

Rhonda gave me a little bunch of wildflowers. "When can you leave this place?"

"Tomorrow." I moved over so Rhonda could sit on the bed.

"You are so tanned!" I couldn't believe how dark Dee Dee had become so fast.

"Wait til you see the beach. It's fabulous." Dee Dee pulled up the leg of her shorts to show me her swimsuit tan lines.

"We have to march every morning," Rhonda said as she handed me a wafer biscuit. It had lemon icing in the middle.

"March?"

"We get up first thing and do exercises on the beach, then we go swimming, then it's breakfast and then we have roll call and march. You'll see. You'll pick it up fast enough." Chip was full of energy.

"We have to wear uniforms in the morning," Dee Dee sneered.

"You don't look sick." Rhonda offered me another cookie. They were excellent. "Why do you still have to be in here?"

"Who knows. It's stupid. I'm just fine." I hoped Rhonda wouldn't become best friends with one of the other girls. I was glad this was my last day. "Where do you march to?"

"Nowhere, just around this square. The Soviet anthem is played and they put up their flag. They say all this stuff in Russian over these loudspeakers. You'll see." Rhonda went over to the window. "The camp is huge! There is a stadium over that way with a track and there are theatres for plays and concerts. You can't see the parachuting from here but there is parachuting—"

"And we'll be doing cosmonaut training. They have a facility here." Chip was so excited. She was loving it. I couldn't wait to get out and see this stuff.

"What is cosmonaut training?" I hoped it wouldn't be boring.

"Cosmonauts are Soviet astronauts. We are going to go and

get to do the tests to see if we can handle space travel, absence of gravity, all the things one needs to be able to do to become a cosmonaut." Chip clapped her hands. "And so much more."

"Wow! Chip, could you talk to the hospital people and see if I can go now with you guys?"

"Wait until tomorrow, Kirsten. They said tomorrow. I don't think my talking to them will do any good. They have to make sure you are healthy before you can join in with the rest of us."

"Are they scared I'll spread germs?"

"Yes, that's why." Chip had fallen into my trap.

"Then why did they allow you to come into the hospital and visit me? What's the difference? Talk to them, please." I made puppy-dog eyes at Chip. She couldn't resist. She was up. She was off!

"Goody!" Rhonda was sitting on the window ledge now, swinging her legs. "You'll be able to come back with us now. I can't wait to show you around. It's hard to believe this is a camp."

"Yeah," Dee Dee agreed. "It's amazing. There are war planes parked on the lawns. Our room opens up over a balcony that looks down over a solarium filled with fountains and plants and there is a grand piano too. There are eight rooms in total to each indoor courtyard like this. Then the common courtyards open up to glass doors and a balcony outside that overlooks the grounds. It's beautiful. This is a *camp*! More like a luxury resort."

"You're pulling my leg."

"No," Dee Dee shook her head. I looked at her hard. Neato. She was telling the truth.

"All of us girls share a room upstairs and the boys are downstairs. We have the balcony. They don't. We are right over top of their room. Our beds are in a row. I saved you one beside me. Oh, Sam threw some chairs again. It was worse than at the hotel. The chairs were lighter so he could throw them further." Rhonda handed me the package of wafers. "Have another."

"Why don't you get dressed?"

I could tell Dee Dee about that, boy oh boy. "They took my suitcase. They gave it back, finally, but only after I promised to stay in my pyjamas."

"They're jerks. They took our suitcases too. They haven't

given Dee Dee her bag back yet." Rhonda turned and swung her legs out of the window.

"They say my other suitcase has been lost now too. It's bull!" Dee Dee's eyes welled with tears. "They won't give me my clothes. That's why I'm in these ugly camp issue shorts!"

"Come sit beside me." I sat beside Rhonda on the window sill with my legs hanging outside. Suddenly there was a ruckus behind us. Babble of Russian. A nurse was standing there clutching her heart and yelling at us.

"I think she wants you to get down." Dee Dee sounded bored.

"Why?" Rhonda didn't move so I didn't.

"Who knows. She probably thinks you are trying to commit suicide," Dee Dee said.

"More likely trying to escape. I think they are scared I'm going to run away or something."

"Shit. They are probably going to nail *this* window shut now, Kirsten," Rhonda said.

I brought my legs around. The nurse pulled me back to my bed. She hadn't stopped yelling. You didn't have to hear the words to know what she was saying. *You could have been hurt. What if you fell. You must not do that. It is very dangerous. You must stay in your bed.* Blah blah blah. These people were driving me crazy. I was going to end up in a sanatorium after this, a real one, for crazies. Another hospital woman came in. The nurse continued harping to her. The other woman took up the harping. Dee Dee yawned and raised her eyebrows. Dee Dee had a skill in that. Her "look how bored I am" attitude was impressively rude. I was going to learn that.

Chip came back. "I tried, Kirsten, really I tried. I'm sorry. They promise that you will be able to leave the hospital tomorrow." The two Russian women started on at Chip now. Chip looked confused. "*Yuni puni maya.*" Wow, Chip was speaking Russian! "We better go now. I think they want us to leave."

"Oh Chip, don't go, not yet!" This sucked. "Chip, every day they say to me that I can leave the next day and then the next day, it is the next day. They may never let me out! Don't go. I hate it here. I want to go with you guys."

"I'm sorry, Kirsten. There is nothing I can do."

"She's healthy. This is stupid." Rhonda made a face at the nurses.

"I'm sorry. We have to go. We'll see you tomorrow. I promise." Chip kissed my cheek.

"Bye." Dee Dee was shaking her head.

"See ya." Rhonda was leaving too. "Keep the cookies. Bye."

"Bye." I said it with my "woe is me" voice. The nurses left too. One of them did a "hmph" noise. Some things you didn't need a translator for.

THEY ARE KEEPING ME PRISONER AGAINST MY WILL.

I packed my bag and had it ready on the end of the bed. I had my clothes out, set for the "go ahead." I spat in the cup beside my bed. I'd been spitting in it all night. I wasn't sure what I was going to do with it yet. But it was for the nurses. All of them. For the ones who left me with my bum bare. For the one who had left me lost outside the treatment room. For the one who had said "hmph." For the one who brought the creamer of water, good thing I was a good pill swallower. For the ones who tried to make me eat food that wouldn't go down. Olga, my doctor and a nurse came in. Good.

The doctor did the usual listen-to-me-breathe. My chest was clear. It never had been full. Feel my forehead. Feel my throat. Look in my mouth. The nurse handed me the pills and the creamer. The doctor spoke to Olga. I swung my legs off the bed. I'd blind them with the speed of my exit. Superman wouldn't be able to keep up.

"You must stay one more day."

I stared at Olga. I hated her. I stared at my doctor. I hated her. I included the nurse in my stare. "Why?" I pursed my lips until they were white so they'd know that I was really angry. Just so there would not be any doubt. It was time to show them my temper. I was known for my ferocious temper. I had modelled it on George's, from the *Famous Five* series.

"You are not better, but soon you will be better." Olga was starting to look worried. I added my famous scowl. It was evil. I had practised in front of the mirror for years. If Hollywood ever discovered it, I'd be cast in horror movies, the possessed child, the demon spawn, Satan's little beauty. I deepened the look. It worked best when I increased it in three separate stages. It took control, great control. The nurse was saying something. I added a stage. The doctor said something. Olga was going to translate but I stopped her by adding the final stage. Olga said something to the doctor. The doctor pretended to look at the charts. I knew she was pretending. She just didn't want to look at me. The doctor mumbled into her charts.

Olga sighed. "You need to stay here. You need more treatment."

I added a noise now. A low growl. I gripped the bedsheets with my two fists. My knuckles even went white. What next? I had to have a finale. It was time to shout! "YOU ARE KEEPING ME PRISONER AGAINST MY WILL!!! I AM NOT SICK! YOU ARE!!!" I jumped out of bed, stomped over to the window and banged my fist on the ledge. The ledge was plaster over cement. My fist just made a small slapping noise. I wanted to punch out the glass of the window. I wouldn't go that far, though. I didn't want to cut myself. My fist hurt. I looked at the peeling, pale yellow paint on the ledge. I wanted to kick something but I didn't have shoes on. It was hard to throw a successful temper tantrum in pyjamas and bare feet. I turned around, leaned against the wall, crossed my arms and gave them the "if looks could kill" look. It was useless. The doctor muttered and left. The nurse followed her.

"It is for everyone's best." Olga was leaving too. I wanted her to leave quickly because I was going to cry and I didn't want them to see. Tears streamed down my face. I didn't make a noise. Tears, fast, like the rapids Big Jim shot in his bright yellow boat. Big Jim. I wished I had Big Jim and his sports camper with me now. I wished I was in my room back at home. I closed my eyes and pictured my room. My sunny room. The tears came even faster so I stopped picturing my room. It made things worse instead of better.

"Misha is here to take you for walk. Get dressed in your clothes and he will wait in hall." Olga was beaming. It was a better offer than sitting on my bed all day. Jean shorts, Canada flag tee and North Stars with sport socks. In the hall I found Olga talking to Misha.

"Misha will have you back in time for your treatment at four o'clock. Do not be late. Have a good time." Olga left us.

"Hi . . ." Misha didn't know how to say anything else in English. He beckoned me to follow him. I did. Down the hall, down the stairs and yahoo outside. OUTSIDE!!! It was sunny. We walked down a paved path. There were not many people about. We walked in silence. "Hi . . ." Misha said it again. He looked at me, waiting for something. He wanted me to say something.

"*Da. Nyet?*" That was it. My full Russian repertoire. Misha took my hand. I was not used to guys taking my hand. He led me over to a flowerbed and touched the petals of a flower.

"*Tsvyety.*" That must have been "flower" in Russian, unless it was "rose" because it was a rose he was touching.

"Rose," I said in English.

Misha clapped his hands and laughed. He looked excited. "*Roza! Da, roza.*"

"No." I spoke clearly. "ROSE. Not *roza*. ROSE."

Now Misha took both my hands. He stood facing me. Holding my hands. "*Rooskeey . . . roza . . . roosiyskaya, roza.*"

"Oh." I got it now. "Roza" was "rose" in Russian. It was so close to English. It was exciting. We continued walking.

Misha held his two fists up in front of him. He held up his first finger, "*Adeen,*" then the second, "*Dva,*" then the third, "*Tree.*" He did it again. "*Adeen, dva, tree, chiteeree, pyat, shest, syem, vosyem, dyevet, dyeset.*" He was teaching me to count to ten in Russian. So that was what we did all the way down to the sea front. For some reason I was finding it difficult to concentrate. I had never had this problem before. I had a really good memory and it worked fast. I could memorize stuff practically instantly. It was something about Misha that was making it difficult. We walked out on the pier. Misha was pointing now, down to the water. I looked over the edge. There were all these jellyfish in the water. "*Medusa. Mee-doo-za!*"

"Jellyfish." I kept telling him the English words for things but it seemed he wanted to teach me Russian and he wasn't interested in learning English. "Medusa." I repeated it because I had to. It was what he wanted. "Medusa" was a neat name for jellyfish. The water by the pier was full of them. I had never seen so many jellyfish at one time in one place before in my life. The Black Sea should really have been called the Jelly Sea. Misha stood behind me, looking over my shoulder. I could feel his chest on my back. I wanted to move but I didn't.

"*Smatryet!*" He was pointing at something else. He sat me down on the edge of the pier with my legs dangling over the side and then he sat behind me with his legs on the outside of mine. He seemed really comfortable but I wasn't. He acted as though this was normal. But it wasn't. He pointed down at the bottom, to the sandy floor of the sea. "*Marskaya zvyezda.*" I did not know what he was talking about. "*Marskaya zvyezda.*" I still did not get it. He tried over and over and finally got up, pulling me up with him. He led me off the pier and down onto the sandy beach beside the pier. The beach ran forever. I had never seen such a long beach. We walked a few steps and then he picked up a dead starfish. "*Marskaya zvyezda!*"

"Oh! Starfish. *Mars...*"

"*Kaya zvyezda.*"

"*Mars-kayas-rizla,*" I repeated. I knew I would not remember it later. We walked along the beach.

"*Krab.*" There was an empty crab shell half buried in the sand.

"*Da. Krab.*" How was I going to tell him it was the same in English? "*Roza*, rose. *Krab*, crab." I clapped my hands to show him it was neat. That it was another word that was almost the same in both languages.

"*Da. Khara-sho! Krab.*" Misha led me further along the beach. I wanted to ask where all the people were. Where were the kids who were at the camp? Why was no one around but us? I'd have to mime it somehow. I stopped. I pointed to him and then I pointed to me. Then I put my hand to my forehead to shade my eyes and looked around in a full circle to show seeing as far as I could see. Then I shook my head "no," to say "nothing." And then I gestured palms–up, quizzical. It was confusing, I knew. So I did it again.

"*Ponyal.*" Misha got it. He closed his eyes, put his palms together and put his head on his hands.

"Ahhhh." I got it. Everyone was sleeping. It was the middle of the day, though. How strange.

Misha led me up onto the grass to a bench where we looked out at the sparkling sea. Misha sat with his legs crossed. Guys at home didn't sit that way. It had something to do with their balls. Guys at home sat with their legs wide open. They wanted you to believe that they couldn't close their legs because their balls were so big. It wasn't true, though. They just pretended that it hurt. Misha took my braid in his hands and twiddled it.

"*Vo-la-see. Volasee.*" I could feel his breath on my cheek. He repeated the word again while playing with my plait. It was either the word for braid or hair. I wasn't sure. I didn't really care.

"*Volasee.*" I said it quietly while looking dead ahead. He then took my hand. It was like touching the electric fence at Squirrel's farm. He played with my hand now.

"*Roo-ka.*" Then he wiggled my fingers. "*Pal-yets. Palyets.*" He looked at me to repeat the words. My throat was dry all of a sudden. I didn't even feel like I could speak. What was wrong with me? My heart was clumping like horse hooves. "*Roo-ka,*" he urged while drawing on my palm. "*Rooka, rooka, rooka.*"

"*Rooka!*" I pulled my hand away and pretended to be excited about getting the words. Then I stood up and wiggled my fingers through the air "And *Palyets. Rooka* and *Palyets!*" I was overdoing it, but it was the only way I could think of to get away. Then I held up my hands, wiggled my fingers and said, "*Dyeset.*" That was ten. "*Palyets.*" And that was fingers. I had said, ten fingers. Misha applauded. I bowed. He patted the bench for me to sit back down. I gave in and sat down. He moved in close to me. Damn. I should have challenged him to a race down the beach or something, the kind of thing I normally did with boys. Misha took my wrist and bent it back and forth very gently. Double damn! Maybe an arm wrestle?

"*Zapyastye*," he breathed. Forget it. I couldn't say it and wouldn't remember it. I shook my head. Now he touched my face. Misha was touching my face. He was way too close and he was delicately outlining my face with his fingertips. "*Leetso*." At least the word was easy.

"*Leetso*," I repeated as fast as possible so he could stop touching my face. Then he touched my lips. No one had ever touched my lips before, not this way. My whole body felt out of control. I wanted to leave.

"*Goo-bee*." It was the funniest word I had ever heard. "Goobee" was lips, in Russian! How could he say it without laughing? I burst out laughing. He didn't understand.

"GOOBEE!?!" I roared. "Goobee!" I slapped my knee. "Goooobeeee!" I punched his arm. I was better at punches than tender touchings. What a dumb word. How could you ever say it romantically? Could you imagine? Kiss my Goobee. My gooby goobee! It was too funny. Misha looked confused. Good. I tapped my watch and reminded him, "*Chiteeree*." That was four. I didn't know how to say "o'clock." It wasn't 3:00 yet but I was ready to go. I felt all shaky, nervous shaky, like I had just finished playing at a piano exam. I'd had enough of Misha. It was strange. He was great to look at; his sandy hair and super dark tan, his brilliant aqua green–blue eyes. Too bad he had to go and be so touchy-feely. I was glad he didn't have his own watch. He looked surprised when I said the time. We walked back to the hospital.

"*Babachka*." He pointed to a butterfly.

"*Babachka*," I sighed out. Other than the numbers, I couldn't remember anything he had taught me. We got to the door of the sanitorium. I looked at my watch again. I pretended to look surprised. Then I laughed. "*Tree*." That was three. I slapped my forehead as if to say "stupid me." I shrugged and walked in anyway. Misha followed me up to my room. We stopped at the door. "Thank you, Misha," I smiled. "Goodbye." He didn't want to leave. I could tell. I played stupid. "Bye. Bye. Thank you so much for the lovely day. Goodbye." I did a little wave.

"*Da sveedanya*." His eyes were gorgeous.

"*Da sveedanya.*" I had heard that word before. It meant good-bye. "*Da sveedanya. Misha.*" I went into my room. He left. Phew! I walked over to the window. It was closed and the room was way too hot. I pushed up. Nothing. I kneeled on the sill and tried to pull up. Brother, not again. Yup. It had been sealed shut.

I had been to my treatment. I still had no idea what they were doing to me. I had been to dinner. I had no idea what they had served to me. The soup was bright purple. It was the colour of grape and cherry Kool-Aid when you mixed them together. This was hopefully my last night in the hospital. The thing was, that was what they had said every day so far. Maybe tomorrow they wouldn't let me go, either. If not, I'd run away. I picked up my pen and writing paper. I'd write to Chip.

Dear Chip: I have run away. They are keeping me prisoner and are never going to let me go. I cannot spend anymore time in the hospital. I do not know what they are doing to me here.

I was not sure what else to say. There were ten beds in the room. They still were all empty. I wondered if I could get around the whole room without touching the floor. I put down my writing paper. I jumped to the first bed. Cooool!

GET OFF ME,
YOU STUPID CAPITALIST.

I was being let go! I couldn't believe it. I could join the others. A nurse with big calves had taken me from the hospital to another building. It was kind of an office building. There was a round table where I was to eat breakfast with three other kids, in this room that looked a bit like a classroom. A whole dead fish on a white plate was set down in front of me. The fish was definitely watching me. It was like one of those paintings you'd see in a gallery, where the eyes followed you wherever you went in the room. A bowl of kasha was set down beside the dead fish. If I didn't eat something, they would send me back to the hospital. If only there was somewhere to hide it, like behind the stove at home. Maybe I could hide the fish in my kasha so that at least it looked like I ate half my breakfast. I looked at the other three to make sure no one was watching me. I slid the fish off my plate and into my bowl of kasha. I tried to bury the dead fish. Its tail was too long—I couldn't get it all in the bowl. A teenage girl looked up at me. She made me think of Mary from Halifax. I put my arms around my bowl to hide what I had been up to. She was frowning at my empty fish plate. Why was she frowning? Of course! There should have been scraps on my plate. I wouldn't eat the whole fish. There should have been bones and the head and the tail. She went back to eating. I slid the fish back out of the porridge bowl and onto the plate. Kasha had stuck to the outside of the fish. It looked even grosser now. I dropped my fork. The girl looked again. She was looking at my plate. She frowned harder. I hoped she wouldn't say something. I picked up my fork from under the table. As I sat up I bumped my head on a ledge under the table. A ledge! I sat all the way up. I looked around. I took my fork and knife and inserted them into the neck of the fish. I closed my eyes. This was awful. I cut. I could feel the knife sink through the fish. I opened my eyes. There was the head, eye still looking at me. Now the tail. Poor fishy. I cut off its tail. Good enough. I looked around to make sure no one was watching again. I took the fish body and slipped it onto the ledge that ran around the underside of the table top.

YES! Now for some kasha. I stuck my hand in my porridge bowl. The girl looked up again and saw me sitting there with my hand in my kasha bowl. She was looking at me like she could throw up. I laughed nervously. She turned away. I quickly took the handful of slop and loaded it onto the ledge. It was not so easy. I scraped it off my hand. I wiped the rest of the kasha off my hand and onto the underside of the table. Voila! Finito. Pretty damn good. It actually looked like I had eaten most of my breakfast. A woman was coming out to take my dishes. She told me what a good girl I was. I didn't know the Russian words for it, but I could tell what she was saying anyway. I used that same voice when talking to Coolit.

Two people in uniforms came to take me somewhere. Their uniforms were light blue shorts, with matching hats. Hats like upside-down paper boats. They had red pioneer scarves on too. We went outside and then over to another building. This must have been the building that Dee Dee and Rhonda had described to me. We went through this series of connecting indoor court-yards, like big hotel lobbies, with plants, pianos and fountains. We came to the last one and then climbed up a set of curved stairs to a balcony. We entered the first room at the top of the balcony. Yippee!!!

"Kirsten! You're back!" Rhonda ran over and hugged me.

"You must have been so sick." Mary was feeling really sorry for me."

"I wasn't sick," I informed her.

"You're back in time for marching." Dee Dee handed me a uniform. "You're supposed to try this on to see if it fits." Wow, my own marching outfit. "We all have to wear them." Dee Dee tossed the hat to me.

"This is your bed." Rhonda showed me to the narrowest bed I had ever seen in my life. "We have to make them every morning just like in the army."

"Yup. And you have to make your pillow into a pyramid, like this." Oksana showed off her bed proudly.

I'd never be able to make a bed that neat. I noticed my hand smelled like dead fish. "Where is the bathroom?"

"I'll show you." Rhonda said and I followed her.

"Hurry. We don't have much time before roll call." Mary was all ready.

"I missed you, man." The bathrooms were at the far end of the balcony. "I didn't think they were ever going to let me out of that stupid hospital. I'm still supposed to go back for these dumb treatments, eh!" I stood in the middle of the washroom. A wave of shock flooded over me. "Rhonda, there are no doors on the stalls!"

"I know. It's awful. And there are no seats on the toilets."

"I don't think I can go like that, without a door." I washed my hands in the sink. A Russian girl and her friend entered. The Russian girl stood up on the rim of the toilet and pulled down her pants. She peed standing on the toilet rim, talking to her friend three stalls down, who was doing the same.

"RHONDA!"

"I know, Kirsten. Too weird. I've been told that because some people from the Soviet Union are so used to going to the bathroom over holes, they can't go, or don't know how to go, sitting down. Bizarre, huh?"

"She is really standing, going! She even has her shoes on the rim. Do you sit on the rim, Rhon?"

"Yeah. I have to. Let's hurry up." I followed Rhonda back towards our room. I wondered if Mary from Halifax stood on

129

the toilet. She seemed to really be into the *when in Rome* thing. Imagine not knowing how to use a toilet. I couldn't believe it.

I was with the whole Canadian group. We were all in our uniforms, waiting to parade around the square. I was nervous. I'd never marched in my life. We were lined up in order of size. That meant I was at the back. I was always at the back or front when lined up according to size. We were lined up two across, except for me. No one was beside me. I was by myself in the back. Adrian and Chip were side by side. Then Jay and Big Karl were together, then Oksana and Alexi, then Dee Dee and Mary, then Rhonda and Little Karl, then Sam and Iggy. And then it was me!

"You start on the left foot. Adrian will say 'left, left, left right left.' You do that on the spot. Then you start moving forward," Sam said this over his shoulder.

"When we get to the flags, only the people in the front look right. We all keep looking forward," Iggy added. This was getting confusing.

"You have to keep two feet away from us." Sam measured with an arm's length.

"No more and no less. You are going to have to take big steps." Iggy demonstrated.

"And whatever you do, listen for when we are told to stop. Adrian will freak out on your head if you bump into the people in front of you." Sam was scaring me. Why was I by myself? They should have let Rhonda march beside me for the first time. They all knew what they were doing. It wasn't fair. All because I was the littlest.

There were several groups in front of us. We marched with our country members. The first groups were off. Marching music was playing. Wow, they marched different—with straight legs like in old Hitler movies. Were we supposed to march like that too?

"Sam," I whispered loudly. "SAMANTHA!" I whispered louder.

"BE QUIET IN BACK!" Adrian roared. I died.

We were off. I couldn't see what the others were doing because I was behind them. I didn't know how to march. We had to go up steps to get to the square. I was on the wrong leg already. I couldn't keep in beat and keep up at the same time. I didn't know how to move my arms. Was it same arm and same leg or opposite arm and leg? I was on the wrong foot again. There were people watching from the outdoor balconies. They'd see me marching all crazy, like a spaz. To top it off, my shoelace was undone. I had to keep watching it so I wouldn't trip. My hat was too big. It kept falling forward over my eyes. I looked like a single Stooge, or Laurel without Hardy, or one Marx brother, or Jerry Lewis. I looked like Jerry Lewis in a war movie. I was watching my shoelace so I didn't see them stop. I crashed into . . . Little Karl? I had marched right between Iggy and Sam and had ended up all the way up the line at Rhonda and Little Karl.

"Get off me, you stupid capitalist!" Little Karl was spitting mad.

"Whoops." I adjusted my hat and moved back into "formation." Adrian and Chip were staring at me. Dee Dee and Oksana were laughing. Adrian told them to "shut up and turn around." Adrian actually looked embarrassed. Marching wasn't something you could just *do*. The music had stopped and stuff was being said over loudspeakers. They were those kinds of outdoor speakers that even if you had understood the language being spoken, you wouldn't have known what was being said. Everybody turned on the spot to face the front of the square. I did what everybody did. Then the Soviet national anthem was played while they raised the hammer and sickle, the Soviet flag. The Soviet anthem was so dramatic. It was like a symphony or something. "O Canada" sucked. No wonder no one ever sang it proudly. I believed practically our whole country was embarrassed by it. I bet our sports teams would do better too if we had a better anthem at the beginning of games. I bet Canadians would be different if we had a better national anthem. "Waltzin' Matilda" was cool too, but in a different way. The Australians sang it instead of their real anthem. "God Save the Queen" was boring. We sang it on Fridays at school instead of "O Canada." More stuff burbled over the loudspeakers, then we were called to "left face" by Adrian. Then it was off marching again. Brother!

We were in our bathing suits with our clothes overtop, walking down to the beach to go swimming. We were on different paved paths from the ones Misha and I had gone to the sea on. This camp was huge! It wasn't like a camp at all. Dee Dee was right about that.

"Here's the camp store where I bought the lemon wafers." Rhonda was counting out some kopeks. "You have to get your stuff now. It isn't open later."

I hadn't brought money with me to the beach. No one had told me about the store. Some kids were drinking water out of a black rubber garden hose that was lying on the grass. I was thirsty so I went over and after a boy finished drinking, I took the hose. I gulped the water.

"*NYET! NYET! NYET!!!*" A big, muscular woman with long hair flew at me and snatched the hose from my hand. She shoved me back to the path. Another Russian kid had the hose now and was drinking. This wasn't fair.

"Oh no, Kirsten, you mustn't drink the water here. You'll end up back in the hospital. Oh dear." Chip had taken me out of the hands of the strong woman.

"But how come they can drink it?"

"Because they are used to it. Their stomachs can take it."

I sometimes drank out of the stream that ran through our property at home. The stream went through farm fields before it got to our house. Sometimes there was white foamy stuff on top of the water. Well, I drank that water (not the foamy part) and I was okay, so I bet I could handle the black rubber hose water.

"I'm glad they let me out of the hospital, Chip. I was going to run away if they didn't."

"Where would you have gone?" Chip asked politely. We were walking again. Rhonda handed me a lemon wafer.

Hmmm. Where would I have gone?

"Chip! Chip!" Adrian was calling. He was behind us talking to some people. Chip left. Rhonda and I continued walking.

"Were all the doctors really women?" Where had Mary come from?

"Yeah. There were no men doctors at all. Every important person was a woman. Oh, except for the man who runs the treatment machine."

"The treatment machine?" Mary didn't know about my treatments.

"This stupid thing they hooked me up to. It was for my sore throat. I don't know what it does."

"Did it work?"

"No." I wished a shorter walk to the beach.

"Well, it must have made your throat better because they released you from the camp hospital," Mary said.

"I was better by the time they put me *in* the camp hospital, Mary. The dumb machine didn't work because there was nothing for it to do."

"They were only trying to help you."

"They weren't trying to help her! They were experimenting on her with some contraption!" Rhonda said. Maybe she was right. Maybe they were using me for some sort of experiment. I was scheduled for a treatment this afternoon.

"Don't be so stupid! Why would they do that?" Mary had a crease between her eyebrows. It was pretty deep at the moment.

"Because the Soviet people are the Soviet Union's greatest resource." Rhon was quoting Adrian. "They wouldn't want to waste their own resources, they'd rather use Canada's."

"It was probably just radiation therapy used to shrink her glands, or cook her tonsils so she doesn't get tonsillitis again. They use radiation rather than surgery. They do it for all sorts of things, acne, ringworm, adenoids." Mary's forehead furrow was turning into a ditch.

Wait a minute, radiation therapy? RADIATION THERAPY? I didn't like this one bit. "Do you really think they were doing some sort of radiation therapy? Or experimentation?"

"Sounds like it." Rhonda handed me a wafer. "I mean, have you ever heard of such a thing for a sore throat?"

"No."

"See?"

"Yeah. It's weird. I'm not going any more. I'm supposed to go this afternoon. I'm not going back to that creepy dentist-chair room. Forget it."

"Good. Ah wow. Look at the water, Kirsten." We were at the beach. It was beautiful. It was sunny and the water twinkled.

"Let's get in!" I dropped my towel and clothes in a pile. Iggy and Sam were already standing in the sea. I ran towards them.

"Wait up," Rhonda shouted after me.

I ran into the water where Iggy and Sam were. I felt stuff sliming around my legs. I looked down. It was jellyfish, everywhere. "OH MY GOD!" I ran right back out of the water. Rhonda and the boys laughed at me.

"You'll get used to them." Sam picked up handfuls of jelly and let the goo slip between his fingers.

"Wait'll you do the crawl." Iggy tossed a jellyfish across the water. "Your fingers go through them, every stroke."

"But don't they sting?" I thought jellyfish were dangerous. People drowned sometimes if they were stung by them.

"Not this kind." Rhonda picked one up to show me. "Apparently the stinging kind are more purple. These are clear, see? No sting. I was terrified at first to go in too. It's okay, though. You will get used to it. Come on. Come with me." Rhonda dropped the jellyfish and took my hand. She pulled me into the water.

"Why are there so many?" I had never seen anything like this. The water was thick with jellyfish, all around my body. I felt them brush past me, float against me, tickle my legs. I was already getting over it. I wasn't ready to pick one up yet, though.

"It's good they aren't the stinging kind."

"You have to watch, though, Kirsten, because apparently they get the odd stinging one here. Watch for purple. We haven't seen one yet."

I looked back at the beach. Dee Dee was lying on a towel. Oksana was brushing her hair. Chip and Adrian looked like they were fighting. Big Karl was reading. Little Karl was too. Jay and Alexi were walking down the beach. It was good to be back with them all.

We had showered off at the beach, then changed for lunch. And now, we were filing into the huge meal hall.

"Sit beside me." Rhonda pulled me several tables into the

room. They were long tables. Bigger than the ones in the camp hospital. Chip and Adrian walked past and went to a smaller table at the front of the hall.

"Where're they going?" Chip and Adrian were at a table for six.

"The group leaders eat together and we eat together. It's great." Oksana sat on my other side.

"So what's on for today?" Iggy sat down across from me and tucked a paper napkin into his shirt. "I hope it's as good as the French toast we got at breakfast."

"You had French toast for breakfast?" I imagined my fish lying under the table, on its ledge. I hoped it had not been found yet, otherwise they might have put together that it was me.

"You mean you didn't get French toast in hospital?" Iggy was holding his knife and fork in his two fists, points up.

Rhonda nudged me. She was shaking her head. Damn Iggy! I had never met anyone who could string me along like that. Then lunch was served. It was right out of a horror movie.

"What the hell is that?!?!?" Dee Dee pushed her chair back from the table with a nails-on-chalkboard screech. Iggy was giggling. They, the horror things, were plunked down all around the table.

"I'm going to be sick." Rhonda turned around in her chair. "I can't look."

"What is it!?!?" Dee Dee demanded.

"Tongues." Iggy's eyes were popping out of his head. "Whole tongues!"

"They must be cow tongues." Jay poked the giant tongue on his plate with his knife. "They're huge!"

"Well, I don't eat anything that can taste me back." Iggy slammed down his knife and fork.

"Shit, they still have the taste buds on them and everything." Jay was still poking his cow tongue. It was the size of a whole roast.

"They're boiled, aren't they?" Big Karl had taken his sunglasses off. "Why are they bright red? Shit, they're bleeding. They served us rare tongue!"

I looked at Mary. She was just sitting, looking at her plate.

Not even Mary was eating. Whole tongues just sitting on the table, no vegetables even. Just whole tongues, skin on, taste buds on and bleeding. Holy gross me out!

"I never thought it could get worse." Oksana had tears in her eyes.

"Hey, Iggy." The tongues reminded me of something I had been meaning to ask. "What does your dad do with the bulls' balls after he cuts them off?"

"Have you never had prairie oysters?" Iggy had pushed his cow tongue towards the centre of the table.

"Prairie oysters?"

"We eat them, of course. What did you think?"

"He's joking, right?" I turned to Rhonda, who was still backwards in her chair.

"No. Not this time."

"You eat them?" I looked at Iggy.

"Well, *we* don't. My family doesn't have cows."

"I thought you were farmers." I'd never heard of farmers without cows.

"Grain. We farm wheat mostly."

"Oh." I *had* heard of that, in school. Prairie farms were huge and I remembered seeing the pictures in my geography book of fields and fields of wheat.

"DON'T CUT INTO IT!" Jay looked like he had seen a ghost. He pushed his plate towards the centre of the table too.

"Can we leave?" Oksana *was* crying now. "Alexi, go ask Chip if we can go back to our rooms. Please?"

"We aren't supposed to get up during meals." Alexi poked his cow tongue with his fork. "Okay. I'll go ask." Alexi was at the head of the table. His chair made a huge noise too when he pushed it back. People at other tables turned their heads and looked at us.

"I have a friend in school who sometimes eats tongue sandwiches. But Heidi's sandwich tongue doesn't look like this tongue." The tongue on my plate hung right off the edges!

"That's because her tongue doesn't still have taste buds, man. It's supposed to be peeled, eh, and I bet she doesn't have a whole tongue," Jay said. He had pushed his chair way far back and was balancing on the back two legs.

"Yeah. It's sliced thin, like salami or something."

"Will you shut up!" Dee Dee snapped a photograph of her tongue and then put a napkin over it, like a white sheet.

"We should try it." Mary was still staring at her plate. She had her knife and fork in hand.

"Go ahead, Mary," Jay smiled with one side of his mouth. "If you can sink your fork through that, then cut a chunk with your knife, I'll give you five rubles."

"I'll make it ten if you put it in your mouth," Big Karl added.

"Twenty if you swallow." Iggy got in on the action.

We all watched. Mary put the points of her fork on top of the tongue.

"I never realized how big a cow's tongue was til now," I said, watching Mary all the time. That was a lot of money.

"It looks bigger out of the mouth cuz you don't normally see a whole tongue. They have taken this from right back at the root. Also, I guess it's relaxed, so it's spread out." Jay put his money on the table. A lot of money.

"The tongue is the strongest muscle in the human body," Big Karl informed us.

"I CAN'T!" Mary's hands were shaking. She put her cutlery down. "I just can't stab it." She was right about that. The thought of feeling your fork sinking through the skin and flesh of the cow tongue was insane. But still, for all that money...

"Get out of here, all of you!" Adrian was standing there. Alexi said *sorry* with his eyes. "Go back to your rooms and stay there! I'll be talking to you after nap time! Go. You are a disgrace!"

Oksana started to bawl. "It's not our fault," she sobbed. "It's not our fault we can't eat bleeding tongues." We all ran out.

"Shit, I forgot my camera." Dee Dee went back.

I did not understand being made to rest when you didn't feel like resting. I had never had forced naps before. Not even in kindergarten. My friend Patty's kindergarten made you take a nap. The kids even brought baby blankets to school to sleep on.

At Orlyonok everybody had to go to their rooms after lunch for a nap. They even made you get undressed. None of us were tired. We were all sitting on our beds, talking about what Adrian was going to say to us and stuff.

Dee Dee ran into the room. "Holy shit, you'll never guess what. When I went back to go get my camera, Adrian was eating our food. He'd gathered up all the tongue and was sitting there eating it."

"I've seen him doing that too," Mary said. We all made gagging noises. "He likes the food. He thinks it's a waste."

"I don't care. They can put tongue down day after day and I'm not eating it." Dee Dee was right. "And Adrian is welcome to our leftovers."

"I'm glad it wasn't prairie oysters." I still wasn't sure if Iggy was telling the truth about that.

"Yeah, I would have thrown up if I had to look at boiled balls," Rhonda gagged. She had her lemon wafers out. I hoped she'd offer one. My Crunchie Bars were long gone.

"What food do you miss more than anything? No, how about this, if you could have anything in the world right now, what would it be?" Dee Dee looked at me. I wasn't ready.

"A Joe & Louis." Oksana actually shouted it. "Think about that chocolate and yummy cream filling."

" A Joe & Louis is your best pick? I thought your parents ran this great Doukhobor bakery." Dee Dee smiled.

"Oh, I thought we needed to pick food that could be shipped here."

"No, any food, from anywhere!"

"Camille's Fish and Chips." Mary was sitting up. She had put her book down.

"Who's Camille?" Dee Dee asked.

"It is the best fish and chip place in Halifax. It's under the bridge. My family goes there every Friday night. It's some good, I tell ya." Mary smacked her lips.

Rhonda went now. "Okay, don't laugh at me, you guys, but I could really go for Swiss Chalet right now. We don't have one near us but we go whenever we're in Alberta. I normally get a quarter chicken dark meat but today, I'd order the half."

"Mmmmm. Swiss Chalet," I agreed. "My mom thinks they put cocaine in the sauce."

"Why?" Oksana asked.

"Because no one likes it the first time they try it, right? And the next thing you know, you are having cravings for it in the night."

"Kirsten, that has got to be true! I have to get two jars of the gravy now." Rhonda was excited. "One for the chicken and one for the fries. I hated it the first time too!"

"Me too," Dee Dee agreed. "Then every time I have been since, I have eaten more and more gravy!"

"Can I add something to my Joe & Louis?" Oksana asked.

"Sure," Dee Dee agreed.

"I'd like a big bag of Hostess potato chips. I mean one of the big bags with the three big bags in it. I want one salt & vinegar, one barbecue—"

"Ohhhh, barbecue." My mouth watered.

"And one plain."

"I don't like plain." Her other two choices were better. But then that's how the big bags came. There was always a plain. I only liked plain chips with dip. I loved dip. "You better have some onion dip with the plain bag."

"DIP!" Oksana yelled. "I WANT CHIPS AND DIP!"

"What about you, Kirsten?" I still wasn't ready. I made a face at Dee Dee and then it came. "Oh, I know. I know. Have any of you ever been to Montreal?" Dee Dee and Oksana had. "Well, I want a Montreal smoked-meat sandwich from Schwartz's Deli. I don't want it lean and I want the fries. I don't normally like fries but today I want a big order of fries and I won't care that I don't know the other people who are crammed in at my table, either. I just want that salty greasy meaty juicy dripping sandwich."

"Gross, Kirsten." Rhonda was looking at me like I was a freak.

Dee Dee stared at the ceiling. "You need an extra order of dill pickles with your sandwich and a Coke."

"What about you, Dee Dee?" Rhonda asked.

"Well, I had been thinking that I wanted a Caesar salad and I still want one but what I really want is a Pizza Nova pizza."

I clapped my hands. "Pizza Nova! Yeah. What on it?"

"Pepperoni—"

"Double cheese." Oksana didn't normally butt in.

"Mushrooms," Dee Dee continued. I'd have to pick those off but I was used to doing that. "Green peppers, onions, olives, tomatoes." It was sounding like what my parents ordered. I didn't like tomatoes on my pizza, either, because they just made it soggy. Though, right now, I'd still be happy.

"Do you think they'd deliver?" Rhonda picked up an imaginary phone. We all laughed.

"My friend's mom makes this cherry cheesecake." Oksana was standing on her bed. "It isn't baked. It is the best! It cooks in the fridge. I guess it doesn't cook but you have to wait."

"My mom makes that too, with a graham crust, right?" Rhonda stood on her bed.

"Yeah, that's the one." Oksana was jumping now. She was the loudest-quietest girl I had ever met.

"Here's to trailer-park cheesecake!" Dee Dee laughed.

"I had it for my last birthday!" I did. I really did. I had requested it.

"I love that cheesecake!" Mary kicked her feet in the air. We all loved that same unbaked cherry cheesecake, with the soft delicious inside. Yummy!

"Ana, get down," Mary whispered in a hurried voice. Chip and Adrian entered. Adrian stood by the door and Chip sat on the end of my bed.

"We have just been talking to the boys." Adrian looked very serious. "The food issue is becoming a grave concern. Chip and I are split on how to deal with this. We are going to talk to you like you are adults. In return we want you to behave that way." I did not know what he was talking about.

"What Adrian is saying is that he wants you to try harder. The Soviet people are trying very hard. The tongue today was a great treat for them. Your reaction was very rude. It's one thing not to like something, but you didn't even try. You should not treat your hosts so badly." Chip made me feel bad.

"Come on, Chip. Whole cow tongues? It was shocking!" Dee Dee was getting mad again.

"Just make an effort, please." Chip was begging.

Adrian wasn't looking at us. He was staring out the window. He hated us. "If you make an effort tonight at dinner, we will see if we can arrange a meeting tomorrow with the camp administration and kitchen. If you behave rudely, though, we can't ask them for favours, can we?" He pulled his beard. "Not that I believe we should do this at all. You should just eat what the others eat. You should experience the Soviet Union in the full. I am disappointed in all of you. You haven't even tried to like anything." With that, Adrian and Chip left.

"Why are you crying, Mary?" Mary's face was all blotchy and tears flooded out of her eyes. Adrian didn't even yell at us. Her crying made no sense to me.

"Because I have tried. I have been trying hard all along. Today was the first day I didn't eat my food. I have been doing everything right and because of all of you I ... I ... forget it!" Mary sobbed. She rolled over on her bed with her back to us and lay there, facing the door, crying.

I was singing Manfred Mann's "Blinded by the Light."

"Repeat the lyric you just sang." Rhonda was laughing.

"Rubbed up like a douchent." I could make the words sound close enough that most people wouldn't have noticed. Or maybe most people wouldn't have noticed because no one really knew the words. It was free time and Rhonda was showing me the camp. I changed tunes. I knew all the words to Neil Sedaka's "Breaking up Is Hard to Do." We had this amazing teacher at school. Mr. Hallett would sometimes say, "I don't feel like history today. Let's sing instead." And we would. He'd go to the piano and we'd spend the whole afternoon singing songs like "Beth" by Kiss, and "Evergreen" from *A Star Is Born,* or "Fifty Ways to Leave Your Lover," and "One Tin Soldier," which was a real lesson, or "Tie a Yellow Ribbon," which was hope, or "That'll Be the Day," which was fun. Mr. Hallett could sing louder than the whole school put together. We'd have competitions in the gym. The whole school singing against Mr. Hallett. Mr. Hallett always won. He never did the songs the school board wanted us to sing, songs like "Kookaburra Sits in the Old Gum Tree." He taught us real songs. Songs about war and peace. Songs that were sung the day the soldiers opened fire on the peace-demonstrating students, during the Vietnam War. Songs about "The Night They Drove Old Dixie Down." I knew all the words to "American Pie." He taught us about the groups and about the times. I learned more in his music class about history than I did in anybody else's history class ever. And it was all from music. He taught us what the songs were about. Songs could be like poetry. They weren't always what they seemed, like "Lucy in the Sky with Diamonds" and "Puff the Magic Dragon." Those songs were about drugs. I was going to have Mr. Hallett for two more years but just for singing and history, not for gym, English or math anymore.

"This is the stadium." Rhonda had stopped walking outside a huge sports stadium.

"Wow." I could not believe my eyes. It was like an Olympic stadium.

"C'mere. I found a balance beam over here."

Outside the entrance of the stadium was a balance beam. Rhonda got up on it and did some stuff.

"Cool, Rhonda." I'd never been on a beam before. My friend Patty Gluck took gymnastics. She was really flexible. Patty could lie on the floor on her stomach and kick her feet up and around in a bow so that she was looking at the back of her heels, in front of her face, on the floor, like Olga Korbut. It was wild. My back just did not bend like that.

Rhonda dismounted. "That's called a round off. You go."

I got up. "I've never done this before." I jumped up and down on the beam.

"Good," Rhonda clapped. "Try a round off."

"Okay." I walked to the end.

"Just like a cartwheel. But put your legs together at the end and twist." Rhonda stood by like a skating coach. At least she had demonstrated. My skating teachers just stood. They never demonstrated. Patty said it was because their bums were too big. They'd lose their balance.

"Wow." I did it. Just like that. My heart was beating fast. It had been scary but it was easy. "How was that?"

"Keep your legs straighter next time."

Some people came over. Rhonda got back up on the beam. She did a cartwheel on the beam this time. I wouldn't be able to do that. Off the end was one thing, but staying on? No way. Then she did a backwards flip off the end. The people clapped. I got back up again and did my round off. It felt good. No one clapped.

"Let's go, Rhon. I want to see the parachuting."

"Okay, that's excellent!" We left the stadium.

It was three in the morning. I was lying in bed. I had stomach cramps and had to go to the can bad. It was probably dinner that had done it. We had all tried hard to eat. I didn't want to go to the washroom by myself.

"Rhonda," I whispered. She just lay there. "Rhon." Nothing. I tiptoed over to her. "Rhon."

"What?"

I woke up way more easily than that. If someone else in the room rolled over in bed, I woke up.

"Will ya come to the bathroom with me?"

"Mmmmm." Rhonda rolled over and closed her eyes. I did not want to walk down that dark hall on my own.

"Rhon?"

She jumped up. "If he takes the pony up Rupert's Pass, I'll kill him!"

What the hell was she talking about? "Rhonda?"

"Oh my God. Did I just say something?" Rhonda rubbed her eyes and shook her head.

"Yeah. You must have been having a dream. You were talking in your sleep. It sounded pretty bad. I thought I should wake you up." This was my usual kind of lie. It was the truth but a lie too. But it was going to work to my favour and wouldn't hurt any-one at all. "Maybe we should go for a little walk. If you go back to sleep right away, you might just go back to having that awful nightmare. Let's go to the bathroom. I have to go anyway."

"Okay. Thanks." Rhonda swung her feet out of the bed,

grabbed her toe socks and started to put them on. They were all the colours of the rainbow. Really cool. They took too long to put on, though, and I really had to go. Toes didn't cooperate like fingers in gloves. "Ready."

We crept out of the room and along the landing to the washroom. I had been holding diarrhoea all night. It had been tough. I just didn't want to use a toilet without doors when I had the runs, especially in front of strangers. It was bad enough for just pee.

"Rhonda, my stomach is really upset. Can you stand outside the washroom and let me know if anyone is coming?"

"Sure. You shouldn't have drunk out of that hose." Rhonda stayed on guard outside. That helped.

I went fast. It was over in seconds. A huge explosion. If I had done that before bedtime when the can was crowded, my life would have ended. I reached for the toilet paper. It was empty. "Rhonda," I called out. Nothing. "RHONDA." I hoped that wouldn't wake anyone up.

"What?"

"There's no toilet paper. Could you get some? Hold your breath." How embarrassing.

"Sure." I heard her banging around. She went from one stall to the next. "Shit!"

"What?"

"There isn't any."

I sat there on the cold rim. I flushed the toilet behind me to get rid of the smell. "Is there any paper towel or anything?"

"No. Let me look around. I think there is a cupboard by the entrance to the showers." Rhonda left. I sat there. I had had it with Soviet toilets. Rhonda finally came running back in. She skidded across the floor in her sock feet. She had a big wad of toilet paper. I watched her slide past my stall. She slid back.

"You will never guess what I found. You know that cupboard before the shower room? Well, it looks like a cupboard but the back wall isn't a wall. I slipped into it and it opened. It's a toilet, Kirsten! There is a little room behind the supplies with a private toilet. There's even a lock on the door." She handed me the toilet paper. Soviet toilet paper wasn't exactly soft. You could probably strip furniture with it.

"Move." I signalled her to get out so I could wipe my bum. "A secret room, you mean?"

"Altogether secret. It looks like a wall, right? I wouldn't have known it opened if I hadn't been sliding and hadn't banged into it. Hurry up and come see."

Rhonda opened the cleaning cupboard door. "See? Mop, broom, cleansers, toilet paper. Just a little cupboard, right? Well, watch." Rhonda went to the back wall of the cupboard and pushed. It moved. It was very dark behind the wall. It took a second for my eyes to adjust. She pushed further. I stepped into the cupboard behind her. Then she walked into a room behind the wall. I followed.

"WOW! This is excellent." This was the best discovery in the entire world. "Rhonda, you are amazing! We have our own private toilet now."

"Yeah, I bet no one knows about this. I'll try it out." Rhonda pulled down her PJ bottoms and sat on the toilet.

"I guess we won't run out of toilet paper in here," I snorted. This was heaven. I reached back into the cupboard that we had stepped through and got some toilet paper for Rhonda. "This sure beats Narnia!"

"My stomach's not great, either," Rhonda moaned.

"I think eveyone in the group has it." I stepped back into the supply cupboard to give Rhonda more privacy. "Too bad there isn't a light in here. It's kind of hard to see. It'll make it hard for wiping. Use lots of paper. Hey, when do we get to go parachuting?" I heard the toilet flush.

"We don't parachute til the last week. I don't think we should tell anyone about this room." Rhonda pulled the wall back closed behind her. "Only go in here when no one sees you. We'll work out a code for daytime use."

"The last week?" That was so long away.

Rhonda opened the door to the cupboard just a crack. "All clear."

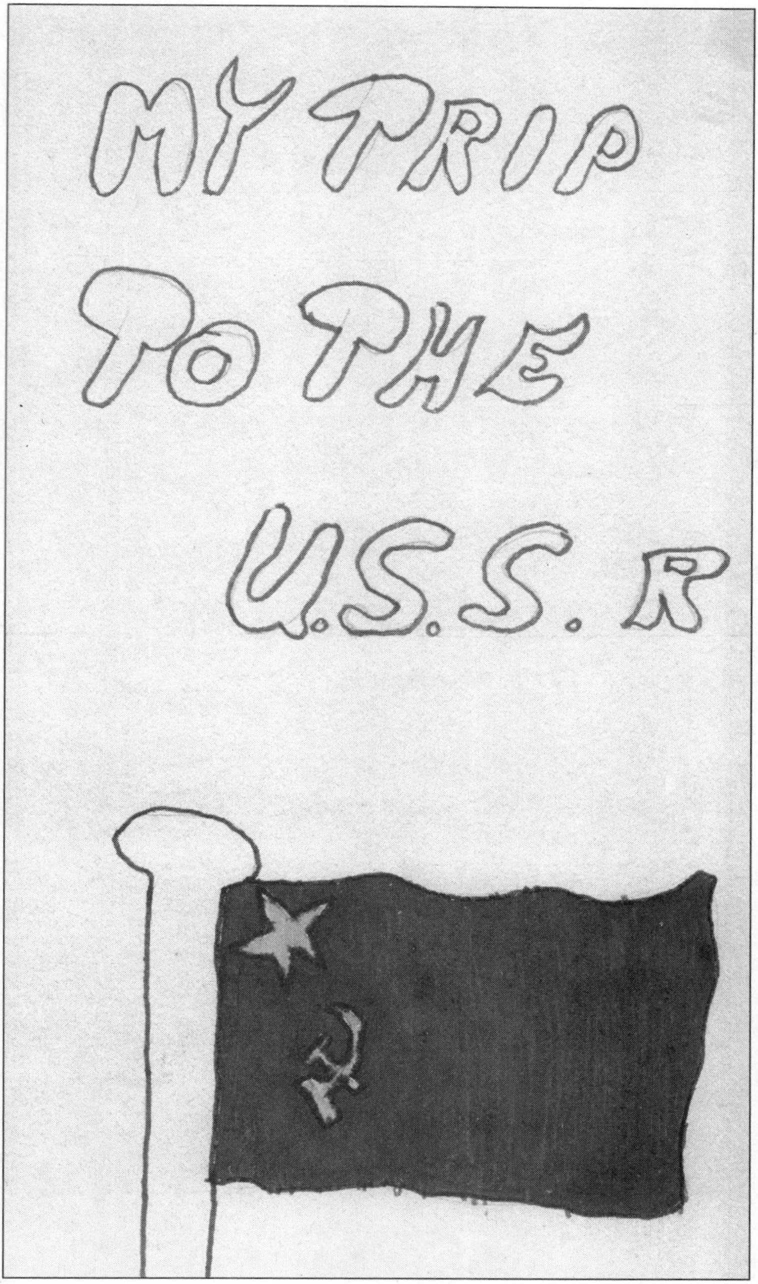
MY TRIP
TO THE
U.S.S.R

Aeroflot boarding pass. Just like a capitalist airline, except there was no first class and everyone was served caviar.

Invitation to the Children's Festival in Moscow, celebrating the Year of the Child, 1977.

The brat in the USSR.

Kirsten with Red Army officers at the Moscow Exhibition.

Red Square: seconds before Kirsten and Rhonda outrun the Red Army and Soviet police.

St. Basil's Cathedral, Red Square, Moscow.

Early morning exercise on the Black Sea. Everyone in camp had to participate. Photo courtesy of Jo-Ann Baran.

Being a tourist in Sochi, famous for its health spas and "Friendship Tree."

Smuggled currency. A ten-ruble note illegally removed from the USSR by
Kirsten.

Censorship won the day. Kirsten's 2nd place
medal in a sidewalk art competition.

Might as well jump—without
permission or safety training.

Ten-hut! Every morning the children of Camp Orlyonok marched and
fell in for roll call.

Kirsten delivering her presentation "Lost in Moscow" at the Canada–USSR Association in Toronto.

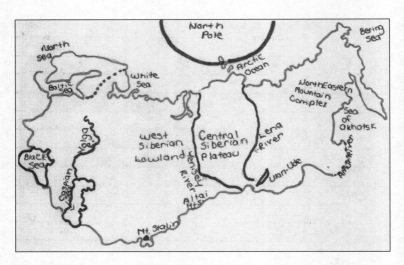

The Soviet Union, circa 1977, by Kirsten Koza.

IT WAS JUST LIKE THE ARMY.

Being woken up by trumpets or bugles was worse than my friend Trisha's clock radio buzzer. I'd never experienced this before in my entire life. It was just like the army. When those bugles blew, you had to jump out of bed, make your bed and get changed for morning exercises in ten minutes flat. I was pretty speedy at stuff normally. But bed making was not easy. I was going to have to get help at this. I watched Oksana.

"Hurry up, Kirsten. They time us." Dee Dee was buckling up her sandals. "Shit, I wish I had my Adidas tennis shoes here!" It figured Dee Dee had Adidas. "I'll probably never see them again. I had some nice stuff in those cases. I had this white blouse with lace all around the neck and shoulders. You'd have loved it."

"Yeah, I have one like that at home." I didn't but I wished I did.

"Dee Dee, you have more in your carry-on, which you still have, than any of us have in our large cases," Mary said. It was the first thing she had said to us since yesterday afternoon.

"Kirsten, hurry up!" Rhonda came over to my bed. "What are you doing?"

I'd never had to make a bed without wrinkles before. My mom

usually made my bed, not because I was lazy but because it always looked so awful when I did it. I could never get the bedspread straight. And I didn't make a bed just with wrinkles. When I made a bed, it usually looked like there was a body still in it.

Rhonda took the blanket off my bed. "Well, that's why it looks so bad. You have to straighten out the sheet. You can't just hide the sheet with the blanket.

"Let me do it. You guys get dressed." Oksana took over and Rhon and I put on our bathing suits with our shorts overtop. You put your bathing suit on because everyone showered at the beach after exercises.

"She has to learn to do it herself," Mary said.

"Kirsten can learn to do it during our spare time so no one gets in trouble for being late or for being a mess." Oksana folded the pillow like origami and had it standing in the required triangle, first try. She was great. "The covers have to be pulled so tight that a coin bounces." This *was* like the army. Just like in the movies.

"I'm telling that she didn't do it." Mary was standing at the door, ready to go. Would she really tell on me? Mary had seemed so nice, a prude but nice. This was not nice. And it was not very grown-up behaviour for someone her age: "I'm telling."

Rhonda spun around. "If you do, Mary MacGregor, you'll be sorry!"

"Why would you tell?" Dee Dee looked at Mary with a "hate-your-guts" look.

"Yeah, what's it to you?" Oksana said.

I was surprised that Oksana had the gumption. She had seemed so quiet at first but yesterday she was shouting about Joe & Louis cakes and jumping on the bed and today she was standing up to a teenager. People could be surprising.

"Quit picking on me! You are all always picking on me! And I am the only one doing what we are supposed to be doing. It's not fair!" Mary looked like she was going to cry again. She headed out the door.

"YOU WAIT!" Dee Dee bellowed. This was getting good. "You know we *all* only leave the room when *everyone* is ready. Stop trying to look like Miss Goody Two Shoes all the time."

"Yeah."

"Yeah."

Dee Dee and Mary stared at each other.

"Okay. Now we can go!" Dee Dee commanded. Mary did a military turn and marched out the door. "Reject," Dee Dee sneered. We all followed. All the rooms were emptying. The whole camp jogged down to the beach. I hated jogging! The boys were ahead of us because their room was closer to the glass doors that led outside. Not because they were better jocks. I didn't think any of them were good at sports, although the Karls said they were going to play professional football. I felt sorry for Dee Dee having to jog in sandals.

"I'm tired," I panted.

"Shhh. We aren't supposed to talk," Dee Dee warned me.

"Why?"

"Who knows? I don't know if it's camp rules or Adrian rules." Dee Dee could barely talk, she was breathing so hard.

"I think it's Adrian rules because we complained so much the first day." Rhonda seemed better at sports than the rest of us. She wasn't breathing quite as hard.

I had had my first migraine headache after a cross-country running race at school back in June. It was ninety degrees outside and humid. The race was really tough. It was two miles. My face was so red afterwards that the teachers at school got scared. Sports always made me go red. The headache started at school. Actually it didn't start with a headache but I kind of lost my eyesight and had spots in front of my eyes. Then I threw up. Then the pain started. Maggie Thompson walked me home from the school bus, even though she lived the other way. I had to keep sitting down. I had never felt so much pain before. By the time I got home I was practically blind. Mom put me to bed and closed my curtains. I couldn't even think of the words to tell her what was wrong. She gave me a 222 and put a cold facecloth on my head. Nothing helped, though. I still had it when Dad got home. It was like someone was chopping my head open with an axe. I almost wished someone *would* chop my head open, just to let the pain out.

"We stand at the back so no one can see us," Dee Dee

whispered to me. We were at the beach. Thousands of us. We stood in rows.

"Move over a bit, Kirsten, so I don't hit you when we do jumping jacks." Rhonda held her arms out to show me the distance.

I held mine out too and stepped away. I hated jumping jacks. Something was called out over the loudspeaker, in Russian, though. People started swinging their arms from side to side, so I did too. Then it was stretch up and then down to touch your toes, stretch up and touch your toes. Over and over. Jay could only get his hands part way down his shins. The Karls could touch the top of their feet. Dee Dee wasn't trying at all. Iggy was really bad. He just put his hands to his knees and that was with bent knees too. Touching your toes was easy. I could put my palms flat in the dirt. I looked down the beach. There were kids as far as you could see. Kids from all over the world touching their toes.

Now it was jumping jacks. I watched the Canadians. Some of our group were just stepping out to the side, not jumping. Jay was just using one arm and one leg. It was funny. I was glad no one was trying. I decided to do goofy jumping jacks. I made my arms go all over and I kicked sand everywhere. Rhonda and Oksana were laughing. I felt someone tap my shoulder. Adrian. I stopped doing goofy jumping jacks and did a few for real.

It was after nap time. We had just finished practising marching for a whole hour. It helped a bit. I could start out on the proper foot now but I couldn't always keep it going. Spacing was tough too. At the moment, all of us Canadians plus our two translators were sitting in the meal hall around our kid table. Four Russian camp people were sitting on chairs in the aisle. They were administrators, I thought, and maybe a kitchen person too.

"They want to know how they can help." Nadia was translating. "What do you eat at home? They will make it for you here if they can."

Chip and Adrian had already lectured us on picking simple dishes. We would have, anyway. I didn't think anyone would have asked for Cornish game hens. Mom stuffed them with wild rice and smothered them in orange sauce, mmmmm. My mom was a great cook. My dad was a great eater. He could put his stomach on the kitchen table. Mom hated that.

"Spaghetti maybe." Jay was looking all mature. Nadia translated.

"Yeah, or macaroni." I had been planning on saying macaroni so I had to jump in there quick before someone else said it and got the credit for it when we were wolfing it down. I loved Kraft Dinner. Maybe they'd get us some.

"They want to know if you eat anything besides noodles." Nadia laughed.

"Could we have something to drink besides tea every meal, every day?" Iggy asked this. "Like maybe hot chocolate."

"Oh, hot chocolate would be excellent!" Alexi nodded in agreement. Everyone nodded. Nadia translated and a camp administrator wrote it down.

"Stroganoff would be good." I was proud of myself for recommending a Russian dish. They'd for sure know how to make that. Beef stroke-me-off, yummy.

"You are such a stupid capitalist pig!" Little Karl was getting very monotonous. "Only an idiot would ask for a dish that was made for the czars." My face started to go red.

"What about hot dogs?" Rhonda asked. "They're easy and I could sure go for one." Nadia translated. The camp people nodded.

"We get these great hot dogs at home! They're a foot long!" Iggy was what my mom would call "effervescing." "You can't find a bun big enough. They probably don't have those here, but they're the best."

"Anything else?" Nadia asked. We had been told not to ask for too many things. So we just shook our heads politely.

"If you could make us those few things at some point that would be just fantastic," Chip smiled. "We thank you so much. We hope that we have not inconvenienced the camp and the camp cooks too greatly."

"Oh no," Nadia translated. "Orlyonok wants to accommodate

you. Their intention has not been to starve you. They say that they hope you will enjoy your meals in the future, starting tomorrow morning, that is."

We all got up. We all said repeated thank yous as we left. The Russians were laughing. Adrian tapped my shoulder. I froze. Oh no. It was going to be about the treatment. They had found out that I had missed it yesterday.

"Don't worry about the beef stroganoff, Kirsten. The administrators wouldn't have cared. Little Karl doesn't really know what he is talking about. The Soviets eat it. All the beef stroganoff was not repossessed by the Soviet government with the rest of the Stroganoffs' belongings." Adrian chuckled. I didn't get it. He put his hand on my back. He was being friendly. It was almost scarier than him angry.

MAKE THEM FEEL
THE SOVIET UNION
IS A GREAT PLACE.

We were so excited about breakfast. This was going to be our first day with the new food. It was all we could talk about while getting ready this morning. And it was also an exciting morning because Rhonda, Sam, Iggy and I were getting to raise the Canadian flag during row call. We had to be taught how to hold the flag, open the flag and raise the flag before morning row call. That meant we got to miss morning exercises. Yes! I still didn't know if row call was role call, row call or roll call. We were getting to march separate from the others too. One on each corner of the flag. We were now standing waiting at the stairs.

"We are very important." Iggy was being serious.

"I know," I agreed.

"We were chosen because we are the best marchers," Sam said. I wasn't so sure about that.

"Do you remember what to do?" Rhonda looked nervous.

"I think so." I hated it when people put doubt in my mind before I had to do something.

"Keep the flag tighter." Iggy pulled his corner.

"Don't pull it out of my hand." I almost dropped the flag. That would have been awful.

"It has got to be smooth. No wrinkles." He tugged again.

"Iggy!" I lost my corner but quickly grabbed it.

"We have to march at the same speed."

"We know that, Samantha." Rhonda was watching for the *go* sign. We were to take our "left, left, left right left" off of her. "Left, left, left right left," she whispered and marched on the spot. It was going to be hard keeping the flag perfect and our feet perfect on the steps. We had two sets of steps, the ones up to the marching square and then the ones up onto the stage where the flagpoles were. Those would be the important steps, where everyone would see us. We marched ahead of the others because we had the flag.

"Jerks." Jay made a face at us as we marched past.

"Stupid crybabies get to march with the flag because they would have cried so much if they didn't get to." Little Karl stuck out his tongue after he said that. If I hadn't been holding the flag I would have pulled his tongue. That'd hurt, someone getting hold of your tongue.

We marched proudly past the others. We put our noses and knees high. We looked dead ahead. We almost fell up the stairs. The flag went in like an accordion and then out.

"Tight," Iggy whispered. We all quickly recovered and kept going. We pulled our maple leaf tight. Around the square we went, keeping our flag as stiff as a board, pulling our corners for all we were worth. The Soviet flag was ahead of us. They made it look so easy. There was another flag marching too. I didn't know what country it was from. I didn't know flags.

"Get ready for the stairs," Rhonda whispered loudly. This was the scary part; up onto the platform. Rhonda and Sam were in front. They started up. Iggy and I pulled tight. Too tight. Rhonda and Sam came right back down the stairs backwards.

"Keep going," Rhonda commanded. Luckily no one fell and no one was hurt. We moved, all four of us, up the stairs with our flag held tight but not as tight. The toughest part of all was raising the flag. In practice we'd done it upside down, then one of my knots had come undone. Sam got to do the hoisting. The Soviets went first. Their beautiful anthem blared. They were so good. Then it was us. We went over to the pole.

"Other way! Remember?" Rhonda hissed.

"No! This way!" Iggy looked pretty definite. I got to stand to the side, thank goodness. I had no idea which way, either. My knot earlier had "relieved" me of tying on the flag. I didn't even tie my shoelaces right. Rhonda had pointed that out. She was right.

"Hurry!" Sam was ready to pull the rope.

"Think about it, Iggy. It makes sense." Rhonda stared at him.

"Yeah, okay. You're right," Iggy agreed. "O Canada" started playing. Iggy had finished. Rhonda had finished.

"Go!" Rhonda told Sam and Sam started pulling. I held my breath. Please be the right way. Please be the right way. It was. After the anthem finished we were all given roses. We stayed on the stage while the next country went. I didn't recognize their anthem even. I wondered if they knew who we were.

Breakfast finally.

"I wonder what it will be?" Oksana rubbed her hands together. We shoved and pushed getting into our seats.

"What!?!? You didn't bring your roses to breakfast?" Jay was being a butt wipe.

"*Roza.* That's what it is in Russian." I used my intellectual voice.

"Jealous!" Rhonda made a face.

"I don't know why they chose you guys. You are the worst marchers in the group." Dee Dee laughed at us. "All you succeeded in doing was making *all* of Canada look *bad.*"

"That's why they were chosen," Jay added. "The Soviets knew that those four would succeed at making the Soviets look *good.*"

"You couldn't have done any better." Iggy said it but Sam was the one who got punched by Jay. I wouldn't have punched Sam. You never knew when he would explode. It was best to avoid Sam. The others really were jealous. We saw bowls coming our way. The fighting stopped. We watched our meals approaching. This was terrific. My mouth watered. I didn't know what for but it watered. The cafeteria ladies were smiling. The kitchen staff came out to watch. Then plonk, plonk, plonk, the bowls were set on the table.

"Oh my God," Dee Dee said for all of us. It was shocking. "Where's the sauce?"

"Plain macaroni!?" Jay said in disbelief. Then they looked up. Then they all looked at me.

"Kirsten, you asshole! You just said macaroni. You didn't say anything about cheese." Jay was going to kill me. Sam still kept looking at his punched arm. I didn't want a Jay punch, or Indian Sunburn, or pinch, noogie, or anything else he might do.

"Way to go, Kirsten." Dee Dee looked truly disappointed.

"But at home if you said macaroni it would come with the cheese. You wouldn't just get a plate of noodles." I was begging for someone to understand, or agree. No one did. It was true, though, if at home you ordered ravioli in a restaurant it came with the sauce. You didn't have to ask for the sauce as well. Same with spaghetti. You'd just say "I'll have the spaghetti" and the tomato sauce would be there. It wasn't fair. You didn't have to ask for macaroni *and* cheese. The group hated me now. Then the hot chocolate arrived. It was steaming hot. It had obviously been boiled because there was a gross skin on the top. Mom did that to custard sometimes and I wouldn't eat it then. The hot chocolate was way too hot to try.

"Ow! Shit!" Jay had the whole brown, hot chocolate, scummy skin stuck to his top lip and he was trying to peel it off. I bet that hurt. Sam smiled.

"Just plain noodles for breakfast." Rhonda was eating. "Who'da thought? Who'da thought you'd have to tell them that pasta was lunch or dinner? Who'da thought you'd have to ask for sauce? You guys do all realize that we asked for *just* spaghetti too. We didn't say anything about sauce or meatballs."

Thank you, Rhonda. It was true. And actually it was Jay who had asked for the spaghetti. He started it. If he'd said spaghetti and meatballs, well, then I would have said macaroni and cheese. No one apologized to me, though. And no one said anything about Jay being the one who had asked for *just* spaghetti. Maybe they'd forgotten. I never forgot stuff like that. I always remembered everything everyone said and who said it and when. My parents hated that.

"The hot chocolate is really strange." Oksana was blowing and sipping. She was right. It was weird.

"Their milk is different, I think. Maybe it isn't from a cow." Iggy had finished his plain noodles. They were really soggy noodles. There was water in the bowl too. They hadn't been drained well.

"That's it. The milk." Jay's mouth was red where he'd peeled off the milk skin.

"Too bad there aren't marshmallows." Oksana held a napkin around her glass so she wouldn't burn her hands. "It isn't as good as hot cocoa at home."

She was right about that. My mom made the best hot chocolate on the street. All my friends agreed. We had this great toboggan hill and everyone in the neighbourhood came to my house to use it and everyone always asked, "Do you think if we get cold enough your mom would make hot chocolate?" Mom made her hot chocolate with tinned evaporated milk as well as regular two percent. She also added extra sugar and tons of marshmallows. Even people who didn't like evaporated milk in the normal way loved it in her hot chocolate. She used Nestlé's Quik, which was sweet on its own but that extra sugar she added . . . oh boy! Creamy, chocolaty, sweet-goodness! And sometimes she did the ultimate and added sweetened con-densed milk but that was only when she had some left over from making cheesecake and if I had not already had it on my bananas at breakfast.

"Hot chocolate and plain noodles! No one at home would believe it," Alexi chuckled.

Shit. I should write to my parents. I hadn't done that yet. I'd write a letter later on, during nap time maybe.

Lunch. We were excited again but maybe not as much, just in case. We were all sitting at our Canadian dining table again, waiting.

"It could be that the macaroni was plain at breakfast because it was breakfast," Rhonda said with hope in her voice.

"It was very gracious of them to try." Mary seldom smiled and the only time we saw her these days was at meals. "Be polite, no matter."

"Maybe we'll get hot dogs, like Rhonda asked for." Iggy was the most eager.

"Here it comes!" Sam called out. We all watched. We all hoped.

"I don't believe it." Dee Dee started to giggle.

"It's not funny." Jay frowned at me.

"Yes it is," Dee Dee snickered.

"Kirsten, you are so dead!" Jay was definitely going to kill me.

"It's the same as breakfast!" Iggy looked confused. Then the hot chocolate arrived. "Exactly the same."

Chip had explained about the hot chocolate. She said that the Soviet milk wasn't pasteurized like our milk, that it was boiled hard to purify it and that was why it tasted different. Everyone knew better than to even touch their steaming cocoa this time.

"This is crazy." Oksana was laughing too.

"Are we just going to get this over and over for the rest of our time at camp now?" Rhonda spooned up some soggy macaroni noodles. "Should we say something about sauce?"

"I think we should," Dee Dee replied. Mary gave Dee Dee a dirty look and Dee Dee saw it.

The thing was, about the sauce issue, I'd never have told any of the others this, but I liked my pasta plain. In a way, to me, this was a stroke of good fortune. I liked sauce and all but on the side. I always had my noodles and sauce separate. Well, except for macaroni and cheese. I did sometimes eat my cheese sauce *on* my macaroni noodles, sometimes. But spaghetti and meatballs, I always had them separate. I didn't actually even like them touching. Mom gave me compartment plates for eating pasta; that way I didn't get any tomato sauce touching my pasta. I'd never have told the others, though.

Rest period was almost over. I had been going to write to my parents but I didn't feel like it now, not with everybody mad at me about the macaroni business. I had played solitaire on my bed instead. I cheated too. I never cheated at games with other people, only at games I played with myself. I shuffled my deck like a poker pro. We were going to be going to some solidarity meeting. I didn't know what solidarity meant. Little Karl would end up calling me a capitalist pig because I'd end up saying something that showed that I was not really a member of this solidarity club. I was not a member of any club. I hated clubs. Mary was putting her uniform on. She wore it all the time now, even when we didn't have to.

"We should have asked the camp to make *blini*, *baursaki* or *grenki*," Oksana said from her bed.

"What?" I was sure she was still sleeping.

"Pancakes, doughnuts, French toast," Oksana explained. "My parents make all those things. Our bakery is Russian, you know. My mom's never eaten meat."

Chip came into our room. "Hello everybody." She was all smiles. "I just thought I'd come and talk to you before the meeting, maybe go over a few things."

"Sure Chip, have a seat." Dee Dee opened her hand to the row of empty beds that were across from our beds.

"We just want to stress a few things about talking to the Soviet Komsomols. They don't have the things that you have at home, like fancy bicycles or cars. They don't get spending money like all of you do, or get to buy clothes like you do, or have private swimming pools and saunas at their houses. What we don't want you to do is rub their noses in it. It is important to them that they feel that the Soviet Union is a great place. Which it is." This bugged me. We were supposed to make them believe the Soviet Union was a great place and not talk about how great Canada was. This sucked. I just didn't get it. Chip was still going on. "Please don't brag. It won't go over well. They have a different set of values here." Hold it, hold it, hold it. If they had a different set of "values," then we should have been able to brag without it bothering them, or, not brag because it wouldn't have been bragging, but tell the truth. Yes, I had a pool and a fantastic bike. So? That was how it was in Canada. If they didn't think bikes, cars and pools were important, then it shouldn't have bugged them that we did and they shouldn't have felt that the Soviet Union was less great because of it. Also I hated lying this way. My grandma would have said it was being modest. But being modest to me was not bragging to Sherry Taggart about how much my jacket cost, because her family was poor, or about not showing everybody in the neighbourhood my regional public speaking trophy. But if someone asked me, well, that should have been different. If someone had wanted to come see my trophy, they should have been able to. It was like that with this, I didn't see why we should have to lie to the Soviet kids. Canada was great. It was a great place to live. We had great lives.

We were sitting in chairs across from the Soviet Komsomols. It was question period. I felt nervous. I still didn't know what a solidarity meeting even was.

A Soviet girl with very out-of-date glasses asked something and then the interpreter, not one of our translators but a man in a uniform, told us in English what she had asked. "Natasha would like to know if you are Komsomols at home." Oh boy, she was asking if we were young Communist Party members?

Adrian moved to answer. Hey, I thought we kids were supposed to answer the questions. "Sadly," Adrian shook his head, "we do not have Komsomols in Canada yet, but maybe someday we will be lucky enough to be like you." My dad would have hated this. This was one of the reasons he didn't want me to go on this trip. He was scared there would be brainwashing. It was okay, though. Dad didn't have to worry. I couldn't understand why Adrian sucked up to the Soviets so bad. It hadn't occurred to me before but I now realized that he really wanted Canada to be communist like the Soviet Union.

"Now it is your turn to ask a question," the interpreter said to us. We all just sat there in silence. I think everyone was too shocked by Adrian's answer. Well, maybe not the Karls.

Big Karl put up his hand. "What do you want to be when you grow up?"

A boy answered. A very tall boy. Their translator translated. "What I want is what my country wants for me. My country, my government, will decide how I can best serve them. If I am excellent at sports, then my country will support me to the extreme to be an athlete. I am probably going to be a basketball player for the Soviet Olympic team. That is why I am at Orlyonok. Because I excel at basketball. I work very hard!"

Hmmmm, I didn't think I trusted that translator, because his answer was nowhere near the same length as the boy's answer. I wished Nadia was around. She'd tell me the truth, what the tall boy really had said.

Dinner. This was just not a good day. It was macaroni *again*. I had been hoping that it would be plain spaghetti. The change would have been nice, but having everyone look at Jay instead of me would have been nicer.

"What time do we leave for this camping trip tomorrow?" Dee Dee asked. What camping trip, was my question, but I saved it.

"First thing." Alexi was draining the water out of his macaroni bowl into his glass.

"I think I am going to have trouble hiking in the mountains in my sandals." Poor Dee Dee. Wait a sec, hiking in the mountains? Why didn't I know about this?

"Do you think they will keep serving us macaroni on the camping trip?" Little Karl had yet do one thing to make me like him. No one answered him.

"Maybe you should see if there is someone at camp here that can loan you some sneakers, Dee," Big Karl said as he handed the big round loaf of bread to Dee Dee.

"Thanks. Yeah, maybe. That would be okay, depending whose sneakers, I guess." Dee Dee did not look too keen. She was probably the type who brought her own bowling shoes to bowling. "But one thing for sure. I can't hike over rocks and stuff in these sandals, especially carrying a backpack." Carrying a backpack? This was sounding like a serious camping trip; hiking over rocks, in the mountains, carrying our stuff on our backs. Wow!

I HOPE THE TENTS DON'T LEAK.

It was first thing in the morning. We didn't have to go for exercises or roll call since we were going camping. We did still have to make our beds, though. All of us girls were in our room packing. We had been given these army-green knapsacks. They were huge! We had been told not to fill them, though, to leave room for our food.

Chip came in with some shoes. "Dee Dee?"

"She's in the can," Rhonda told Chip.

"Oh. Well, could you get her to try these on and see if any of them fit? I'll be back in a few minutes. I have to go see the boys." Chip dumped the running shoes on the floor and left. There were four pairs altogether.

"Dee Dee isn't going to like any of them." Oksana picked up a pair of high-cut, black basketball shoes.

"Holy shit! She's never going to wear those." Rhonda was laughing at the shoes. "Look at these ones. They don't have laces. Slip-ons like kindergarten kids wear."

"Where did Chip dig these up from?" Oksana was laughing too.

"I think those ugly laceless ones are Sonya's." I was pretty sure I'd seen her wearing them.

"How dare you be so rude!" Mary shoved her marching hat on her head.

"I wouldn't wear that on the motorboat if I was you. You might lose it." Rhonda turned her back on Mary and picked up a plain pair of white canvas—well, off-white because they were pretty dirty—runners. "I bet these are the ones Dee Dee picks. Even if they don't fit. They're the only ones I'd wear, if I had to."

"Yeah, but they look like baton twirler shoes," I snickered. Baton twirling was just about the stupidest pastime I could imagine doing. The Bellamy sisters up the street from me did it. They competed. What a waste of time! My mom always said you should pick hobbies or sports that you would still do when you were an adult. I somehow couldn't see my grandma twirling a baton with her friends. The worst thing about majorettes was their outfits. I wouldn't be caught dead.

Dee Dee came into the room. She looked upset. "I wish there were doors on those stalls! It's inhumane!"

I wanted to ask what had happened but I didn't. Dee Dee wasn't really the type to talk about stuff like that. "Hey, Dee Dee—"

Rhonda cut me off. "There's a Chip delivery for you." She pointed to the shoes. Oksana, Rhonda and I all muffled giggles. Dee Dee just stood there, staring at the assorted runners. She reached for the dirty white ones.

"I told you, I told you, I told you!" Rhonda exploded.

"What?" Dee Dee looked confused.

"We knew you'd pick those ones." Oksana could be shrill sometimes. She was no longer "the quiet one."

Dee Dee sniffed the off-white shoe before she put it on. "Like I have a choice!"

"I think you should wear Sonya's." I was laughing really hard.

"You ungrateful witches! You have no right to laugh at Sonya's shoes! She has been so generous to loan them! You make me SICK!" Mary heaved her backpack up and stomped out of the room. If Mary had been different, she'd have made me feel guilty.

"Why is she wearing her uniform all the time now?" Rhonda took her toe socks out of her backpack and put sport socks in instead.

Dee Dee was walking around in the majorette sneakers, test-ing them. "She told me that clothes set people apart, that uni-forms make them equal or something. She thinks we should all wear our uniforms all the time. She wants to be just like the Soviets. These runners aren't much better than my sandals. Their sole is paper-thin."

Chip breezed in, smiling as usual. "Well, Dee Dee? Do any of them fit?"

"These are the closest." Dee Dee hadn't even tried on any of the others. "They're a little small, but I think they'll be okay."

"Wonderful!" Chip picked up the unwanted shoes. "I'll go tell Olga." Olga? Surely not the Olga from the hospital. I didn't remember her wearing those shoes. I didn't remember her feet, actually. Now I was going to be caught for missing the treat-ments. Shit. "Oh, by the way, everyone, could you please meet outside the kitchen, in the meal hall, with your backpacks, in five minutes?" Chip left.

We all stood outside the swinging kitchen doors. It wasn't just us. There were a group of Italians and lots of Soviets. We were being made to fill our bags with potatoes. I hadn't been given mine yet.

"You have to admit, macaroni would have been lighter," Iggy teased Jay. Jay gave Iggy a wedgie. Just a little one but still. Iggy's pants were so loose now it was pretty easy for Jay to pull the jeans right up Iggy's crack.

"Aw man!" Iggy pulled his pants back down. "I was just joking."

"Iggy, I think we need to put another notch in your belt." Adrian came over. He didn't say anything to Jay for being so mean.

Iggy undid his belt and handed it over to Adrian. "Rhon," I whispered. "Look. You can see Iggy's butt crack."

"Why do you think I would want to see that?" She looked anyway. She laughed.

I was pushed over to the potato table. My bag was filled. There must have been a dozen massive potatoes shoved in my knap-sack. "I thought we were just going for two days."

165

"Yes, two days," a fat woman said. She was Russian. I was surprised she spoke any English. I had to be more careful of that. Sometimes I said things, assuming they wouldn't understand.

"Well, I won't eat this many potatoes in two days." I wasn't whining.

"We share burden. Everyone equal."

"Yeah, but I'm not going to eat all these, so I don't see why I should have to—"

"KIRSTEN!" Adrian came at me holding Iggy's belt. It scared me. He'd never have hit me. He wasn't even threatening. But just someone coming at you holding a belt, you know. I grabbed my knapsack. I could barely lift it now, with all the shit I'd been given. I didn't even like stupid potatoes. Stupid Adrian. Stupid fat woman. My bag hit the floor and I dragged it over to the next food line. Onions.

We were in three long, red and blue wooden motorboats, roaring across the Black Sea. There were about twelve people in each boat. Cool water kept splashing inside the boat from the waves. I couldn't help smiling. It was great! The boats were going to take us around the coast and drop us off. Then we were going to have to hike up a mountain and set up camp. There were two Komsomol leaders in our boat, Moyseen and a different Nadia. They were boyfriend and girlfriend. You could tell they were leaders because of the funny pointed elf hats they were wearing before boarding. It seemed the name Nadia was as popular in the Soviet Union as Karen was at home. I had three Karens in my grade six class. There were a lot of Natashas in the Soviet Union too. Moyseen was a huge hunk! I couldn't stop looking at him. He kept smiling at me with a "what a cute little girl" smile. Nadia kept smiling at me too. She was pretty like Dorothy Hamill, except without the haircut. I wished I was Nadia. No, not really. I just wished I had Nadia's place but was me still. Moyseen, Moyseen, Moyseen. I liked his name too. Moyseen. They were younger than Chip and Adrian, who were in their late twenties, but older than Dee Dee and Jay. Maybe Moyseen and Nadia were eighteen or twenty. It was so hard to tell. The Russian young people looked younger than us but the old people looked older than our old people. Then there were the Italians. The Italian kids looked like grown-ups. They all smoked too. The Italian sixteen-year-olds looked like twenty-year-olds. And fashion. Boy! Their fashions were way ahead of ours in Canada. I didn't realize that until Dee Dee told me. I figured they just had different styles in Italy. The Italians all looked like they had just stepped out of a magazine. The Italian girls had been wearing wedge high-heeled sandals with their jeans earlier. Dee Dee said that meant we would be doing it next year. None of us Canadians had heels here. And none of us wore heels with jeans. We wore our sneakers. I didn't think I'd be wearing heels with my jeans next year even if it was the fashion. I'd never be able to run away from Doggie Dogdirt and his clods of earth or whatever he might decide to throw at Patty and me. I'd be dead. It was like what my dad said to Mom about bears, when we were camping up in Killarney Park. He said, "Rosemary, I don't have to run faster than the bear, I just have to run faster than *you*." Well, I could run faster than Patty right now and I wanted to keep it that way.

"Kirsten, come get your backpack!" Chip couldn't see me and I was hiding. I was hoping that the boat would leave with my pack before anyone realized. We were on shore now, unloading the boats and getting ready to hike up the mountain. The mountains weren't huge like the Alps or Rockies. They were old and worn like the ones in Killarney Provincial Park.

"KIRSTEN!" I could see Chip. She was looking all over for me. I had no choice. I couldn't believe I was going to have to lug those stupid potatoes and onions up a mountain. "KIRSTEN!" I stepped out from behind Moyseen.

"Oh, Chip."

"Where were you? I have been looking all over and calling and calling."

"You were? Oh. Gee. I didn't hear you. Sorry." I picked up

my knapsack. I couldn't even get it around to my back, it was so heavy. Chip helped. The straps were too long and it hung down below my bum to the back of my knees.

"This is no good." Chip pulled it off me. "We have to adjust this. Hmmmm."

"What?" I crossed my fingers. Maybe mine was broken. Maybe the stuff would have to be taken out and divided up among all the other people.

"This is as small as it goes. Sorry. I guess you'll just have to hang on to the straps at the front to keep it up." Chip walked away to help Sam. My dad would never have let this happen. Equipment always had to be perfect.

"How am I going to climb a mountain if I can't use my hands because they are holding onto my knapsack straps?" No one was with me. I said it out loud anyway. The motorboats were leaving. We all waved goodbye to the drivers.

"My family doesn't go camping." Dee Dee's backpack fit way better than mine did, because she was tall.

"My family does. We go on canoe trips in the wilderness. Canoeing's better than carrying backpacks," I sighed.

"I wonder how far we have to go." Rhonda's pack didn't fit great, either, but better than mine. "Jeepers, look at Mary."

"What is she doing?" Dee Dee's mouth dropped open.

Mine had too and no wonder. Mary was carrying everything. She was over with the fat Soviet woman who had filled my bag with potatoes earlier. Mary was loaded up with huge pots and maybe an army tent. She had a pack on the front and one on the back too.

Our leaders were yelling at us in three different languages to start moving.

"Pull it tighter!" We were at the top, on a small plateau that joined two mountaintops. Rhonda called it a saddle. We were setting up camp. "Tighter!"

"All right, Rhonda!" I grunted. Rhonda wanted us to have the "best tent." We had already missed having the first set up, or the second, or the third, so now we were going for the tightest, most secure, best-looking tent. The Canadian boys had the first tent up. The tents were huge. They slept six or more. They had a big metal pole in the middle. I could almost stand up in it. I had a pup tent at home. I bought it from Canadian Tire with pennies we saved in a three-foot-high, plastic, brown, Canada Dry bottle-piggy bank. My pup tent was orange and light blue nylon. These tents were army-green canvas.

"Let me bang it in!" Rhonda took over my tent peg. The ground was so rocky it was near impossible to bang them in. Rhonda drove it in deep. "How you doing, Ana?"

"Got this one right down, Rhon!" Oksana was on the other side. I couldn't see her.

Mary was over with the Russian cooks, making lunch. I guessed it was going to be potatoes and onions. At my friend Tara's camp in Algonquin Park, they made this stuff over the campfire with bananas, chocolate chips and marshmallows wrapped up in tinfoil. Sounded terrific. We wouldn't get that here.

"KIRSTEN!" Rhonda was standing with her hands on her hips. Who made her boss today? "If you aren't going to hammer pegs, you can at least pull the string tight."

"Move!" Dee Dee was hitting my shoe. "I have to put the peg in here." I moved.

Everyone was standing around our tent, clapping. All the countries were clapping for us. The Canadian girls had won "Best Tent." Rhonda, Dee Dee, Oksana and I, the best tent-setter-uppers in the world! Now it was lunch. Or that is what I gathered from the cook banging the pot with her ladle. Mary did not help us set up our tent. She did not even come over to look at our tent.

"We get to go swimming after lunch!" Sam was wearing his tin bowl like a hat.

"We set up our tent way faster than you did!" Iggy already had his lunch. I could see in his bowl. It was a mess of blahiyuck. Potatoes, onions, kasha, water. No thanks.

"Fast is not as important," Rhonda scorned.

"It is if you are trying to get out of the rain!" Iggy did a raspberry. There was potato on his tongue. Gross. Sam had his spoon stuck to his nose now. What a couple of morons. Rhonda and I left.

"I'm not eating." If Rhonda wanted to, she could, but I really had no desire to eat the potatoes and onions I had lugged up the mountain. Not cooked like that. Ashes and smoke were blowing our way from the campfire too.

"Me neither. Let's go sit in the tent!" Man, Rhonda and her tent!

"Okay. Maybe we should get ready for swimming." I was glad that we didn't have to have a nap while camping. And because we had to go all the way down the mountain to get to the sea, we were allowed to go swimming right after lunch too.

Dee Dee was in the tent. She was crying. "This sucks," she sobbed as we crouched into the tent. Well, Rhonda crouched. I could practically walk upright.

"What's wrong?" Rhonda sat down beside Dee Dee on her sleeping bag.

"I have my period! And in case you have not noticed, there aren't any toilets around here! No outhouses, nothing!" Dee Dee blew her nose. Her eyes were all swollen.

Poor Dee Dee. This was really awful. I didn't have my period yet. None of my friends did. Though Betty Lil'Canoe pretended to get hers last year at school. She didn't, though. No one got their period like that. She wore sanitary pads every gym class to show off. Well, my mom said you got it only once a month for three to seven days. Betty was getting hers every week and that was just not possible. All the girls in my class wanted their periods. I did and didn't. Dee Dee was an example of why I didn't.

"Are you using pads or tampons?" Rhonda asked this. I never would have, but Rhonda knew what she was talking about because she got her period.

"I only brought tampons because of swimming and things. They're easier and took up less room in my bag. But now ..." Dee Dee could barely speak. "I mean, a napkin I could have changed in the tent but what am I supposed to do about a tampon? What if someone sees me? What am I supposed to do with it after? What am I going to do?"

"It's a good thing you packed them in your carry-on. Man, Dee Dee, who knows what they do for tampons in Russia? Wow, look at your toothbrush. I mean, it had already been used …" I was trying to show her things could have been worse. She made a "throw-up" face at me. What had I said?

"We'll hike with you into the woods and post guard." Rhonda had a good idea there. "We'll have to do that for each other for going to the bathroom anyway. There is no way I want to get caught by one of the boys with my pants down. Just bury your tampon, Dee Dee. Stick it under a rock or something."

"Yeah," I agreed, though I had been planning on holding poo and peeing in the sea. I could hold poo for days. I held it for an entire week when my family went camping last summer. So did Muzik, my Siamese cat. He wouldn't go without his litter box. There was sand around the campsite and everything. It should have been the perfect litter box, but he just wouldn't. I held it because I had such a hard time going anywhere but on my toilet at home.

The sea did not look like the same sea that we arrived on. There were whitecaps now and the waves were pretty big. The beach here was all stones like in England. I always thought that was funny in England, how they called it a beach but there wasn't any sand. The English may have called their beaches pebbled but I called them bouldered. You could buy candies in England that looked like the pebbles at the beach. They really did. They tasted okay but not great. I always wondered why rock candy, the pink, hard, peppermint-tasting sticks, was called rock. You could buy rock at the same places you got the pebbles. I thought that was funny. Rock candy always had the place name written on the inside all the way through it. Like Brighton in England or Niagara Falls in Canada. How did they do that?

"There are jellyfish here too!" Rhonda was in already. "Hello! Earth to Kirsten. What is with you today? You coming in?"

"The waves must have brought the jellyfish. There weren't any when we arrived." I was standing knee-deep in the water but the next thing a wave crashed right into me, up to my shoulders.

Iggy was standing a couple of feet away from me. I could see his bum crack again as his bathing trunks weren't staying up well anymore. There were jellyfish at my ankles. I picked one up. I walked over to Iggy, pulled open his trunks and dropped it inside.

"What the hell?" Iggy's face went blank. He couldn't believe what happened. Rhonda was behind him now. She picked up two monster jellyfish and dropped them into the back of his shorts. Then Iggy screamed. I could never have screamed like that even if I was being murdered. It was a girl-in-a-movie scream.

"HOLD HIM!" Rhonda shouted. Sam and I obeyed. She stuffed more into his trunks, down the front now. Iggy was wriggling like hell. We were laughing like maniacs. You would have thought the jellyfish were the stinging kind by the fuss Iggy was making. Then he splashed deeper into the water. So we picked up jellyfish and started hurling them at him.

"Christ, you guys! I got one in my ear." Iggy was banging the side of his head like when you got water in your ear, but it was jelly in his.

"ASTANAVEETSA! STOP!" A Russian Komsomol leader was yelling at us. "STOP!" She looked very upset, like she could cry. God, Iggy wasn't hurt or anything.

"Shit, you guys!" Iggy had his bathing suit off now and was emptying the jellyfish out of his trunks. He was deep enough in the water that you couldn't see his weenie.

"Those are living creatures you have killed!" The Komsomol girl was standing in the water in her shoes. "When you pick up, you rip, when you rip, it die. You have killed gentle animals!" I'd never thought of jellyfish as living before. I just thought of them as blobs of jelly floating in the water. This girl made me feel shitty. "Do not pick up and throw. Very cruel." She waded back out of the water in her shoes.

"Who cares," Rhonda said quietly. I cared, though. I wouldn't throw them any more. I'd try not to let my hands rip through them any more when swimming, either.

"There is Chip, Chip, looking for some dip in the store, in the store, in the store. There is Chip, Chip, looking for some dip in the Quarter Master's Store. My eyes ar-re dim, I cannot see. I have no-ot brought my specs with me. I have no-ot brought my-e, specs, with, me." Songs around the campfire. If only there were marshmallows to toast. The Russians started singing a song now. It was beautiful but not the type where everyone could join in. Moyseen and Nadia were holding hands. Sonya and some man I'd never seen before were sitting very close. There was lightning in the distance and faint rumbles of thunder. The Komsomol girl who yelled at us about the jellyfish earlier had a beautiful singing voice. You could pick hers out because she was singing in harmony. Whenever I tried doing that on my own, it just sounded off key.

"Raindrop." Oksana showed us her knee where it hit.

"I hope the tents don't leak." Dee Dee had just moved over to our side of the fire as the sparks were getting bad on the other side. The wind had really picked up.

"Another one." Oksana tapped her nose. I hadn't been hit yet.

"Mary is still over there helping the cooks clean up after dinner, eh?" Rhonda nodded towards the kitchen tent. "Do you think she is going to sleep over there too? She hasn't even moved her sleeping bag into our tent yet."

"She hates us for some reason." Oksana shrugged.

"Nah, that's not it. Mary's upset at Sonya, because Sonya's sharing a tent with that man," Rhonda said. "Sonya's engaged to some other guy. But it isn't like they are the only people in the tent, so I don't get it."

"I'm tired." I hoped it would rain harder so they'd make us go to our tents.

"Yeah, me too," Oksana agreed. The Italians were singing now.

"Raindrop." Rhonda had been hit.

"Sssssh." A Russian girl with the whitest skin I had ever seen (except for the skin on the albino I saw in the parking lot at Shoppers World once) hissed at us. "Sssssh."

"Was that for pointing out that it is raining, or for talking?" Rhonda asked. The White Russian gave her a dirty look. We sat and listened to the Italian group sing.

"All right, everyone, it is time to batten down the hatches!" Adrian had obviously been waiting for the Italians to finish so he could say this. I'd been hit by quite a few drops myself now.

"AGGGHHHHHH!"

I had been sleeping for maybe an hour. I didn't know who had screamed. Maybe it was all of us. The thunder was right on top of us. Lightning and thunder happening exactly at the same time.

"We are going to die!" Oksana was sitting up, rocking back and forth with her hands over her ears. Another flash and crack. The wind was vicious too. The tent was blowing like mad.

"We are on a fucking mountain. We are practically the highest thing!" Rhonda had her flashlight on. You didn't need it half the time with all the lightning.

"The metal pole is not good!" I shouted as loud as I could.

"Yeah, if the lightening is going to get anything, it is the pole!" Dee Dee was wearing her sleeping bag like a hood.

"We need rubber!" I screamed right after I said this because of the huge bang. The lightning was so constant that the tent remained brilliantly lit for minutes.

"I have never seen anything like this in my life!" As Oksana said this, a huge gust of wind shook the tent but it hung on.

"Our running shoes!" I yelled.

"Yes! Everyone tie your running shoes around the pole. We'll be able to ground the lightning that way. Just like rubber tires on a car." Rhonda was already tying her sneakers around the metal pole in the middle of the tent. I followed. I tied as quickly as I could. I didn't want to be touching the pole too long. Crash. I screamed. Done. My shoes slid to the bottom of the pole. Oksana went next and then Dee Dee.

Someone was unzipping the front of our tent. "Hello! Coming in." It was Chip and the Italian girls. "Their tent has come down," Chip bellowed as everyone came piling into our tent. "Actually it didn't just come down, it was blown right away."

Suddenly there was a horrific crack of thunder at the exact same time as the brightest lightning bolt probably ever to exist. The hair on my body was standing on end. We were all screaming as if we had been hit.

"Shit, a tree at the edge of the campsite has been hit." Chip was struggling to close the zipper.

We all squished together and held hands. One of the Italian girls was crying. The little chubby one named Gina. She was my age. I hated storms but they were so exciting that I loved them too. Though this one was a bit beyond what I loved.

"The Canadian boys have lost their tent too. They have joined the Russian boys," Chip hollered.

"Yahoo Rhonda!" Dee Dee clapped her hands but you couldn't hear her over the gale.

"Chip, I'm scared!" Oksana's eyes were like saucers. Eyes like *flying* saucers!

"We are all scared, Ana." Chip crawled over the bodies and put her arms around Oksana. The wind hit the tent hard again.

"We're still holding!" Dee Dee screamed. "I sure am glad that we didn't aim for *first* tent set-up."

"Tie your running shoes around the pole." Rhonda pointed to our decorated tent pole. The Italians understood and took their shoes off and added them to our pole. Our tent unzipped again. It was Mary.

"The kitchen is gone!" she yelled as she crawled in. "So is the boys' tent and, ah, I see the Italian girls are here. The Italian boys are now without a tent too. They have had to get into the Soviet boys' tent." Mary moved into a corner. It was getting pretty crowded in our tent. It made me think of a small yellow storybook I had when I was little called *The Tent*. "Bill led Ted to the tent. Ted led Al to the tent" and so on. I hoped our story wouldn't end up like that story, though. An Italian girl with a haircut like a boy tried to close the zipper. She couldn't. Then we saw it was because someone else from the outside was trying to open it. It was a Russian girl.

"Come in!" Chip yelled. "Welcome. *Dabropazhalavat... Fkhadeet ... um... fkhadeetee.* Yes that's it, come in, *fkhadeetee!*" The Soviet girls pushed into the tent. We were about to make the *Guinness Book of World Records* for the most people to ever fit into a tent. There was lightning. I timed it. It just stayed light. It was constant. I could see my watch. The thunder was deafening. It stayed light. It was light for three minutes and ten seconds without a break. This was unreal!

The "Morning After." We sang that song with Mr. Hallett in music class. It was one of those mornings after a storm when the sun was brighter than normal and the sky bluer. We were looking for stuff that had blown away in the night. Like all the tents except for two. The Russian boys' tent and our tent were the only ones that had remained standing. We had been first and second place for best tent. The judges of that contest were bang on. People were photographing the tree that had been hit. The tree was only as far from our tent as home plate to first base.

"If any of the tents had been closer to that tree, the people inside would have been electrocuted because the electricity goes through the root system of the tree." Big Karl whistled after he said this, a whistle to say, that was close.

"The cooks can't make breakfast because all the wood is wet." Iggy and Sam came over to inform me of this. Why they thought I'd care about potato and onion.

"What are they fighting about?" I pointed to Moyseen and another Komsomol.

"The sea, apparently," Iggy shrugged.

"What about the sea?" Why would people argue about the sea?

"The waves are too big and the boats won't be able to come get us." Now, this was more interesting than wet wood. If I'd crossed a campground to give someone the exciting dirt of the morning, it would have been rough sea dirt, not potato dirt.

Adrian and Chip and the Italian leaders were over with the arguing Komsomols.

"Democracy in action," Little Karl said in passing. He said it in his typical sarcastic, sneery, snobby voice. For some reason he always pointed these comments at me. I didn't know why. I didn't even know what the hell he was talking about. What did a group of arguing people have to do with democracy? The argument continued. All of us kids just stood and watched. Three different languages going at it. Then it ended.

"Canadians over here!" Adrian called us over to the front of our tent. The Italians went to near the burnt tree and the Soviets stayed by the soggy firepit. "We are going to have to hike over the mountains. If we wait any longer we won't be able to get over the mountains before nightfall. There is a road on the other side of the mountains and the Komsomol leaders say a bus will be sent to meet us. This is what they do in the case of high seas or bad weather. We can't stay here as we don't have enough food and most of the camping equipment has been blown away or destroyed."

"How far is it?" Good point, Dee Dee.

"It will take us the entire day." Adrian's face was pretty serious. He was not even pretending that it would be fun. I almost wished he would pretend. It had been really hard climbing up to the campsite. I had been one hundred percent exhausted from that and if I was going to have to do that sort of thing for a whole day, well, I didn't know if I could.

The sweat was pouring off me. Why did it have to be so hot? I had no idea it would be so hot when we set out in the morning. The family Von Trapp didn't look like this escaping across the mountains in *The Sound of Music*.

"Boys, slow down!" Adrian was puffing. We had already climbed over the mountain we had camped on and were getting near the top of the next one. "You have to be able to keep this up for the rest of the day and if you wear yourselves out now, you will regret it and *no one,* get this, no one, is going to carry you."

"We won't get tired." I hoped Little Karl would end up eating those words.

"Slow down anyway. We can't afford to have you slip and hurt yourselves." Adrian's forehead was dotted with drops.

"Uhhhgh." I couldn't get up the rocky ledge. It was like stepping from the floor in my room to the top of my dresser, which I actually could do by using my arms, like getting out of the pool. If only I didn't have a stupid, too-big knapsack on that kept pulling me back down the mountain. I felt as if a bungee cord was attached between me and a tree at the bottom.

"Take it off, Kirsten, and put it on the ledge. Then climb up." I did what Chip said. It worked. We continued going up. "We can rest at the top for a bit," Chip gasped. "We'll have to." We continued. I wiped sweat out of my eyes. It burnt worse than the sea water.

"Fuck!" I had slipped and scraped my knee because of being blinded by sweat.

"WHOSE LANGUAGE?" Adrian stood above looking down.

"Kirsten's." Little Karl was going to be lucky if he got out of these mountains alive. "She swears all the time."

It was true. I'd got in big shit in grade four from my teacher Mr. Darlington, for telling Michael Greene to fuck off. Mr. Darlington would never have known if Michael Greene hadn't told on me. So I told Michael Greene to fuck off again later, after I'd been bawled out by Mr. Darlington. Michael Greene's head was too big for his body. I figured when he was born the doctors didn't massage it back into shape. Or it was the head massager's first day.

"I don't want to hear language like that out of your mouth again." *Fuck off, Adrian!* Saying it in your head wasn't quite as good.

Finally the top. I dropped my stuff by a flat rock where Dee Dee was already sitting.

"Awww. My feet are killing." Dee Dee was taking off her fairy twirler shoes. She wiggled her toes. "I'm scared I'm going to pop out the front of these things."

"My feet hurt too." I had had the feeling all morning that there was a blister happening on the back of my right heel. That was my big foot. My right foot was a half size larger than my left foot. It was really hard to buy shoes.

"Take off your shoes." Dee Dee was airing her toes, spreading them wide.

"Yeah, that looks like it feels good." I took off my North Stars and socks. Yup, there was a blister all right. Huge. On the back of my right heel. I always got them there, which was weird because you'd have thought that my smaller foot would have been the one that would rub in the shoe.

"You should pop that." Dee Dee was nuts if she thought I was going to do that.

"No!" Rhonda came over with some water. "Never burst a blister during a hike. It's there for protection." She handed me the canteen. "This is it, the end of the water, all we get." I had a sip and gave it to Dee Dee. I put my socks back on and then my shoes.

"I should never have taken my shoes off." I could barely get my right one back on. "What has happened to my feet? Oh God. Shit. My right heel kills just touching the back of my shoe now!"

"Yeah. You shouldn't have taken your shoes off. You never do that." Rhonda actually did seem to know a lot about this camping and hiking stuff.

"Dee Dee told me to," I mouthed to Rhonda.

"Dee Dee is from Toronto," Rhonda mouthed back. "What's wrong with Mary?"

"She was bitten by some disgusting insect, on her back." Dee Dee handed back the canteen.

"Moving out!" Adrian yelled this but he was still sitting down. I wondered what Miss Dilly would have said about that in our body language class in grade five. If I remembered right, that was saying one thing with your mouth but your body was saying the opposite about how you really felt. I bet Adrian just really wanted to swear like me.

We had to wait for the buses. That had caused more arguments about whether they were even coming. Then there was panic—maybe the boats had been sent after all and maybe the sea had only been rough where we were and not at Orlyonok. We sat on the roadside for half an hour. Then there was panic that we had come down out of the mountains in the wrong place. Then the two buses arrived and the excitement ended. Nobody was singing on this bus trip. Nobody was even talking. We had all also tried to keep whole seat rows to ourselves when we loaded on board, instead of sitting beside one another like we usually did. I took my shoes off now. My sock was stiff with blood. My blister had popped on its own. I had to peel the sock away from the back of my heel. It made my blister bleed again. My head was bursting too. I still had my vision so I hoped it wouldn't be a migraine. Even if I did get one, there was no way I'd tell anyone because there was no way I'd go back to that unsanitorium. Next thing they'd be giving me treatments of the brain. Shit, spots in front of my eyes. Shit. I needed to get a 222 in me before it was too late. I needed codeine!

"I don't even want dinner when we get back to camp. I just want a shower and bed," Dee Dee moaned from the seat behind me.

"Maybe they'll give us a *good* dinner, though, because we've missed ours and we aren't eating at regular mealtimes." Rhonda had been talking about hot dogs for the past hour. I couldn't join in their conversation. My head. I had 222s in my suitcase in our room. Mom had given me some just in case. Hurry up, bus. I wished I'd brought them camping.

"These winding roads make me feel sick to my stomach." Iggy opened his window wide and stuck his head out.

"At least there isn't any food in your stomach to throw up." Dee Dee had her feet up on the back of my seat. They smelled. I didn't say anything, though. You couldn't very well tell someone older than you that their feet smelled. My head. My head. I closed my eyes.

We had had our dinner. It had been beef stroganoff. Sadly, it wasn't enough like beef stroganoff that you got at home that I could point it out to the others. The noodles were stroganoff kind of noodles and there were stringy bits of beef in it but there was no sour cream and wine sauce or mushrooms or onions or anything to make it taste good. But still, stroganoff is what it was. We were now sitting in one of the camp's indoor theatres. We were about to see a human circus. If it had been just a plain old regular circus, I would have stayed in my room. I hated circuses with animals.

"How's your head now?" Rhonda had seen me swallowing a 222 in the room before dinner. I had to tell her about my headache but made her promise to keep it a secret.

"The pill is starting to work," I whispered, but still looked around just to make sure no one was listening.

"You know how you said you didn't want anyone to know because you don't want to be sent back for treatments? Well, I was thinking, maybe the headache is from the treatments they were giving you in the first place. Maybe they've done something to your brain."

The lights went out. It was black. You couldn't see a thing and then the circus began. Why did Rhonda have to leave me with a thought like that? Acrobats. No, this headache was like other headaches. There was nothing different. The men looked like they had huge balls in those leggings. Massive bulges between the tumblers' legs, massive. This was just a regular bad headache. Nothing was wrong with me. Look at those balls!

IT DIDN'T REALLY LOOK MUCH LIKE A FORT. OH WELL.

We were having a sandcastle-building competition. The whole world was competing. We walked halfway down the beach to case out the joint.

"Here," Jay selected our spot. No one argued. What was to argue about, anyway? It was as good a place as any. All the sand was the same. Perfectly clean, no stones or sticks or weeds, just the odd dead jellyfish. The beach was raked every day. We stood in a circle around Jay's stick in the ground and stared at the sand.

"What are we going to build?" Rhonda asked.

"I guess some sort of castle." Jay poked his stick in deeper. "It's a sandcastle-building contest, so I guess a castle."

"Maybe we should make it something more Canadian." Big Karl crouched down and ran the sand between his fingers. "It will need to be wetter."

"What about a fort of some sort?" Alexi sounded doubtful.

"Yeah, that's a great idea!" Big Karl stood up. "We don't have castles in Canada and I'm not counting Castle Loma." He looked at Dee Dee with his Castle Loma comment. Casa Loma was some rich guy's dream house in Toronto, not really an old castle at all, but it was beautiful. Big Karl squinted and scratched his chin. "A fort ... now, that is very Canadian and served the same purpose as early British castles before they just became monuments to display the royalty's wealth. I think that's a great idea!" Big Karl was starting to sound like Adrian.

"Me too! I think it is a very good idea." Little Karl was trying to look professional, surveying the sand like Big Karl and Jay.

"It will be hard to build a fort without Popsicle sticks."

Everyone laughed at Iggy's comment. I bet we all had had someone in our classes at school who built a fort out of Popsicle sticks for a Canadian history project. It was Colin Tate in my grade four class who built a Popsicle-stick fort. He said it was Fort George at Niagara-on-the Lake. It was pretty awesome. It had everything. His mom did it for him. She did all of Colin's projects. You could tell. Colin gave out Laura Secord chocolates to everyone in the class when he presented his project because Laura Secord led her cow to tell the soldiers the Americans were coming; that was before she made chocolates. I now knew the chocolate gifts were smart because no one complained that Colin's mom did his project for him like we usually did. I bet his mom realized she'd gone too far with the fort when they had to rent a van to bring it to the school. That was when she probably realized it would take Laura Secord candy to shut the rest of us up, or to stop us from beating Colin up at recess. I liked Laura Secord butterscotch suckers. But the first two sucks always tasted better than the rest. The butterscotch tasted better on the outside of the sucker, it was different somehow.

"... there." Jay had outlined the fort with his stick in the sand. I had missed exactly what we were doing.

"What are we supposed to do?" I whispered to Rhonda.

"Carry water up."

"To build a lake?"

"No, to make the sand wet."

"Where will the lake be, though?"

"There isn't a lake. What are you talking about a lake for?"

"Forts are always on water, or have rivers or oceans nearby." Well, all the forts I'd been to had that, anyway.

"Well, tell Jay."

"Um, Jay." I didn't like talking to Jay. "We should build a river or lake or something by the fort." My heart was beating.

"Okay." That was it. He didn't make me feel like an idiot. Weird. "Kirsten, Rhonda, Iggy and Sam are in charge of excavating a pond beside the fort."

This was great—we were working as a team, no fighting, just working together. Nobody was being rude about anyone else's ideas or suggestions. Nobody was making fun of anyone. We dug. We built. We hauled water. We filled. We smoothed. We patted. We wetted. We were finished and in good time.

"More water in the pond!" Iggy yelled. It was a problem, keeping it filled. Rhonda and I ran back and forth with two more bucketsful of water.

"There!" Big Karl stood back and admired our work. I had to say it wasn't great. It didn't really look much like a fort. Oh well. We'd made something, anyway.

We put our Canadian team sign up beside our mound and hole. I once ate a bag of crisps on a picnic bench outside a pub in England called the Mound & Hole, or was it the Hound & Mole. No, you couldn't tell what our fort was if you didn't already know. Then all the teams were called down to the far end of the beach. It was the start of the judging. We would all move down the beach in order, viewing each country's project. We walked down the beach together to the start of the judging.

"Shit," Jay muttered as we passed a futuristic city with road ramps in the air and onion-towered skyscrapers, all made from the same sand that we had used for our fort. It was like *The Jetsons,* this city. The kids were just finishing up on it. You could hear them talking in Russian. What was with these super-human Soviet kids and their solar inventions, solidarity meetings and futuristic cities? We continued walking. We were all silent. We got to the end of the beach. We were at the first castle. It was made by Soviet kids too. It was Neptune the sea god and mermaids and Greek stuff and it looked like a carving at a museum.

"This is embarrassing," Dee Dee said quietly to the rest of us.

"These people are going to see our fort," Jay whispered. We moved to the next sand sculpture. That was what these were. I didn't know why it had been called a sandcastle competition because there weren't any castles that I could see. These were sculptures. Holy Canoli. It was the Kremlin. You could tell, not just tell, it was perfect. Everything was there.

"We should go remove our sign," Big Karl hissed. "I don't want people to know the fort is ours. Do you guys?"

"Skip that, they'll still know." We were standing in front of a life-size statue of Lenin. "This is nuts, man!" Jay had his arms crossed and his sunglasses down his nose. "We have to send someone to destroy the fort. We can't let them get to the fort!" Jay was right. We all looked at each other. This was bad. Very bad.

"Who should go?" Dee Dee asked. This was scary.

"Kirsten," Jay said. The others nodded.

"Why me?" My heart was in my throat. The whole big lump of it.

"Because you are the smallest and no one will notice you. You have to get to the fort and knock it down before the rest of the world gets there." Jay was serious. They were all serious.

"Okay." I was a good soldier. I would do it. I would get back to the fort and destroy it before it fell into enemy hands. I would do this for Canada. *O Canada, our home and native land, true patriot love, in all our sons command, with glowing hearts, we see thee rise, the true north strong and free.* I ran down the beach, as fast as my legs would carry me. I looked back. Everyone was looking at the next sculpture, no one was looking at me. *We stand on guard for thee, O Canada, we stand on gua-ard for thee.* Faster, Kirsten. I ran in the sand. I got to the fort. It looked worse than I remembered it. The pond was empty and the sand on the outside of the fort was drying out and crumbling. It was the crappiest castle on the beach. I started to kick in the walls. Quickly. I kicked like a fiend. I kicked the beaver the others let me mould by the pond. You couldn't tell what it was, even, and it was way too big. I kicked its head off. The beaver could have eaten the people who lived in the fort, it was so big. I jumped on the beaver and caved in the pond. Then whistles blew. I looked up. It was too late to run. A hand came down on the back of my neck. I was pulled away from the fort. The fort lay in ruins. I had completed my mission. People from all around the world were looking down the beach at me. I was hauled away. Captured, yes, but successful.

I was sitting in an office with three uniformed Russians looking at me. I'd say nothing. They'd get nothing from me. Adrian entered.

"We do not understand. We thought this was a child from another country destroying the Canadian contest entry but it seems she might be a Canadian. Is she one of yours? We can make her say nothing but *ya nee paneemayoo Rooskeey.*"

Adrian nodded his head but you could tell he didn't want to. "Yes, she is one of the Canadian group." He looked at me. "What were you doing?"

"Destroying the fort." I knew he knew that but that was all he'd get.

"Why would you do that?" Adrian asked. I'd never let them know it was because the fort was so bad. I'd never tell. I would take the fall.

"Because the others wouldn't let me help build it," I said it in a pretend whiny voice. Maybe they'd send me back to Canada, a disgrace, a cheater, a spoilsport, a traitor. I'd know I was a hero in my heart, that I'd sacrificed myself for the good of my country. Adrian was looking at me funny. Had he seen me this morning, hauling sand and building the fort? Had he seen the finished fort? He might have. He might have known I was lying. I put my chin up and put on my tough look. I crossed my arms like Jay.

"Kirsten, I want you to go back to the dorm room and stay there." I got up and looked defiantly at the Soviet camp leaders. I turned with a military turn and marched out. Adrian stayed. The door closed behind me. I stopped. I couldn't hear what Adrian was saying. I headed back to the camp building where our room was.

I was sitting on my bed. It was just before lunch. I was screwed. I knew it. Adrian had not been back to see me yet.

"Way to go, Kirsten!!!" The others came into our room. All of them. Boys too. "You did it!" Jay clapped me on the back. He was gorgeous.

"The fort was an absolute ruin. You'd have never guessed it was a wreck even before you'd smashed it. No one would have guessed what it looked like before." Dee Dee handed me a Russian chocolate bar.

"Adrian came back to the beach. He said that he didn't know what had gone on and that he didn't believe you when you said that you had wrecked the fort because we wouldn't let you help build it." Oksana gave me a box of lemon wafers. This was great.

"Yeah, thanks! That was a good cover, Kirsten!" Alexi was smiling and nodding.

"You were great!" Rhonda grinned.

"Great!" Big Karl gave me the thumbs-up sign. This was cool.

"Mary!" Oksana warned. In walked Mary.

"Hi, Mary." Jay hated her. "Congratulations on your team's sculpture coming in third this morning. I was just wondering why you decided to join a Soviet team rather than build for Canada?"

"Well, I'm glad I did, seeing as how one of your own teammates sabotaged your entry." Mary gave me a really dirty look.

"You shut up!" Oksana confronted Mary full on. "Don't you say one thing about Kirsten!"

"Yeah!" All the others put in their backing.

"What is this? This is strange. Defending the person who wrecked your beautiful fort. That is what you said, wasn't it, Dee Dee? Oh no, what has happened to our beautiful fort? I think that's what we all heard down at the beach; how wonderful it had been; that a battle had been raging; that you had even built sand flames. Hmmmmm. Very strange. And now you all stand in defence of the 'naughty little girl'...." Mary did the in-quotes thing with her fingers. She just made peace signs with both hands and bent her fingers fast. That meant quoting. I'd start doing that. It looked cool.

"Give it a rest, Mary," Dee Dee sneered.

"You guys are cheaters. You are an embarrassment!" Mary marched out.

"The cheating isn't embarrassing. The fort would have been embarrassing." Iggy scratched the top of his head. We all laughed. We laughed big. The fort had been terrible!

I was allowed to go to lunch. Well, I guessed I was allowed because no one told me otherwise. Chip and Adrian didn't say anything else to me about wrecking the sandcastle. We entered the meal hall, all of us together. There, set out on all the tables, was the most glorious sight. Bottles of milk. Cool. Frosted. Dew dripping. Glass bottles of milk like you'd get in England. We ran to the table. This was the first thing at camp that had made us run to the table. Stuff usually made us run away.

"God, I don't believe it." Jay had a milk bottle in hand.

"Moo!" Iggy grinned.

I grabbed up my chilled bottle. I couldn't wait. Milk. Beautiful milk. I gulped. There were chunks in my mouth.

"Shit." Jay held the bottle away from him. "It's sour!"

I thought I was going to heave. There were curdled blobs in the milk and it was thick. Almost as thick as—

"Is it yogurt?" Alexi was shuddering.

"This is gross! It's sour and chunky." Jay didn't know what to do with the bottle.

"I can't believe they put out sour milk! God, it smells like vomit." Dee Dee hadn't tasted it. Lucky Dee Dee. It was bad enough when you took a gulp of tonic water, thinking it was going to be Sprite. But taking a gulp, expecting milk and getting—

"Buttermilk!" Iggie gagged. "I think it's chunky buttermilk."

It was after lunch and nap time and the second competition of the day was about to start, a sidewalk-drawing competition. We had all been given chalk and were to create pictures on the paved walkways of Orlyonok. I was sitting on the ground, staring at my chalk colours. Not a big selection. White, blue, yellow, pink, green and red. I'd never seen red chalk before. A whistle blew. The competition had started. Hmmmm. We were supposed to draw something with the theme of "peace and world unity." Hmmmm. I looked around. Iggy had two pieces of chalk shoved up his nose. He was trying to crack Sam up. It worked. Iggy stuck two more pieces of chalk in his ears. What a goof. Got it. Got my idea. I'd draw a picture of Satan making friends with an angel. The biggest symbol of peace there could possibly be. Peace between heaven and hell. I had white chalk for the angel and because I had red I could draw the devil. If I'd been in Canada he would have been a pink devil because we didn't get red chalk at home. I wanted to ask Rhonda what she was drawing but we weren't allowed to talk. I started drawing. I outlined and then filled in. I drew the angel without her wings. Then I drew Satan. I wrapped his tail around the angel's legs. They held hands. Then I drew beautiful angel wings behind them. Someone tapped my shoulder.

"Hello, Kirsten." It was Olga from the hospital.

"Hi, Olga. How are you?" I was nearly done my work of art. I was really happy. I was a pretty good drawer. My mom was excellent. That was where I got it from. My dad sure wasn't. I asked him to draw a horse once and it looked more like a dog.

"Kirstyonushka, I think maybe you should change drawing." Olga was crouching beside me. Change my drawing ... why? This was utterly confusing, the last thing I would have expected. Was it bad? I thought it was good. "It is very good. But topic not so good. Deetadeetadeetadee." She tapped her fingers on her thigh. "You make into something else, yes? You change. Good girl, yes?" What the hell? This was an excellent drawing! A great symbol of peace. "You must change this." Olga was being stern now. She was not suggesting I change it; she was telling me to change it. Her voice was starting to shake now. "You make into something else. You do now!" She stood up. I looked at her stupid baton-twirler shoes. They had been Olga's shoes that Dee Dee had worn. Poor Dee Dee. Olga stayed behind me. I just did not get this.

"Okay, Olga. Sure." I looked at my picture. Without an eraser it was going to be difficult. Even if I had had an eraser, erasing on pavement would not really work. Got it. I'd make the angel into a Soviet space capsule and I could make the devil into Superman, an American symbol, but he had been invented by a Canadian. Superman would be helping the Soviet cosmonauts make it to the moon. I could draw stars behind them on the black Tarmac. I started. The angel wings became the rocket's fins. I filled her all in, in white. I made her face a cosmonaut looking out a window. I turned her halo into a star caught on the point of the rocket ship. I gave Satan—now Superman—a cape and changed his legs from red to blue; they looked a little purple, oh well. The drawing just was not as good now. It never was if you had to make such big changes. My first one was artistic. This one looked like something a nine-year-old would have come up with. Stupid. I added a CCCP to the Soviet rocket ship that used to be an angel. I used the red to do it. I used yellow for the stars in the sky. Olga should like the CCCP. I drew the moon at the top right and the earth at the bottom left.

"Very good, Kirsten." She had been standing there all that time. It was hard to draw with someone over your shoulder, watching like that.

I was sitting in the dinner hall with my "comrades." I looked at the medal I had won for my stupid drawing. The Soviets had got it wrong, though. They thought that the Soviet rocket ship was giving Superman a ride to the moon. I didn't know why they thought Superman would need the lift. Second place in the camp drawing competition for *that*! My other drawing was so much better.

"Dee Dee? I don't get it. I had drawn something else first but Olga made me change it. It was way better." The writing on my medal was in Russian. It had a pin on the back. It was like an army medal, not like a school award medal.

"What had you drawn?" Dee Dee had a big mouthful of hot dog. Well, kind of like a hot dog—more like the wiener kind you got at an Oktoberfest. Not a sausage, though, a wiener.

"The devil making peace with an angel."

"You drew what?" Little Karl opened his mouth as wide as he could and stared at me. There was brown bread in his teeth. "Did you hear that?" he said to his big brother.

"Religion is not allowed in the Soviet Union," Dee Dee explained. "When the Communists came in, they made the whole country into atheists. They tore down synagogues, cathedrals and churches. Practising religion is against the law."

"Your drawing was against the law!" Little Karl made a *sheesh* noise.

"Oh." I was not religious. My family had never gone to church or a synagogue. My dad's family was Jewish but my mom came from a long line of agnostics and atheists and pagans. My parents didn't tell me what to believe. I'd been to a church with my friend Squirrel before. It was interesting at first but then it was boring. I didn't believe there was a God or a heaven or hell. But my drawing should not have been against the law. How could a simple drawing be illegal? I wasn't even thinking about religion when I drew what I drew. What if I did believe in devils and angels? I was mad about being told to change my drawing. It almost made me want to believe in devils and angels and heaven and hell, just so I would have had reason to fight for my drawing. I got like that. When someone told me to do something it made me want to do the opposite. Like the room thing; if my mom said to clean my room, even if I wanted to clean it, I wouldn't because she had told me to. If I was like my friend Squirrel, who went to church *every* Sunday, poor Squirrel, and was told I could not go to church, that would make me mad. But how could they tell people not to go to church? It would make some people want to go more, if they were like me. How could that be a law, anyway? And why was it a law? "You mean going to church is against the law here?"

"Yup." Big Karl had a whole wiener on his fork. "Religion causes too many problems. It starts wars. It makes people hate each other."

"Hmmm." He was right about that. Look at Ireland and look at Israel. I sometimes pretended to watch the news to be grown-up and those countries were always in the news. Maybe this was better. But still, telling people what they had to think. I mean, if I was *made* to go to church, then I wouldn't want to. You couldn't suddenly make me believe in God, so how could you make someone who believed in God just suddenly stop, though I'd tried to do that a couple of times. People got really upset about religion. You just ended up in stupid fights. My drawing was hurting no one. You should be able to draw anything you wanted. People should not tell you what you could and could not draw. I had been in trouble for my artwork before. I got in trouble in grade five from a supply teacher because I had covered my desktop in pencil drawings of naked people, mostly women. The supply had called me a "dirty little girl." I had to stay in at recess and clean all the desks in the class. My mom said it was right to give me trouble for drawing on the desks but it was not right to give me trouble for drawing naked people.

Wow. I was hit by a horrible thought. All my favourite holidays came from someone's religion, like Christmas and Chanukah, Seder and Easter, and what about Hallowe'en? We celebrated them all in my house and in big fashion. Did this mean there was no Santa Claus and no Easter Bunny in the Soviet Union? What about trick or treating? No trick or treating? Wow! Awful! I couldn't think of any fun holidays that didn't come from a religion. Even Valentine was a saint, so that would be out. Gosh, so would St. Patrick's Day. The Soviet Union maybe was not such a fun place to live. I had noticed in Moscow that hardly anyone smiled. People at camp smiled but they were kids mostly, kids having fun. Hey, at the Soviet Friendship Centre in Toronto they had painted eggs for sale. I was sure they had been Easter eggs. Hmmmm.

"I hear the kids from the Middle East are getting sick from the food but they aren't getting sick because it's so bad, they are getting sick from gorging on it. They think it is fantastic. Apparently they are going to be given five small meals a day, to try to get them to eat less at a sitting." Dee Dee was looking at the new table of kids. "Check out the acne too, that boy needs an introduction to a face cloth."

The Middle Eastern kids had arrived yesterday. I didn't know if they were from Iran or Iraq. I knew it had to be one and not the other because one I thought was the enemy of the Soviet Union and was friends with the United States. And the Soviet Union and the United States couldn't have the same friends, for some reason.

"They were all puking after lunch." Jay smothered his bread in apricot jam. Even though the jam was sweet it didn't cover up how sour the bread was. The jam was new since we'd complained about the food, not that we had asked for it. Chip had, on our behalf. It was the same brown paste stuff we'd had in

Moscow. It seemed they only had one brand of jam here in the Soviet Union.

"Their food must be really awful where they come from if they think this food is fantastic." Iggy had to turn around to look at the Middle Eastern kids.

"Iggy, turn around. Stop staring." Alexi kicked Iggy under the table. You could tell because you could see Alexi's body move and then Iggy winced.

No Christmas. Life without Christmas.

SOMETHING SECRET.
SOMETHING WEIRD.
SOME SORT OF
COMMUNIST PARTY MEETING.

It was after morning exercises, roll call and breakfast. We were getting ready to go swimming. I quickly wrote in my diary: *July 29, place: Camp. Special day seems like every day. Komsomols are a group of young people being trained mentally, physically and politically.* I had found that out yesterday. I reread yesterday's entry.— *Made sandcastle and our group lost that contest.—Drawing competition—all the kids who thought they could draw in Orlyonok. I came in 2nd in that and won a medal.—Good day.* My parents would like this.

"Coming to the can?" Rhonda winked at me. That meant she wanted to use our secret washroom. It took two because one had to post guard and give the okay for the other to enter and exit, without being seen.

"Yep." I closed my diary and shoved it under my pillow. Rhonda and I walked along the balcony. People were coming towards us in their bathing suits. Maybe the bathroom would be empty. Three Italian girls said *Ciao* to us. The Italians had toothpaste that tasted like black currant. It was excellent.

"You can go first because it was your idea." The truth was I wanted Rhonda to go first just in case mine smelled really bad. I did the main bathroom check. There were girls brushing their teeth. I watched them, then signalled Rhonda to enter the closet. A few minutes later there were the two taps on the closet door. I gave the one tap back. That meant wait. The toothbrushers were leaving. I waited. Then I gave the two taps, for all clear. Rhonda came out and I stepped into the wardrobe, then into Narnia. That was more of our code talk for the secret can. Narnia was my idea. I went quickly. It was so much easier in private. I finished, jumped up to pull up my jeans and, whoops, fell into the back wall of the room. I felt it move. I did up my pants and then pushed the wall a little harder. It moved some more. This was weird. I went back into the wardrobe and knocked for Rhonda. She gave the all clear.

"Get in here, Rhonda. There is something you have to see."

"That is awful dangerous, Kirsten."

"Believe me, it's worth it."

Rhonda came in. I motioned her to follow me into Narnia. "Watch." I pushed the wall at the back of the room and the wall moved a little.

"This must lead somewhere else." Rhonda squished in beside me. "Push." We pushed together and the wall moved straight out about a foot. Then we felt the wall moving back in towards us. So we pushed harder. The wall moved back out. Then the wall started to move back closed again. So we pushed really hard and it opened. The reason it had kept closing was because as we were pushing it open, two guys in uniforms were pushing back at us.

"Holy shit!" we both said together. We were standing in our can, staring out at some secret hall. There was a shiny wood floor and at the front of the room was this huge bronze head of Lenin. Everything was gold and red and important-looking. People were doing something at the front beside a podium. There were chairs neatly in rows. And red wall hangings.

Suddenly there was commotion. We had been seen. Someone yelled at the two uniformed guys. You knew what they were yelling even if you didn't speak the language! "Hey, who are those two girls standing in a dark little room beside a toilet?" We were being pushed closed again. The wall was pushed back shut, leaving us standing beside our toilet in the smelly cleaning cupboard.

"Let's get out of here!" Rhonda pulled me. We were not even that careful coming out of the closet. No one was there to see us.

"We have to tell someone now," I said as we rushed back to our room. "Dee Dee and Oksana maybe. What do you think was going on in there, Rhonda?"

"Something secret. Something weird. Some sort of Communist Party meeting or something. Something we were not supposed to see. An out-of-bounds place."

"Damn!" No one was in our room. They must have gone to the beach already. "You know, Rhonda, those guys weren't just Komsomols. They were army or something."

"Yeah, I know. That was bigger than kid stuff." Rhonda and I rushed down the stairs to the fountain and piano court. Smash, crash. Holy shit! A kid just jogged right through the glass door in front of us. He stood four feet away from us with jagged spikes of glass sticking out of his leg and stomach. There was blood coming out of his stomach, blood coming out of his leg. The piece of glass sticking out of his leg was a foot long. Then he screamed. He must not have seen that the glass door was closed, they kept the glass so clean. He must have thought it was open. The blood was very red on his white T-shirt. People ran past us to him. Grown-ups. We didn't move. We just stood there. The boy was maybe sixteen. Someone pulled out one of the pieces of glass. Another person yelled "*nyet.*" Blood spurted like a fountain from where the glass had been. Someone pushed down on the fountain and kept pressing. The boy was lying down on the floor now, with the glass sticking straight out of his stomach. He was lying down on shattered glass. Glass and blood all over. A stretcher came and he was taken away. Rhonda and I just stood there.

We had been to a movie in the camp's outdoor movie theatre. It was some sort of sixties Soviet mystery with a car chase on a mountain road. There was some kissing too. I didn't really know what was going on because it was all in Russian and there wasn't even any English writing underneath to let you know. There wasn't any popcorn, either. It was fun sitting outside, though. We were now back at the dorm building. I was sitting at the piano beside the fountain. I played "Nadia's Theme," which was also the music to *The Young & the Restless*. Some Soviet kids clapped. They recognized "Nadia's Theme" but that was because of the Olympics, not because of the soap opera. I hated soap operas. They were boring.

"Play something else, Kirsten." Rhonda was leaning on the side of the piano. I wished she wouldn't because it kept moving. It was a grand piano but it was on wheels. I started to play the theme from *Rocky*. Rhonda ran up the stairs. She was being Sylvestor Stallone. She did the dance at the top of the balcony just like Rocky did in the movie. We were killing time before bed. We were going to go to the secret room after lights out, Oksana and Dee Dee too. The Soviet kids didn't know who Sylvester Stallone was. I played the theme from *Welcome Back Kotter*.

"I bet Kirsten likes Horshack." Little Karl walked past the piano into the boys' room. Horshack? Horshack was the biggest nerd on *Welcome Back Kotter*. He was a retard, with a stupid laugh. Iggy did the laugh as he walked past. It was kind of like a seal. I stopped playing.

"Come on, Kirsten, this is great. What others do you know?" Oksana asked.

"Ummmm. The Salada Tea commercial?" I started to play it. It was actually a song called "The Homecoming." It was very pretty. Everyone knew it as the Salada Tea commercial, though. I played it at a recital once. I got bored so I went into "You Are the Sunshine of My Life" by Stevie Wonder.

"Kirsten, you are going to go to hell for doing that!" I opened my eyes. It was Mary.

"You can't go to hell in the Soviet Union." I closed my eyes and swayed my head like Stevie's again.

"You still shouldn't make fun of blind people." Mary headed up the stairs.

Mary was finally asleep. It had taken her ages. Because my bed was beside Mary's, I was the one who had to check on whether she was asleep. I was sitting up in bed. It was pitch dark. Mary was snoring. They weren't fake, either. They were real snores. She said the reason she snored was because she had something wrong with her adenoids.

"Let's go," I whispered. Dee Dee and Oksana would not be able to believe the secret room behind Narnia. I couldn't wait to show them. They were going to like Narnia too.

Rhonda was shining her flashlight through a sock; that way it wasn't too bright. "Follow me," she commanded. I grabbed the back of her PJ top, Oksana grabbed me, and Dee Dee, Oksana. We were off. Down the hall we tiptoed. We stopped. Rhonda shut off her flashlight.

"Do you think the boy who went through the glass lived?" Oksana was tugging so hard on the back of my baby doll top that the front of it was strangling me.

"Who knows." Rhonda started to move forward again but with her light off.

"Maybe his ghost will haunt here."

"There are no ghosts in the Soviet Union." I was choking. "Ana, stop pulling so h-cuh-ard."

"Sorry." She loosened up. We were at the bathroom. No one was inside. Rhonda turned her light on full.

"This way." I opened up the cleaning closet. Rhonda flashed the light in.

"Just looks like a normal cupboard, right?" Rhonda stepped in and went to the back wall. "Well, watch." She pushed. It moved open and there was our wonderful toilet.

"Wow! Ahhhh! Excellent!" Dee Dee shoved passed me and touched the toilet with her hand, like you would the crown jewels, if you were allowed to touch them. "How long have you known about this?"

Rhonda and I looked at each other. We couldn't let Dee Dee know that she could have used this private toilet the whole time she was on her period. I had wanted to tell the others but Rhonda wouldn't let me. I felt crappy.

"Since this morning," Rhonda lied. It was partly true. The

next part was true anyway. We had discovered the secret, *secret* room this morning.

"Now watch this." I pulled Dee Dee out of the way so that I could get to the back of the room, beside the toilet. I pushed on the wall. Nothing. I pushed harder, with everything I had. "Shit."

Rhonda came in beside me. We both pushed. Nothing. "For crying out loud! They've sealed it! Christ!" Rhonda shone her light all around the edges of the wall.

"They're really into doing this here. I mean, first there was your window back in Moscow and then Kirsten's window at the camp hospital and now this," Oksana said.

"The secret room is amazing, some sort of special ceremonial room and something heavy-duty was going on in it today." Rhonda pushed again. "No way."

"Maybe there is another way to get into it." Dee Dee sucked her cheek. "I doubt people traipse through the girls' bathroom, the cleaning closet and then this toilet when they're graduating from Komsomol to KGB agent."

"Shall we?" Rhonda had that look you got when playing Truth, Dare, Double Dare. She was daring us.

"Why not?" Dee Dee looked at the toilet. "I wish you'd found this four days ago."

"I'm in." Oksana was playing with a pimple on her chin. I didn't get pimples. I hoped I never would.

"I just don't get where this secret room is, because if you think about it, you would think that there would be another row of dorm rooms on that side," I pointed through the wall, "like there is on our side."

Rhonda checked that no one was in the bathroom. "All clear."

"So let's go over to the other foyer and go up the stairs and check out the first room," Dee Dee said and we went down the stairs and then past the glass door that the boy had walked through. The broken glass was all gone and the blood had been cleaned off the floor. They had not put in a new door yet, though.

"I hope he didn't die," Oksana whispered.

"There was a lot of blood, Ana." I didn't think he could have made it. Not with the spurting, not with the jagged piece sticking out of his stomach like a pirate's blade. When I was four I fell through a glass greenhouse in England. The glass split my kneecap open. When I looked down I could see the white bone through the blood. I screamed. Grandma didn't drive so a neighbour had to rush us to the hospital. I had lots of operations and was lucky to keep the bottom half of my leg. My mom was in Canada and Grandma didn't tell her. Grandma didn't want to worry her. I wondered if someone had phoned this boy's mother. We were in the next fountain court or foyer. The piano was at the other end, opposite from ours. So were the stairs. Like *Alice Through the Looking Glass*.

"Ohhhhh. It's backwards here. Their washroom is on the other side of ours." Rhonda slunk ahead of us up the stairs. We followed. I wished we were wearing black. We moved quickly down the balcony. Yup, there was the bathroom like ours. So where was the secret room? This was weird.

"There's the cleaning closet." Rhonda flashed her light. Dee Dee opened the door. It was full of supplies like ours. Dee Dee went to the back and pushed. Nothing happened.

"You know, I don't think this wall moves. It's concrete blocks. Look." Dee Dee stepped to the side so Rhonda's light could hit the back wall. There was no secret toilet here, not to mention a secret, secret room.

"Damn!" Rhonda shut off her light. She was conserving her batteries. She always did that.

"Maybe there is some other way. Like around the back of the building. Maybe you get there through an outside entrance," I said. Oksana and Dee Dee looked at each other.

"Are you guys telling the truth about the secret room?" Dee Dee grabbed Rhonda's flashlight and beamed it at us. From one to the other.

"Of course!" Rhonda snatched the light back from Dee Dee.

"Let's keep looking." I couldn't think of any other way to prove it to them.

"I wanna go to bed and I don't wanna get caught walking around camp at night." We had lost Dee Dee. She closed the cupboard door.

"Let's just see if we can find some secret stairs or something. You have to see this room. It is unbelievable!"

"You're right, Kirsten. It's absolutely *unbelievable*. A secret room on the other side of a toilet in a cupboard? Ridiculous! You read too much!" Dee Dee left the bathroom. Oksana shrugged her usual shrug and followed. Rhonda and I were left standing in the other kids' washroom.

"Tomorrow is Soviet Labour Day, right? So it's a day off. Maybe we should look then, while the others are at the beach or something. I think Dee Dee is right about getting caught wandering around camp. I think inside is one thing but if we get caught outside, I don't know." Rhonda flicked her flashlight on again. We left the loo.

"Tomorrow." I wished I was tired. I liked nighttime stuff.

THIS WAS NOT LIKE A SCHOOL TRIP TO AN APPLE ORCHARD.

It was Labour Day. We were tidying our room before going to some State nut farm to pick hazelnuts, all day. Labour Day was not a holiday in the Soviet Union.

"Kirsten, are these yours?" Dee Dee kicked my pink Marks & Spencer underwear across the floor.

"Kirsten, is this yours?" Oksana threw a sports sock at me. It was mine.

"Kirsten, you're a pig!" Dee Dee threw the other sports sock's mate at me. "Gross. Your socks are disgusting! At least keep them over there on your side." The next thing, her pillow hit me on the side of my head. Hard. I grabbed it and ran out of the room with it. I dropped it off the balcony. It just missed Iggy, who was coming out of the boys' room below.

"Thanks. I could use an extra pillow!" Iggy ran with it back into the boys' room.

I went back to tidying. Tidying to me just meant shove it out of sight. So I shoved everything in my suitcase as fast as I could and closed it shut, boom.

"Kirsten, you should throw garbage out." Rhonda handed me the pail. I opened my case again and pulled out a few candy wrappers and some used Kleenex left over from when I was sick. There, boom. Done.

This was not like picking strawberries with my mother. This was not like a school trip to an apple orchard or maple sugar farm. They really wanted us to work. They expected it. All the Soviet citizens did farm labour on this day. Rhonda and I were sitting on the grass under a hazelnut tree, though Rhonda said they were filberts. We had with us our empty bushel baskets, which we were supposed to fill not just once, but over and over. It was almost like a nut-picking contest.

"Here, try one." Rhonda had peeled me a nut fresh from the tree.

"Hey, you kids, get out of that hazelnut tree." That was from the Jello pudding commercial. "Hey, you kids, get out of that Jello tree." I put the nut in my mouth. "Mmmmmm." I wondered if they'd be good warm, like chestnuts. "It doesn't taste like hazelnuts at home.

"Filberts." Rhonda ate hers. "You're right. Maybe they are dried when we get them."

"Or roasted like peanuts. Have you ever had that hazelnut and chocolate spread called Nutella?" I had always wanted to try that. It looked great but Mom wouldn't get it. She said "there is no way we are spreading chocolate on our toast in the morning." I didn't see how jam could be any better for you.

"I've seen the ad on TV but my mom won't buy it." Rhonda's mom would probably get along with my mom.

"*KTO VEE!?! KTO VEE!*" A Soviet worker woman was yelling at us. Another was watching with fists on hips.

"What is she saying?" Why'd Rhonda ask me that? The only Russian I knew was Misha's touchy-feely Russian. All the kids in our group except Mary had refused to take the Russian language classes at camp. It had made Adrian furious and sad. The Russian woman stooped over and pulled Rhonda out from our tree cave. The other grabbed the empty basket. This was freaky. I pushed myself deeper into the cave, right up to the trunk of the tree. Now they were yelling at me.

"*As-taftee meenya!*" I shouted. "*As-taftee meenya!*" The women marched off.

"What did you say?" Rhonda lifted the branches.

"I don't know exactly. I heard a kid say it over and over in the hospital. It made the nurse go away." I crawled out, dragging my basket behind me.

"Let's get out of here. Let's go pick nuts somewhere." Rhonda was right. There were so many people at this nut farm. We'd just mix in for a bit somewhere else. Rhonda and I jogged a few rows of trees over and started picking.

"I can't imagine I'll fill one of these." I couldn't reach very high on the tree and the lower branches did not seem to have as many nuts.

"Who cares? Pick a bit and then we'll go hide somewhere else." Rhonda peeled another nut and popped it into her mouth.

"What do you think those women were saying to us?" My arms were hurting from holding them over my head.

"I am more interested in finding out what you said to them," Rhonda giggled. "Maybe you told them to go to hell."

"I don't think so." What did I say? I could be dead meat. "I might have just said bring me the bedpan."

Rhonda laughed really hard. "Oh my God, you're funny!" She clutched her sides. "My stomach hurts."

"My grandma says nuts make your stomach hurt. Maybe you shouldn't eat so many."

"You are so funny!!!" Rhonda kicked over her basket. "Whoops." She couldn't stop laughing.

A nut hit the top of my head. I looked around. Maybe it fell out of the tree. Then another one caught me right between the eyes. This was war. I saw the enemy but pretended not to.

"Rhonda, pick your nuts up and put them back in your basket," I whispered.

"Why are you whispering?" A nut caught Rhonda on the rump. "Hey!"

"In the tree behind you. Don't look." I was still whispering.

"Pretend you don't know where the nuts are coming from. Then on three we'll nail them from two sides."

"Here." Rhonda gave me some of her nuts. "Okay?"

"One, two, three." We ran and attacked the tree behind us. We pelted the tree with nuts. Sam and Iggy screamed. Sam fell out of the tree. We beaned him as he tried to run away. Now there was more Russian shouting. A Soviet man said something to a woman, who ran off. Some little old lady started picking up the dropped nuts and filling her basket with our nuts.

"Hey!" Rhonda yelled. "She's stealing our nuts."

Then there was Adrian. Adrian and Sonya and ten Soviets. "You are a disgrace!" I'd heard those words too many times. Adrian was really mad, beyond his usual vein-bulging purple. "This is not play! You are here to work but, oh no, you spoiled brats don't even know what work is. This is the food of the people. This is not to be wasted. These nuts aren't your toys! The Soviet people pay for you to stay here and this is how you repay them? One day of work, just one day."

"Adrian, Adrian." Chip was there, phew. "Not here—"

"Not here? Then where? These ungrateful shits were throwing precious food!"

"Adrian, they just don't understand." Chip was standing between Adrian and us.

"They will work for the rest of the day and THEY WILL WORK HARD." Adrian turned to Sonya. "How much does an average Soviet picker pick in a day?"

"Thirteen baskets." Sonya didn't even ask anyone. Thirteen baskets. These were big potato baskets and we were picking little nuts. Thirteen, yeah, right.

"You will pick thirteen baskets!" Adrian had spit in his beard.

"Adrian—"

"Shut up, Chip!"

"Adrian, please—"

"I told you to shut your mouth!" Adrian stared Chip down. Then he turned and walked away. Chip just stood there with her back to us. This was awful.

"C'mon!" Rhonda pulled me.

"Shit, you guys, what happened? Why was Adrian yelling at

Chip like that?" Dee Dee must have arrived during their fight. I
hadn't noticed her.

"That was bad." Iggy picked up his dropped nut basket. "Hey,
that old woman took all our nuts! Where'd she go?"

"We'll have to start from scratch." Rhonda picked up her
empty basket. Then she dropped it and kicked it three times. I
had an uncomfortable feeling in my stomach. I didn't think it
was from the nuts.

Some people did pick thirteen baskets. We didn't. We had started
bringing half-full baskets back and dumping them but we were
caught by a guy in uniform who stood there counting baskets all
day and making sure they were full. I didn't get it, though. I didn't
understand why the people worked so hard and tried so hard.
Mary picked tons too but there wasn't a reward or a medal for
this. Chip and Adrian didn't talk to each other on the bus ride
back to camp. Rhonda and I brought a stash of nuts back with
us. Mary said that wasn't allowed, that the Soviets would never
do that.

We were all now standing on the steps waiting to go into the
Friendship Club. The door opened. We were invited in. This was
not like the Soviet Friendship Club in Toronto. No way! We
were standing in some kind of photo gallery. The pictures were
awful.

A man started to speak. He spoke English but he was Russian.
"The Soviet Socialist Republics have many humanitarian projects around world. What you see is but some of our works. We
help nations combat their starving and suffering. We will show
you some of our projects. This—" He stopped by a poster-size,
black and white photograph. It was a picture of a five-year-old.
"This is what the Americans did!" The five-year-old was missing
an arm. His little body was a mess of scars. "This was the Vietnam
that *you* did not get to see. This is what the Americans did! And
this!" He pointed to the next picture. There were heaps of bodies. Families. You could tell they were families. There were children and old people. They were dead. They were bombed and

partly burnt. Eyes opened, eyes black. When people talked about getting a knot in your stomach, well, I now knew what it was. Inside my navel, behind my navel, every time the man said "Americans" I felt the knot get tighter. This could not be. I knew some Americans. They wouldn't do this. There was a family at my school that had moved up from Florida. Nora was a grade behind me. Her family was so nice. Her uncle fought in the Vietnam War. I met him. Her uncle did not burn children. Her dad moved to Canada so he wouldn't have to fight in the Vietnam War.

"Napalm!" The man pointed to a naked little Vietnamese girl. She looked like my baby sister Fiona. This picture was in colour. He turned the picture over, like a page in a giant book. The little girl's back made me want to scream. She didn't even have a bum crack anymore. I'd never heard of napalm.

"The Americans dropped napalm onto innocent villages because they think that these simple people pose threat to democracy, pose threat to mighty United States of America!" We looked at the little girl's back. I wished this picture had been in black and white too. We moved on. We moved to different countries. "The Soviet people want to help nations who are starving. Nations in need. The suffering children! Rather than let Soviet Union help, this is how United States of America would prefer things to remain." The picture was of a starving brother and sister in Afghanistan. Their eyes were the largest part of their bodies.

"It's because of American foreign policy and their insidious behaviour regarding Vietnam that I joined the Communist Party," Adrian told the man. Chip took Adrian's hand.

We walked through room after room of photographs. Photographs bigger than posters. It was different seeing them big than small like in *Time* magazine. And *Time* didn't show photos like these. Not like these. Never in my life. "The Americans prefer these people dead!" "Rather be dead than red." Maybe that is what that meant. I'd heard it often. I didn't know this, not any of this before. That little Vietnamese girl looked like my baby sister.

We lay in our beds back in our dorm. I wrote in my diary. *I am glad that I am Kirsten and am not starving or anything horrible.* "Rhonda? Do you think they will show pictures like that to the American kids at the other camp?"

"I don't know."

"If the boy who crashed through the glass died, do you think his ghost would be here or in his country? It would be awful if he couldn't go home." Oksana sounded teary.

I didn't know what else to say in my diary. I put it down. "Rhonda?"

"I don't feel like talking." Rhonda rolled over on her stomach. No one was talking. No one was sleeping but no one was talking.

THE NEXT THING, SOME GUY PULLED DOWN HER BIKINI BOTTOMS.

We were all waiting on long, wide steps near the Cosmonaut Training Centre. We were waiting to have our pictures taken for the Orlyonok Book. We were in our regular clothes—tomorrow we were going to have a photo in our marching uniforms. The Italian group was there too. We were all going to be photographed together. It was very hot outside. The sun was bright. We'd be looking into it for the picture. I hated that. I couldn't open my eyes looking into the sun. I'd look squinty in the picture.

"Let's sit down." Rhonda's voice was tired, because of the heat probably. I was tired from the nightmares I'd had about broken glass and blood. Dee Dee had had nightmares too, about the Turkish army invading. The border lights at night freaked her out. Oksana, Dee Dee and I joined Rhonda on the sidewalk below the stairs. Little Karl was sitting a few steps up on the stairs, facing us. That was when I saw. He was sitting with his legs open and you could see his bag hanging down his right shorts leg.

"Dee Dee!" It was hard to whisper. "Dee Dee, look at Little Karl. You can see his balls."

Dee Dee looked right up after I said that. She stared at Little Karl's stuff. She slapped Oksana. "Ana, don't look now but look in a second." Dee Dee was trying not to laugh. "Just look at Little Karl's right kneecap."

"Oh my Gawd!" Oksana looked away, then looked back again quickly. Little Karl spread his legs wider. You could see right up. "Why isn't he wearing underwear?" Oksana nudged Rhonda. Oksana started to laugh. "You say it." She looked at me.

"Rhonda. You can see Little Karl's prairie oysters," I spat out.

"What are you laughing at?" Little Karl made a face at us but he didn't close his legs. "What's your problem, Koza?"

"Oh Darwin, get over it already. Everyone knows you like Kirsten," Dee Dee scolded.

I almost fainted. No, he didn't. Little Karl hated me. Why else would he always be so mean?

"All right, everybody, let's form rows on the stairs. Shortest people in front, tallest at the back." Sonya snapped her fingers.

Chip and Adrian had had another blowout after the photos. It was nasty. Because of how badly Adrian treated Chip, we had decided to talk to Chip about it. The shitty thing was that I was elected spokesperson. The reason was because I knew Chip from before. I didn't really, though. Not well enough to tell her to leave Adrian or anything. We had asked Chip to join us at nap time for a talk. We hadn't told her what about.

Chip came in cheery and smiley. Oh no. "Hello, girls."

"Come sit here, Chip," Dee Dee beckoned. We were sitting on the empty bed across from Mary's, closest to the door. Mary had refused to be present in the room for this talk, she said this was the final straw, that she'd now have nothing to do with us or to say to us for the rest of the trip. Chip came over and sat. Everyone looked at me. Drats!

"Yes?" Chip looked around at us.

"Kirsten has something she wants to talk to you about. Something that has been bothering her." Thanks, Dee Dee. It wasn't even true, really. It did bother me that Adrian was nasty to

Chip but I'd never never, never have talked to her about it. If my mom could have heard this or seen this, she'd have killed me.

Chip looked at me. "What is bothering you, sweetie?"

"We don't like the way Adrian yells at you and stuff. Don't let him." I blurted it out a hundred miles an hour. I spoke super-fast when I was really nervous.

"You shouldn't let him treat you that way." Dee Dee looked serious and grown up. I tried to look like her. "Continue, Kirsten." Man! Why me? I didn't even agree with the next part.

"We also think that you should get married, that living together is wrong." I blurted that out even faster. Chip looked at me with bug eyes, and no wonder. She knew my parents didn't get married until I was seven, that they had just lived together before that. Who was I to have said this? It didn't even make sense with the first part, the "don't let Adrian treat you that way" part. *Don't let Adrian treat you badly; marry him.* What kind of sense was that? It was Dee Dee's idea to add the "marry him." She kept going on and on about it. I wanted to tell Chip that she should not go steady with Adrian any more, that he wasn't nice. This was just nosey, though, all of it.

"Well, I don't really think this is any of your business." Chip even said that sweetly. It still made me go red, though.

"It is upsetting for Kirsten that you aren't married because she is so young," Dee Dee said. I swallowed. That never made the lump go away, though. Chip knew about my parents. She must have really thought I had gone cuckoo.

"It is, is it?" Chip looked at me.

"Why do you let Adrian yell at you so bad?" Rhonda asked. I was glad Rhonda brought the important thing back up, the real problem. The other marriage shit was just getting in the way and was making us look like dummies.

Chip held her hands in the prayer position. She was thinking. She was so calm. But that was not real. She was faking calm. "I don't think I want to talk to any of you about this." Chip was still being so polite.

Man, I felt awful. I felt sick inside, sick sick sick. Why did I not stand up to Dee Dee? It was wrong for us to tell Chip to marry Adrian and to lecture Chip on living with him. Why couldn't I just stand up for what I believed? Why wasn't I like Mary? I was weak! I was horrid! I was more worried about being popular and "in" than doing the right thing. I hated myself. I'd never forgive myself or forget this for the rest of my life. I hoped Chip would, though. How could we face her after this?

I quickly finished up writing in my diary about yesterday's events. It was really hot again today. I closed my diary. I was sitting on the cool tile floor beside my bed. We had had our other photos, the ones in the marching uniforms, after roll call. We had said "syr" instead of "cheese" because "syr" was "cheese" in Russian. It wasn't going to make for good smiles because of the "r," which pleased the Soviets because they didn't like you smiling in photos. Photos were serious stuff. It was so incredibly hot we were getting to spend more time at the beach today.

"Let's boogie." Rhonda's bikini wasn't as small as mine. Mine was definitely nicer. Mine had one pink triangle over my right boob and one blue one over my left. and the whole thing stayed on with tied strings. The bottoms matched the top. I had a pink triangle on the front, over my crotch, and a blue one on the back, over my bum. It was really sexy. Really grownup. It was the best thing in my suitcase. It looked great with my tan too. We were all tanned like a Coppertone tanning lotion ad. Dee Dee said she had brought dark tanning oil with her but it was in her lost luggage. I loved the smell of coconut.

"Look!" Rhonda said as we went down the stairs. I could not believe my eyes.

"The guy who walked through the glass," I yelled. I was so happy he wasn't all alone in the hospital any more and he wasn't in a coffin. Now he was in a wheelchair doing doughnuts by the piano.

Dee Dee and Oksana were behind us on the stairs. "Gee," Dee Dee said. "Do you think he'll be in that thing forever?"

"He's not dead. Who is he, anyway?" Oksana asked.

Some girls were giving him flowers. That was nice of them.
He was really cute, actually. Hey, what was it to those girls? They
weren't even there when it happened. "We should say something
to him, Rhonda."

"Yeah." Rhonda and I walked over to his wheelchair.

"Hi," we both said. He just looked at us. There was no expres-
sion. Maybe he didn't recognize us but the thing was, I felt like
he should. I felt like I had gone through the whole awful thing
with him. He looked back at the girls who had given him the
flowers. They spoke some other language, I didn't know what it
was. I felt weird standing there. The other girls were flirting with
him. It wasn't fair.

Rhonda and I decided to sit somewhere else on the beach, not
our usual place. We sat right near the edge of the water, down
where our fort had been.

"This is great." Rhonda shielded her eyes. The sun was bright,
all right. Rhon lay back in the sand.

Some guys and girls were fooling around in the water in front
of us. "Did you see that?" I pulled Rhonda back up into a sitting
position.

"What?"

"Those guys are pulling those girls' pants down in the water."

"Get out."

"Watch." There were screams and the girls came running out
of the water, laughing, giggling, holding each other's hands.
"They're French." I recognized that language. There were more
French guys sitting about twenty feet behind us. I looked back
at them. They looked older than our guys. They had hair on their
bodies. One of them actually had hair on his back. Gross. Black
bushy hair on their bodies. I turned back around so they wouldn't
see me staring. "It's interesting down here."

"Yeah," Rhonda agreed.

The guys who had been pulling the girls' pants down were
still in the water, calling the girls to come back. Suddenly
Rhonda was picked up. The hairy-back guy had picked her up

in his arms. He carried her towards the water, the way a man would carry a woman in a movie. The way a prince would carry a princess. He sure looked like a man with all that hair. Rhonda screamed and kicked her feet. I was not sure she liked it. I would have liked it. I followed them into the water. I didn't want to miss the action. The guy fell and took Rhonda down with him. She stood up and wiped the water back from her eyes. The next thing, some guy pulled down her bikini bottoms. There were other guys under the water, looking. Rhonda screamed louder and pulled up her pants. I went over to her. The French girls came back and someone else's bikini bottoms were pulled down. There were more screams and different guys underwater looking. Rhonda had it happen again.

"I'm getting out of here. Come on." Rhonda started back for shore. No one pulled my pants down. No one wanted to. If they had they would have been surprised. I had lots of pubic hair, not such a little kid after all. I wished someone had pulled my pants down. I wished some big guy had carried me into the sea. Guys loved Rhonda, everyone thought she was beautiful. It hurt.

After swimming we went for a walk, Rhonda, Oksana and I. We decided to walk around the track in the stadium. We each walked in a different lane. The track was blue and made of rubber or something.

"Kirsten! Kirsten!" I looked around. Holy shit, it was Misha!

"Let's run," I said to Oksana and Rhonda.

"Who's that calling you?" Oksana asked.

"It's Misha. Don't look. Don't look. Just keep walking." I was panicking, I didn't know why.

"He is really cute, Kirsten. Christ, is that the guy from the hospital, the one that took you for a walk and visited you in your room?" Rhonda was staring.

"Kirsten!" he shouted again from behind us on the track. He was with some friends.

"Turn around, Rhonda," I commanded.

"KIRSTEN!"

"Run," I ordered, and Oksana, Rhonda and I ran right out the other side of the stadium. I just pretended not to hear Misha. My heart was racing. What was wrong with me?

"Kirsten, Misha is absolutely the most handsome guy at this camp." Rhonda pulled me to a stop.

"Why couldn't we talk to them?" Oksana asked.

"Because ... Forget it." I frowned. I didn't want to talk about it. I didn't know what to talk about, anyway. I didn't know why I ran from Misha. It was confusing. It was weird. He made me feel weird. He *was* handsome.

NOW I WAS REALLY
CONFUSED ABOUT COMMUNISM.

I had tried to write in my diary but the bus we were on kept bumping and jiggling. We were on our way to visit another camp. I wished we didn't have to take buses everywhere. I wished Scotty could just beam us to the other camp. Captain Kirk was gorgeous. Mom liked Spock. She was a freak. She married Dad when I wanted her to marry Mr. Dressup. When I was little I liked the *Mr. Dressup* show way better than *Sesame Street*. *Sesame Street* was for babies. I was reading *Green Eggs and Ham*, on my own, when the kids on Sesame Street my age were learning their ABCs or to count to ten. I wrote in my diary: *We saw a cartoon last night in the outdoor movie theatre. It was not funny. Then we watched* Sinbad. *It was funny but it was not supposed to be funny.* The bus started moving again. I put my diary in my purse. There was no point writing.

"This is a camp?" I looked at the high, jagged wire fences. The buildings were rows of wooden sheds. There wasn't even grass, or trees. This was like prison. No, this was like *Hogan's Heroes*.

"Ssshhh," Jay hit my shoulder. "Don't be rude."

I didn't mean to be rude. It was just what came out. Now I was really confused about communism. I thought being communist meant everyone was equal. This camp was not equal with Orlyonok. This was worse than probably the worst camp in Canada.

We were being taken on a tour. Two camp grown-ups were leading us into the main camp building. It was like a school but made out of wood. Maybe being made to go to camp every holiday was not such a great thing. Who'd want to go here? This was jail. This was worse than the army. This was how I imagined POW camps. My Grandad Field spent four years in different camps during World War II. Gram said that's what made his heart bad and why he died young. We stopped in something like a classroom. There was a smell in the air that made my nose itch. Dee Dee had a snobby look on her face.

"This is a regular Soviet Pioneer Camp," Sonya translated for one of the camp grown-ups. I thought this was going to be a camp for bad kids. "Orlyonok is a special camp."

I put my lips near Rhonda's ear. "I'm glad we weren't sent to a regular camp."

"You can say that again."

"I'm glad we weren't sent to a regular camp." Rhonda hit me. We walked into another, shabby, classroom. There were some kids in it sitting around a table. They looked at us with mistrustful eyes. The camp grown-ups spoke to them in Russian. The kids looked at us with even more suspicion.

"The children here have many activities," Sonya translated. "This is an art class." This was bizarre. How could you have an art class with no art supplies? There weren't any paints or pastels or paper or pencils or macaroni noodles, even. Just an empty table. We followed the grown-ups back out. The kids watched us leave. They didn't smile or wave or anything.

"Next we will go see the dormitories." Sonya ushered us out of the dusty building. No one said much. It was depressing at this camp. The weirdest thing of all was that the camp grown-ups seemed proud of it. A group of Young Pioneers walked past us on the gravel. One of the camp grown-ups yelled something to one of the boys.

"Ivan has invited us to see their dorm," Sonya translated. I didn't think so, that was not what went on. Ivan led the way. We crunched along behind him and up the steps into one of the cabins. It smelled worse than the school building. This was not just dusty, this was musty. Dee Dee was holding her arms really close to her body. She looked like she was in pain. We all crowded into the middle of the dorm. Ivan spoke in Russian to the camp grown-ups, who were smiling way too hard.

"Are we supposed to say how nice this is or something?" Rhonda had her lips near my ear now. "Because it's not. It sucks."

"This is wonderful!" Adrian beamed. The camp grown-ups smiled even harder. Their smiles looked like they hurt. And that was that.

"You have been invited to stay for lunch," Sonya announced. Oh no. Oh big no no no. Not good. This would not be good.

We sat in fear at a long dining table. Chip and Adrian and Sonya were at the grown-ups' table. We were alone at our table, just the Canadian kids. The Soviet Young Pioneers stared at us. There was not the same noise as at Orlyonok. Something was wrong here. The grown-ups were served first. Camp kids carried the food to the big people's table. You couldn't see what was in the bowls. Kids headed our way now. Kasha. Runny kasha.

"This is like *Oliver Twist*." I moved my spoon through my bowl.

"Yeah, but I bet you won't be asking for more," Big Karl sniffed.

"What do you know about *Oliver Twist*?" Dee Dee gave me one of those "look down on" looks. I hated those.

"We read it this year in school."

"You did not. You're in grade six." Dee Dee wasn't eating and actually I *was* in grade six, seven coming up.

"We did too. Just four of us. The smart group. We read it in Mr. Hallett's class." He was our cool singing history teacher.

"You read Dickens?" Why was Dee Dee making such a big deal out of this? I decided I shouldn't mention that I'd read *Jane Eyre* on my own time, for fun.

"And I've seen *Oliver*, the musical, four times on TV," I said.

"Well, I can believe that." Dee Dee was not being very nice to me.

"I don't think we should drink the water." Jay put his water glass back down and smiled at me.

"No kidding," Dee Dee snapped. "I wouldn't touch anything here. I can't believe they brought us here." No one said anything else the rest of the meal. Nothing else was served either. Just kasha.

THE WORLD
IS A STRANGE PLACE.

We were on a five-hour bus ride through the mountains, going to Sochi, a spa town. We wouldn't be going to any spas, though. The scenery was incredible.

"Sonya! Sonya!" The bus driver called Sonya to the front. He was on the bus radio. There was commotion.

"What's going on?" I asked Nadia, who was in the seat beside me. Nadia jumped up and ran down the aisle of the bus. The bus was pulling over and Sonya was on the radio now. "What's going on?" I asked Rhonda, who was sitting behind me.

"How should I know?" Rhonda was leaning forward with her head resting on the back of my seat.

Then Sonya screamed a low, animal scream. The bus driver opened the door and Sonya stumbled off. We were high up on a mountain road. Sonya leaned on a cement guardrail at the side of the road and she screamed. The bus driver and Nadia went to Sonya. Nadia put her arms around Sonya. Sonya clutched Nadia's shirt and fell slowly to the ground, pulling Nadia down with her. We all watched out the bus windows. Nadia rocked Sonya back and forth. The bus driver knelt down beside them. He spoke in soft tones. Nadia looked up at us and said something to the bus driver, who took her place holding Sonya. Nadia climbed back onto the bus. She stood at the front and took a deep breath.

"There has been a tragedy. Sonya's best friends and fiancé have been killed in a car accident. Sonya loaned them her car for the weekend. They went off a cliff on a mountain road."

We all just sat there. We looked over the edge of the cliff our bus was parked by. It was easy to imagine. There were thousands of treacherous turns on these roads. And many turns had no guardrail at all. I bet everyone was picturing the same thing. Sonya came back on. She didn't look at any of us. She sat near the front and pressed her face against the glass. The bus driver slid back into his seat. He picked up the radio microphone and said something into it. Nadia came back and sat down with me again.

"She blames herself. I told her it isn't her fault but she blames herself." Nadia looked at the floor.

"Why does she blame herself?" Rhonda asked.

"Because it was her car. They weren't experienced drivers. Ahohhh." Nadia let out the saddest sigh I had ever heard.

The bus trip took us only four-and-a-half hours instead of five. It was 6:30 and we were at a fancy restaurant in Sochi. I didn't know they had them in the Soviet Union. There were red table-cloths on all the tables, even, and mirrors on the walls. Rhonda, Iggy and I were at a table for four with a boy from the Middle East. The chairs were like steak-house chairs. The boy from the Middle East was the one with the worst acne scars I had ever seen. Dee Dee was right, he needed some pimple products. At least he didn't have any fresh pimples or whiteheads. He was handsome except for the nasty scars. I wanted to ask him if he was from Iran or Iraq or Afghanistan, but what if I picked an enemy country? He was very excited about being in the restaurant. A waiter arrived and we were served a meatball kind of thing for an appetizer.

"This is excellent! Try it," Iggy said.

I tried some. I was scared it was going to be made out of kidney or something gross so I only took a little nibble. "This is wonderful!" I spread my cloth napkin out on my lap with a flick and a flourish. I grinned at the guy from the Middle East. "Mmmmmm!" I said to him and pointed my fork at the meat ball.

"Mmmmmm. Kubeh," he said back. He had a great smile. Big and warm. The contagious kind.

"If kids ruled the world there would be no war," I said to Rhonda. "Kids just make friends. We can communicate with any other kid in the world without speaking the same language." I passed the water jug over to the boy from the Middle East. He thanked me. "See. I know he said thank you, even though I don't know the words in his language."

Then Rhonda pointed at his face and touched her own. Then she gestured a palms up "how" or "what"? What was she doing? That was rude. Was she crazy?

"Kabooom!" he answered. Then he tapped his water glass and flew his fingers through the air, going "chsh chsh chsch." And tapped his face.

"Shrapnel," Iggy said. Why did Iggy know about shrapnel?

"Shrapnel," the boy repeated. "Chsh chsh chsh." The sound of breaking glass and pieces of metal. He touched his face. "Shrapnel."

The world is a strange place. The waiter took our plates.

"Canada?" The boy from the Middle East said to us. We all nodded "yes." "Canada," he said again and did a thumbs-up sign. He grinned. We grinned.

"Canada," I stopped. "No...," I shook my head, "kaboom," I said.

"Canada." And he did the thumbs-up sign again. We all nod-ded and did the thumbs-up back.

So this was Sochi. I had never heard of Sochi before but it was supposed to be famous. It was the most famous health resort and hot-spring place in the world, according to the Soviets. Sochi was famous for its healing hydrogen and sulphuric acid spas. We were outside some museum for some famous Soviet writer named Nikolai Ostrovsky. I hadn't heard of him, either. We were waiting for Nikolai's friend to show up.

"*Helen had a steamboat.*" Rhonda and I were playing a hand-clapping game. "*The steamboat had a bell,*" I flubbed. That was supposed to be crossed arms and I hit my lap. "*When Helen went to heaven, the steamboat went to hel-lo operator please give me number nine and if you disconnect me, I'll kick you in, behind the IRON curtain there was a piece of glass.*" We sang the "iron curtain" bit real loud. "*When Helen sat upon it she hurt her little ass-k me no more questions and tell me no more lies and that's the end of Helen and her dirty little lie lie lies!*" End of song. Rhonda was a bit off-key.

"Rhonda, where is the iron curtain exactly?"

Rhonda jiggled her finger in the corner of her eye. She didn't know, either. "Probably at the border or somewhere like that."

I pictured a huge iron curtain running along the Soviet border. "It must be heavy if it is made out of iron."

"Yup. Here he comes finally." Rhonda got up off the paving stones. A very old man was coming towards us. I got my camera out so I could take a picture of him, this friend of Nikolai Ostrovsky's.

The old man had glasses and a bald head. He stood beside Moyseen. I snapped a photo. I got Moyseen too! Nikolai Ostrovsky was crippled. The old man remembered everything about him. Everything. I picked a bead off my shoulder bag. I'd have to stop doing that soon. There were palm trees all over Sochi. I loved palm trees. I'd have to get more photos of them. I pretended to be listening. I put on my very interested face.

Maybe because the day had been really, really boring, they decided that we'd like to go to a dance. Well, we just weren't going to dance to this kind of music. No way. Dee Dee, Oksana, Rhonda and I stood on the stairs of a huge bandstand where people were dancing. We were outdoors at a park. The dance floor was crowded. Three of the Italian girls pushed past us. They went onto the dance floor to where Little Karl was doing the robot. They thought he was just like Michael Jackson.

"This is atrocious," I declared.

"Kirsten, where do you get those words from?" Rhonda laughed at me. Her vocabulary wasn't as good as mine, nowhere near.

"She's right, though. This music sucks!" Dee Dee wore her bored look.

"Come on, you girls." Chip came at us from the dance floor, clapping her hands and wiggling her bum. My mom danced like that too. Too much bum movement and not enough footwork.

"Passé." I curled my top lip up.

"I only dance to disco," Dee Dee informed Chip.

"You're missing out on the fun!" Chip bum-wiggled back into the crowd.

"Bring out the accordions, more accordions!" Dee Dee called and applauded. She was being sarcastic. "I feel like we are in a tacky Greek restaurant."

"What is with this music?" Rhonda had her hands on her hips and was leaning on one leg. She looked cool so I did it too.

"Yeah, what is with this music?" I made sure I didn't tap my toe or move at all to the music, which was tough for me. Little Karl was dancing up a storm. It was tough to stand still when there was music but I was doing it. This "having a crummy time" was great!

COOL PEOPLE SIT AT THE BACK OF THE BUS.

Another long, barfy bus trip. We were going to a garden to look at plants and trees. I couldn't stop yawning. We were up until after midnight last night at the dance, which I didn't think even was a dance. That was what I put in my diary too, that it wasn't even a dance. And the dorm room was horrible, hot and uncomfortable.

"Why do you think Sonya is still with us? Isn't she going to her friends' funerals?" Sonya hadn't said anything for two days. Nadia was doing all the translating. Sonya just sat looking out windows or staring at her red slip-on runners.

"Maybe they don't have funerals in the Soviet Union," Rhonda answered.

"Of course they do," Dee Dee said. She was in the seat in front of us, sitting with her back to the bus window.

"Have you ever been to a funeral?" Most of my friends at home had. Rhonda, Dee Dee and Oksana, who was in the seat behind us, all said yes.

"I haven't," I frowned. "I want to, though."

"Why would you want to go to a funeral? That's crazy," Dee Dee said.

"I guess to know what they do to the bodies and stuff."

"You're a weird kid, Kirsten." Dee Dee twirled her earring. She had an infection in the pierced hole. My earrings were getting pretty smelly too from wearing the same pair and we had no alcohol to clean them with.

The friendship tree. After walking down paths looking at plants, flowers and bushes, we got to the friendship tree. One hundred and twenty-six different countries in the world had grafted different trees onto the friendship tree. The friendship tree was citrus, so I doubted Canada had made a graft. The friendship tree had oranges, grapefruit, kumquats (my Gram liked those, gross), tangerines, lemons and something called pummelos. Plus more. It was all started back in the thirties.

"Kinda strange." Rhonda was looking at gifts that people from around the world had sent to the friendship tree.

"Yeah. Really strange." There were letters and postcards too, addressed to the friendship tree. Some guy from Brazil had sent the tree a carved statue of a bull. What would a tree do with that? "Do you think the tree minds that most of this stuff is made from wood?" Rhonda laughed at my question. But I wasn't being funny.

Nadia told us how soil from Tolstoy's grave and Tchaikovsky's grave and from the place where Pushkin had a duel was all sent to the friendship tree to be placed at its base. She told us the tree was a symbol of world peace and goodwill and "solidarity," that word again. It kept coming up. She told us about the different people who had grafted buds on the tree, like Ho Chi Minh, the President of the Democratic Republic of Vietnam, the Soviet cosmonauts, Gargarin, Komarov, somebody and somebody else and a famous pianist from the States whom I'd never heard of, Van Cliburn; and then some dead people too, who didn't actually make the grafts themselves but others did for them, like Charles Darwin and Louis Pasteur.

Back on the bus. I was sitting beside Jay at the back. The back of
the bus had a long, high bench seat. There were five of us on it. I
shouldn't have been sitting there. I knew that. The back of the
bus was the worst for making you throw up. I wouldn't, though.
I was sitting beside Jay. My feet didn't touch the ground. We
banged into each other when the bus swerved around corners. It
made me fall into Jay. I liked that. It was an excuse to touch him.
Arm to arm. Someone at the front had started "100 Bottles of
Beer on the Wall," but they started at five hundred. We booed at
the back. Cool people always sat at the back of the bus. Nerds sat
at the front. I was getting the hang of being cool. I hadn't danced
last night to the accordion music and I had booed a singsong just
now.

"Quit it." Jay looked at me. He was irritated. It was because I
had pressed into him going around the curve in the road. Big
Karl was on the other side of Jay. Oksana was to my left, and Dee
Dee was beside her, at the window.

"Is the friendship tree closer to camp or further away from
camp?" Oksana wanted to know how long it was going to take
to get back to Orlyonok. I didn't want to think about that.
Instead of sending bad kids to reform school for a couple of
years, they should just put them on a bus. At home, when we
went on long car trips, Mom always made sure there was lots for
us to do and tons to eat. Licorice shoestrings were great on car
trips. I'd tie mine in knots. We did macramé last year in school.
Mine looked awful.

"Make them shut up!" Dee Dee was talking about the 489
bottles of beer on the wall. She was right. Then I got the idea. I
saw an Italian girl at the front of the bus sleeping with her head
on the shoulder of the person next to her. That would be nice,
to rest my head on Jay's shoulder. The only way I'd get away with
it would be if I pretended to be asleep. I started. I let my eyes
close in bits and then open again. I let them shut slowly again.
Then I started to let my head drop. Then I pretended to wake
up. I jolted up like you did when you were falling asleep sitting
up and caught yourself. That was the worst at school. When you
started to fall asleep and you felt like your head dropped a foot
and then whirled around. I did that once in geography class. I

was tired because we had been to a family dinner in the city and didn't get home until after midnight. I was sure my head didn't really move huge amounts but it felt like it did. Nobody noticed me but I felt like I was whipping my head around like a spaz. Anyhow, this time I tilted my head to my right shoulder. I stayed like that for a while. It felt like forever. Then I gradually leaned closer to Jay. Finally a bend in the road helped me tilt the rest of the way so my head was resting on his arm. It felt great. My head was on Jay's arm. Something was happening around me. I wanted to look but if I opened my eyes I'd have to move my head off Jay's shoulder. I wondered if Jay was pointing me out to the others. That was what it felt like. Then a Soviet Komsomol named Nadia, a different Nadia from all the others, came and got me. She "woke" me gently and took me to her seat in the middle of the bus. She made cooing noises. She let me lie on the bus seat with my head on her lap. I wasn't tired and now I couldn't see out the window. This sucked! It was embarrassing too. Jay and Big Karl must have pointed me out to everyone on the bus. Jay had probably been making faces at me, that was what had been going on. I wondered for how long I should fake sleeping. Sometimes I faked sleeping back in Canada. I faked I was sleeping when I wanted my dad to carry me in from the car late at night. I'd pretend to go to sleep before we'd gotten home. It always worked. Dad always carried me in. Fiona did it too now. Pretended. She scrunched her eyes too tight, though. You could tell she was pretending. Mom carried her. Soon I wouldn't be able to do it any more. I figured this year would be my last and then Dad would be saying I was too big. Fiona was lucky. She had years and years left of faking she was asleep and being carried to her bed.

I LEAPT OFF THE BOAT BEFORE ANYONE COULD TOUCH ME.

A huge festival was taking place, to bring rain for the crops. It was pagan and ritualistic. We had to go through Neptune initiation. We were on this motorboat that was decorated in sea things and paper rings like you made in the early grades of school. We were being taken out to sea, then we had to jump out of the boat, or be pushed and swim into shore.

"I just don't know." Iggy was petrified. He didn't swim so well any more. "I used to be able to float for hours!" Iggy put his head in his hands. I'd done lifesaving for a few years now but you weren't supposed to actually touch a drowning person because they could pull you under, so I wouldn't be able to save him.

"It's because you've lost weight," Big Karl said.

"He should swim better because he weighs less." Oksana was clinging to a seaweed-covered pole. It wasn't real seaweed, just seaweed decoration.

"Nope, Ana. Fat floats. Skinny people sink." Big Karl was skinny. Actually we were all skinny, except for Iggy, and you couldn't call him fat any more. Chip was freaking over our weight loss.

"Why aren't Chip and Adrian doing this?" Oksana asked.

"I heard they went skinny-dipping last night, that all the camp leaders were down here swimming *naked*." Dee Dee was watching the shore nervously.

"Go on!" Jay moved his sunglasses down his nose.

"Ask them if you don't believe me. Adrian will be glad to tell you all about Neptune nudists." Dee Dee shaded her eyes to look at the shore. The people in costumes were getting smaller. Neptune had a long flowing beard and trident. He was surrounded by sea nymphs and mermaids. "They're going to be waiting a long time for us to swim in. Tell them to stop the boat."

"Excuse me," Jay yelled to the driver. The Soviets laughed at us and gave the thumbs-up sign. "Excuse me, but we think this is far enough!" The Soviets laughed louder. Jay was an awful swimmer. He mostly dog-paddled and at times did sloppy head-up crawl, always in sunglasses. Swimming was my best sport. I'd swum a mile before. This would be a piece of cake for me, except for the waves.

"They know what you are asking!" Dee Dee said. She sat on a crate and crossed her legs. "I'm not moving. They're going too far on purpose!"

"Duh da." This would really get Jay and he deserved it. "*Duh da*," I chanted a little louder. "*Duh da, duh da, duh da, duh da.*" That theme from *Jaws* was great!

"KIRSTEN!!!" Everyone in the group shouted at me. I wished I'd seen *Jaws*.

Then the boat stopped. It was time to jump in or be pushed. Dee Dee was screaming and clutching the crate. They were going to have to throw her in attached to the box. They did too and she went crashing over the side, yelling.

I leapt off the edge of the boat before anyone could touch me.

"Do you think there are sharks out here?" Oksana shrieked to Dee Dee.

I started to do the front crawl towards the shore.

"Everyone stay together," Big Karl ordered. "Kirsten, wait!" I stopped and treaded water. Jay dog-paddled over to us.

"Watch," Iggy said. He stopped swimming and started to sink.

He surfaced. "That never used to happen before." Sam splashed Iggy in the face.

"Something touched me!" Rhonda looked terrified.

"It was probably a jellyfish," Big Karl said.

"No!" Rhonda swam into the centre of the group. "It was big. It was hard. Let's get out of here."

"I'm scared," Oksana wailed.

"Why isn't Mary here? She should be out here." Dee Dee sounded annoyed. "Besides which, Mary's on her period."

Jay laughed at Dee Dee's menstrual remark. I didn't get it.

"I don't get it," I said.

"From *Jaws*, you idiot. The first girl eaten is on her period!" Rhonda started to do a fast crawl towards shore. She put her head up and yelled, "Sorry, Karl. Gotta go!"

I followed her. I wasn't waiting around, especially with all those flailing swimmers. My crawl was neat and fast, no big splashes. I'd be first to shore. I passed Rhonda in two seconds. I was on the Caledon Swim Team. We did this thing in practice where if someone was swimming slower in front of you in your lane, you grabbed their ankles and pulled them underneath you and passed over top of them. Something bumped into me under the water. I looked around. Rhonda was ten feet behind me.

"Rhonda?" I swallowed some salt water. "Rhon!?"

"What?" She stopped.

"Something hit me. Something big!"

A wave went over Rhonda's head. "What?" She hadn't heard a word.

Then I felt it again. Something passed by me in the water. "We gotta get out of here. There is something big in the water. It has run into me twice now!" I was careful not to tread water with my legs. I just sculled, my hands on the top of the water. I didn't want to look like bait bobbing in the water for a hungry shark.

"Shit!" She was beside me now. "Go under and look."

Maybe it would be better to see what it was. "Okay." I held my breath, then went under. I couldn't see. The water was murky. It was usually clear. It must have been the waves stirring things up. I came up. "I can't see anything. The water is cloudy."

"We shouldn't be in cloudy water. That is exactly what sharks like, so they can creep up on you. Let's get the hell out of here. Don't splash." Rhonda was scared. I felt sick. "Oh my God, something touched my foot!" Rhonda grabbed my arm. I was going to cry. I didn't want to die.

"Maybe we should float, not let any part of us hang down." I hated the feeling of my feet and legs pointing down, just waiting to be grabbed.

Rhonda started floating on her back. Her toes pointing out of the water.

"We'll scull in. Maybe the sharks won't notice us," I said.

"I'm scared." Rhonda looked at me.

Something touched my hand. It was Rhonda's hand. "I'm *really* scared," I said.

"I'm glad you're with me," Rhonda coughed.

I looked over my shoulder to check on the shore. It was closer now. People waved and shouted at us. Then my bum bumped the bottom. "Holy crumoly, we can touch now, Rhon." We stood up. It was shallower at this end of the beach than where we usually swam. We stood up on the sand bar. The water was only at our knees, unless there was a wave and then it was at our shoulders. "Let's run!" I yelled and we did. We ran right into the middle of the festival. We were greeted by the Neptuners. Things were hung around our necks and we were taken over to Neptune the Sea God. I didn't know what was going on but it was fun. There was singing and cheering. This was a blast!

I would have thought on Neptune Day one might have been served seafood in garlic butter. We weren't. We were going into our room for forced rest period.

"Who are they?" Oksana said as we walked into our room. There were girls on the empty beds opposite our beds. Our room wasn't "our room" any more.

"Hello," Mary greeted the new people.

"*Bonjour*," said a brown-haired girl with bangs down to her eyes.

"They're French," Rhonda said.

"*Oui*. Chantelle, Margaux *et moi. Mais elles*," the girl with bangs, at the window, pointed with her thumb to the two girls at the far end of the room. "*Elles* ... uhhhhh, *Allemagne?*"

"Deutschland," the tall girl on the bed closest to the door answered. She didn't even look up. She was unpacking her bag. Her hair was very short.

"*Est-ce que tu parles anglais?*" I asked the girl with bangs.

"*Je pensais que vous étiez Canadiennes. Vous parlez français, non?*"

"*Non*," Dee Dee answered.

"*Un peu*," I said after. "*Comme ci comme ça*." I did a "so-so" gesture with my hand after saying that. I was glad my dad had taught me a couple of things because if it had been up to my French teacher at school all I could have said were numbers to seventy-two, because that was as far as the Bingo card went.

One of the German girls said something to the other German girl, in German, and tossed a bag of coffee beans to the other girl's bed. The girl sniffed it and made an "ah" noise and tossed it back.

"They brought coffee!" Oksana walked over to the German girls. "Why did you bring coffee?" None of us in our group drank coffee. Only grown-ups in Canada drank coffee.

"You since in Soviet Union drink coffee?" the German girl half mimed.

"No," we all said.

"*Deswegen*." The girl with very short hair, smelled her beans. "*Gut, ja?*" They also had sleeping bags with them and camping pots and plates. When someone told them they were going to camp, they must have not understood. A language problem for sure.

"Gitanes?" the French girl with a frizzy perm asked us. We didn't know what she was talking about. Then she pulled out a package of cigarettes. "*Fumer*. You?" This wasn't good.

"No," Mary said. "No, you will get in trouble."

"Yeah, man. I don't think there is smoking in the rooms." Dee Dee went to the door and looked out. The French girls didn't look like they cared. They parked themselves by the open window and lit up. Smokers and coffee drinkers. We Canadians were so different. Milk drinkers and cookie eaters. That was what we were.

It was nine o'clock at night. I knew it was 9:00 because I kept looking at my watch. It had been 9:00 for ages. We were in the amphitheatre again, this time watching a movie about soccer.

"Do you think they are from East Germany or West Germany?" Rhonda could do nothing but talk about the new girls.

"What's the difference?" I really didn't see why it would matter if they were from the east half or the west half.

"Well, East Germany is communist so I was thinking that is probably where they are from." Rhonda knew more about this than I did.

"Oh." I stared at the movie screen in the same way one would stare at wallpaper, just something to look at while you talked.

"But then I was thinking that maybe it would be West Germany that the Soviets would want here because the East Germans wouldn't need to be taught about communism."

"Are East and West Germany two different countries?" I had always just called Germany Germany before.

"Yeah. They are separated by the Berlin Wall."

"Oh." What was with communist countries and their iron curtains and walls?

"The French girls are pretty bad, eh?" Rhonda pulled one of her knee socks up. The elastic was going. "They're underprivileged kids and their trip was paid for."

"I like them more than the German girls." The French girls had been friendly, even if they did smoke. The German girls had been rude.

"Dee Dee hates the German girls."

"I know." Was it me who didn't like the German girls or had I just said that because Dee Dee had said it? Maybe the Germans weren't rude, maybe they just didn't speak English.

"The German girls are snobs," Rhonda said.

"Yeah, they're snobs." I stared at the screen.

WE WERE BEHIND
IN CANADA, WAY BEHIND.

We were supposed to be going on a hydrofoil this morning but the waves were too big. A speedboat had been sent for us instead. Hydrofoils were popular in the Soviet Union. I'd never been on one before. I was disappointed although yesterday when Rhonda and I were playing hooky from sports day, she gave me her toe socks.

"Nice socks!" Little Karl butted in front of me and climbed into the boat. He made it rock really badly so I had to wait before I could step on. Dee Dee was wrong. He hated me.

"At least we don't have to jump out of this one and swim to shore." Dee Dee plunked down beside me.

"Too bad it's not a hydrofoil," I griped. Jay stepped over me to get to the back by Alexi. The cool people sat at the back of boats as well as buses.

"Iggy, why weren't you at sports day? Where were you yesterday?" Dee Dee asked. Iggy made a face at her and mouthed "shut up." He sat beside Sam. Sam's tan was really dark. He didn't have a shirt on. I hadn't noticed before but he was black as black could be. Not what you'd expect from a platinum blond. My cousin Andrew from Chingford, England, was a platinum blond but he just went red from the sun. Even his scalp went red. You could see it shining right through his hair. Andrew promised to take me to the desert someday but he never has. He promised that when I was four. He probably thought I'd forget. I never forgot stuff like that, though.

"*Dobreye ootra! Darageeye droozyah!*" The motorboat driver welcomed us. "*Kak deela?*"

"*Kharasho,*" Mary said back.

"What did you say?" Oksana asked Mary.

"Good," Mary snipped back. She could have told us what the man had said. She was being difficult on purpose. Oksana stuck her finger up her nose when Mary wasn't looking and looked right at Mary when she did it. We all laughed. Mary looked back at us and we all made straight faces like nothing was going on and then when Mary looked away Oksana did it again and we laughed even harder. If the rest of us had been taking the Russian lessons like Mary, we'd have known what he said. I was hit by a pang of envy. The boat was pulling away from the dock now. It moved away slowly and then the driver gunned it. The waves were pretty big. We got splashed from the whitecaps. We all screamed. This was great!

"Where're they taking us?" Rhonda yelled.

"Who knows, but we aren't due back til this afternoon for cosmonaut training," Dee Dee yelled back. Cosmonaut training? Now, why didn't I know about this?

We were at the astronomy place. There was a huge magnetic tele-scope. My dad took astral physics at university. That was before he sold bras, dentist's chairs or office furniture. Dad pointed out the constellations all the time but he knew their numbers. I knew the dippers, of course, and Orion with his big belt. I knew how to find HR 424, the North Star, too. We followed the translators into a little theatre. There were going to be slides about stars. I loved the plan-etarium in Toronto, by the Royal Ontario Museum. The chairs in the planetarium were great. It was like lying in a dentist's chair. The movie camera at the planetarium was very sophisticated. It looked like a giant alien ant. I liked to sit near the camera in the middle of the theatre. You sat looking up at the ceiling and went on journeys through the stars. I wondered why Dad would rather sell bras? He could tell what type of bra a woman was wearing right through her clothes. Mom hated that. He said, "Different makes give you different shapes." He knew just from the shape of the woman's boobs what she was wearing. He was right too, all the time. Poor Mom. My mom never wore bras, never. My friend Patty said that my mom would end up with boobs like the women in *National Geographic* because of not wearing a bra.

"Neato." I couldn't help saying it. The slides being shown weren't just about stars. They were about the research the Soviet kids did at this observatory. Imagine that, being eleven and being able to talk about your research. There were some pretty nifty things about the Soviet Union. You weren't allowed to draw a picture of Satan, you might even have an art class with no supplies, or have to pee in a paved hole, but at the end of the day you could have science classes at a real observatory and not just for one day on a school trip, either. They showed pictures of Soviet kids in their science classrooms at school. Not even high school kids at home got stuff like that. No wonder Soviet kids were developing solar cars. I had thought the films shown at the Friendship Centre in Toronto were exaggerations. I was wrong. The person showing the slides talked about opportunities and how important Soviet Youth was to the nation's future. I felt jealous. At Credit View, my school, the only experiment we had done was to put sugar in hot water and put a piece of string in the water and then watch over the next few days as the sugar made crystals on the string. We were behind in Canada, way behind, and I had been wandering around the Soviet Union thinking how far ahead we were because of our jeans. At my school we didn't have labs. We didn't really have anything. The kids in grade eight had to be shipped to another school once a week to take Shop and Home-Ec classes, even. I didn't want to take Home-ick, anyway. I wanted to have classes at a real observatory. I wanted to take cosmonaut training, though at home that'd be astronaut training. I should defect from Canada. Canada didn't even have astronauts.

At the Cosmonaut Training Centre, we were taken into this big room with all sorts of rides, like at a fair. We were going to get to see if we could handle space travel.

"That is a gyrosphere." Adrian answered Alexi's question. "It creates the sensation of absence of gravity." Adrian was on top of the world! It was because of Sputnik that he became interested in the Soviet Union in the first place.

"Cooool." Alexi stood by the strange device. It was a chair attached to two massive metal rings. You could tell everything would spin every which way.

"Later," a Soviet military scientist said to Alexi. He led us past a Soviet space capsule, down to the far end of the room. "Who would want to try this first?"

"Rhonda and me, Rhonda and me!" I jumped up and down with my hand held as high in the air as it possibly could go. Rhonda pinched me. I didn't even know what we were going to be trying. "Pick us! Pick us!"

"Yes, yes, two fine young candidates." Nadia had to translate that for the scientist. He led us through the door, leaving the others behind. We were in a crazy round room with diagonal black stripes down the white walls.

"The zebra room," Rhonda giggled. "Groovy, man." She was pretending to be stoned. The man sat us on chairs in the very centre of the round room. Then he left. "This better not be some joke." Rhonda leaned back and crossed her ankles. "Some stupid thing to see how long you can take being in a closed space." Then the room started to spin. It got faster and faster.

"HOOOOLD ONNN!" I screamed to Rhonda and clutched the sides of my baby blue, cafeteria-style chair.

"TOOO FAAST!" Rhonda hollered back. The room spun faster and faster. It was a blur now. We laughed and yelled. I definitely wanted to be a cosmonaut. Then the room started to slow down. Black and white stripes. Black and white stripes. Black. And. White. Stripes. It stopped. The door opened.

"Now walk out here," the military scientist ordered. I got up and fell over. Rhonda staggered towards the door and missed it. I tried to stand up again and instead fell right to the ground. The others were laughing at us. I looked at their faces crowded around the door. The room seemed to still be moving. We stumbled through the door. Rhonda pulled me over and the others screeched with laughter.

"The room was spinning so fast, you guys!" I couldn't stand up yet.

"The room was not spinning." The scientist was grinning.

"It was so." Rhonda was trying to climb up my body.

"*Nyet.*" The scientist tucked his shirt in tighter. "No, the floor did not move one centimetre."

"What do you mean?" This was crazy. I had never been so dizzy.

"Just the walls turn. Floor stay still." The Soviet scientist stood with his feet planted and his hands behind his back. "You have..." He looked at Nadia and said something. Nadia finished for him. "Failed the first test for space travel. A cosmonaut has to be able to walk out of the room as straight and fine as he or she walked into it. He must still be able to perform fine motor coordination. Who would like to try next?"

Little Karl's hand went sky high. "I would." He just wanted to outdo us.

"Can I go too?" Sam didn't raise his hand. It looked cooler if you didn't raise your hand. I'd remember that. The boys entered the room. I could stand up now but I still had to hold on to Chip so as not to fall over and I still couldn't walk.

"That is incredible." Alexi was standing by the little door.

"Stand away, please." The scientist threw a switch and the walls started to revolve. Slowly at first but then faster and faster. You could hear Sam laughing inside the zebra room. Little Karl didn't make a sound. I knew he wanted to be able to walk out of the room without a stumble. I hoped hard that he'd fail like we had.

"OHHHHH GROSSS!" That was Sam. The room kept going round and round. "Stop. Stop this ride. I WANT OFF!" Oh no, Sam was going to start throwing the chairs! "Ahhoh! Please! Stop!" What a wuss he was being. Rhonda and I were standing fine now. We looked at each other. What was wrong with this boy? The room slowed, slowed, slowed. The scientist opened the door. We all moved in close, to see. Sam was trying to leave the room. He was stumbling around in circles. "Get me out of here!"

Little Karl was still sitting in the chair. He was covered in puke. This was the best day of my life!!!

I was strapped into the chair on the metal rings. There was a nuclear device on my throat. The scientist was laughing. Then my teeth all came loose. If I could get the straps off, I'd be able to fly away. I liked flying. The straps got tighter. One of my front teeth fell out of my mouth. I opened my eyes. I was lying in bed. I looked at my watch. It was tough to read. I thought it was ten after three in the morning. I'd woken up because of a nightmare. I wanted to wake Rhonda up but was scared she'd get mad. I would even have woken Mary up if she'd been here, but she'd gone into the hospital to have an adenoid treatment, so I just lay quietly in the dark.

DON'T BE A FRAIDY CAT.

We were down at the beach. Volleyball nets were set up and Rhonda, Oksana, Dee Dee and I were playing. The other team was serving.

"Rhonda. I've decided that today is the day," I declared.

Oksana bumped the ball high in the air and Dee Dee spiked it over the net. "Nice one," Rhonda applauded. "Today is what day?"

"*The* day." I adjusted my ball cap and whispered, "Parachuting." I nodded at her. "I can't wait anymore. I'm going." The ball came to me. I volleyed it right over the net. I knew you were supposed to set the ball up for one of your teammates but I liked just sending it straight over. "Today is the perfect day! Everyone will be down here all day playing games. No one will even know."

"Only if you don't tell them, Kirsten."

The ball came back over to us. Dee Dee and Oksana crashed trying to get it.

"Call the ball!" Rhonda yelled at them.

We'd only ever seen the parachuting tower from a great distance before. You could see it standing tall above an old forest from way down at the game fields. Rhonda and I stood now at its base. We were surrounded by people from who knew where, but not from Canada. We watched some jumpers.

"How high do you think it is?"

"Ow," Rhonda winced. A girl was limping away from the parachute pit. "Maybe twenty storeys. Are you sure you still want to?"

"Look. Look. Look at him!" A boy flapped his arms like a bird as he glided gently to the ground. "It isn't as high as the Toronto Dominion Centre. It's higher than a water tower, though. I still want to."

A Komsomol on the ground unhooked Bird Boy from the parachute. "Not everyone falls so softly," Rhonda said. Bird Boy bowed and strutted away. The group he was with applauded and cheered. "Some of them really crash. We should go for the lessons first. Learn how to fall and shit." Rhonda looked a little white. There was a yell from the tower. The next jumper was coming. Rhonda needed coaxing.

"Rhon, it will be great. Fantastic. Think of the view from up there. Think of what you can tell people back at home. This will be way better than the zebra room. Come on!" I tugged her arm. Her hand came out of her pocket. I grabbed her hand. It was sweaty. "Let's just tag along with this group. The Russians won't know if we should be here or not."

"We will get in big, big shit if we are caught."

"Everyone is down at the beach and we are way up here. We are practically a mile away. Come on, Rhonda. Don't be a fraidy cat."

"Who you calling a fraidy cat? I'm not scared! Not scared of jumping ... just scared of getting in trouble. Ah ... who cares. Let's do it!" Rhonda pulled me now. We followed people to the bottom step of the tower. We looked up. Shit. We had to climb a metal ladder all the way up. Vertical. Way up!

"It's a long way to climb, Rhonda. Oh no, my camera!" I'd brought my camera with me today and there was no way I'd be able to parachute with a stupid camera. I didn't know what to do. I felt a tap on my shoulder. I jumped. It was a teenage guy.

He gestured to my camera, to the top of the tower and then to me. Wow, he was going to take a picture of me with my camera. I gladly gave it to him.

A Komsomol stood at the bottom of the ladder. He narrowed his eyes at us.

"Just look like you are supposed to be here." I frowned at Rhonda. "Try to look serious. We shouldn't look too excited."

"You're right. Look cool." Rhonda bobbed her head.

"Not too cool, though, because then you won't look like you are from wherever those people are from. They don't look so cool."

I watched Rhonda put her foot on the first rung of the ladder. She turned her head and I gave her the "silent scream" face. She punched me and then started up. I followed. I wasn't expecting the ladder rung to feel so awkward in my hands. We were about the same height off the ground as the high-dive board at the public pool back home.

"What the hell are we doing?" Rhonda whispered.

"Having an adventure!" I yelled back. I heard a cough. The Komsomol leader at the bottom was saying something to another Komsomol. I took a hand away from the ladder and gave them the thumbs-up. The Komsomol started yelling at me. He gestured that I was to keep two hands on the ladder. The teenage boy below me on the ladder made a face at me that clearly said I was dumb.

"Stop drawing attention to yourself," Rhonda hissed down at me. "Stop goofing around. Act normal."

Act normal, what was that? We were climbing again. "I'm excited!" I called up to Rhonda. "Slow down."

"It's a long way, Kirsten. We have to keep moving." Rhonda was good at this, probably because she did the uneven bars at gymnastics. I couldn't. I could barely get across a set of monkey bars. Two years ago I smashed my face on the ground when my hands slipped off the monkey bars at recess. I had the worst bleeding nose any of the teachers had ever seen. My arms just weren't that strong. And my hands were always sweaty. I could not climb the rope in gym, either, like some girls in my class could. I'd never be hanging from the edge of a cliff to save my life.

"Shit." There was grit or something in my eyes from Rhonda's shoes.

"What?"

"I got something in my eyes. Your shoes are dirty."

"I keep getting stuff in my eyes too." Rhonda kept climbing. "It's rust and paint flakes from the ladder."

There was a throat-clear below me. I looked down at the boy who'd made a face. He sighed. "I've got something in my eyes," I said to him. He stared at me with a blank face. I felt tears running down my cheeks. It was the stupid stuff from Rhonda's shoes doing it. I could barely see the boy any more. He probably thought I was being a baby. I tried to wipe my eyes on my sleeves but it was tricky while holding onto the ladder. I kept climbing blind and blinking and panting.

"Phew." Rhonda had stopped. "It's hot today." She looked over her shoulder at me. "Oh boy, wow!" She looked up again. "I don't think I can look down any more."

I looked through my foggy eyes toward the ground. "This is as high as the trestle bridge at Forks of the Credit near my house." My mom had to crawl across that bridge. I could walk but trains used the bridge so you didn't want to go too slow. Some of the railway ties were pretty far apart. You had to jump then. You sure didn't want to slip between the ties onto the road way beneath. This was harder. My arms were tired. Rhonda was climbing again. I wanted to rest. My hands hurt from the rungs. I heard a rude comment from below me. People were waiting for me to get going. It was like when you come last in a running race and everyone is watching and waiting at the finish line. I went to step up but I was too exhausted and wasn't ready. My foot returned to the step it had come from.

"OYYYA!!!" It was the boy below. I felt a mushy lump under my foot. I was on the boy's hand. It was his fingers, I knew it. I quickly removed my foot and tried to go up. I pushed. What was that? It wasn't the ladder. My foot was on the boy's head. There was a squeak. And then louder squeaks with stops and longer squeaks. It was familiar noise. It was the sound of sweaty hands and tightly gripped thighs on a firepole. There were other noises too. Exhales. And foreign swear words. I didn't want to look down. I had to look down. My hands were greasy. I held my breath and looked over my shoulder. The lineup of people following me up the ladder was now about ten feet lower than it had been a few seconds ago. They weren't spread out any more, either. They were tightly packed together, sharing the same space on the ladder.

"What the hell was that?" Rhonda had frozen on the ladder. "Kirsten, you still there?"

"Yeah." I was panting heavily. "It wasn't me, it was the boy below me. I stood on his head."

"Oh my God, is he all right? Why did you stand on his head?"

"I thought it was a step. I was on his hand ... and I had to get off and ..." I was trembling all over. I couldn't look down any more, either. Sometimes you heard stories about kids who climbed water towers and fell to their deaths. You weren't supposed to climb up stuff like this.

"Keep going, Kirsten. Just keep climbing. It is probably only ten more minutes until the top."

Ten minutes. That was a long time. A routine at figure skating was a couple of minutes and that was a long time. "Don't go so fast, okay, Rhon?"

"Okay. My hands are wet anyway. They should give you chalk at the bottom."

A soldier at the top helped you off the ladder and onto the platform. Wow, it was really high up. I thought it looked high from the bottom but that was nothing to how it looked from up top. I wanted to say sorry to the boy I stepped on but the way he looked at me stopped me from saying anything. The soldier's Komsomol helper started handing out harnesses. The other people seemed to know what they were doing. They barely needed assistance. There were eight of us jumping. One of them was a translator, we didn't know what he was saying to the other kids, but we watched. The harness strapped between your legs. Mine hung down to my knees, though. The other people's harnesses fit snug at the crotch. Mine hung a yard away. It wasn't right. The helper fiddled with it and then shrugged his shoulders. The soldier handed him another one for me to try. It wasn't any better. My heart was pounding. The soldier pointed at a boy and yelled.

The boy went to the gap in the rail that ran around the platform. The soldier clipped the boy to the parachute, shouted again and the boy was gone. I craned my neck to see. Then the next guy was there, a really tall fellow who'd been ahead of Rhonda on the ladder. He was shaking. You could actually see him quiver. The soldier screamed in the boy's face and then hooked him onto the chute. The tall boy clutched the handrail. The soldier peeled his white fingers off the rail, one at a time. Then the Komsomol helper booted the tall boy on the behind. The tall boy screamed. It was a scream of utter terror!

It was me now. I wished I hadn't been standing so near trying to see. I wished I could have watched some more people. I tripped over to the platform exit. This was the only way down. You could not climb down that ladder. The soldier grabbed hold of me. He hooked me up. I had gone and done it now. I looked at Rhonda, who had moved to the far side of the platform, like she was thinking of other ways to get down. We should have taken the lessons. I didn't know what I was doing. The soldier stared into my eyes. I didn't know what he was thinking.

"Hold here." The soldier put my hands on the shoulder straps of my harness. I was surprised that he spoke English. I guess the Russians had figured out that we weren't with the other kids.

I clutched the shoulders of the harness. "Why hold here?"

"Because it for big man. One-hundred-eighty-centimetre man. You fall out if you do not hold." I felt my eyes pop right out of my head. This sounded all too familiar. It was like the backpack, just like it, only my life did not depend on the backpack. The soldier hit my knees. "Remember bend knees. GOOOOOO!" He screamed at me. I didn't want to be booted on my bum and off the edge like the tall boy so I leapt.

"HUHHHHHHH!!!" The air came out of me and came into me at the same time. Falling. Weird. Dropping like a stone and floating, no, not floating, plummeting. Pass-out feeling. An endless jump off a diving board. Feet where head was, feet where head was. Stomach in mouth. Speeding towards the earth. *Wwwwwhack*. The chute caught. I started to breathe. I looked around. I looked down between my legs. The earth was getting closer. I could see the mountains and the Black Sea. Floating down towards the sandy field. Wow-wy! Bend my knees, he'd said. I bent them. That was like in skating. You had to bend your knees when you landed from jumps. I hoped the landing wouldn't hurt. I couldn't believe how much of the camp you could see from up here. It was a huge place. I looked up to see if I could see Rhonda but all I could see was the big, white parachute. I liked the noise it made, like a giant kite. I held tight onto the shoulder straps, which were not at my shoulders at all but were now above my head. The crotch was tight in the crotch now, though. I hoped the landing would not be too rough. I was as tall as the trees now. Closer to the landing site. Blowing away from the landing site and back around towards the metal tower. I hoped I'd land before blowing hard into the tower. I was skimming over the patchy grass and sand, still floating. If I let go of the straps I could flap my arms like the boy. I could see people watching. I let go of the shoulders and flapped my arms out straight, three times. Then I quickly grabbed the shoulder straps again so I wouldn't fall out. No one cheered like when the boy did it earlier. I wasn't sure I was even going to hit the ground. Some guy was running underneath me. He jumped up and grabbed my ankles before I smashed into the tower. He pulled me down and I barely touched the ground. I ran five steps. I was down.

"Thanks, mister. I don't know what would have happened if you hadn't grabbed me. I don't think I'd ever have touched the ground on my own." I couldn't stop talking even though he didn't know what I was saying. The man helped unhook me from the parachute and from my harness. My legs felt shaky but not from the landing. My bum muscles hurt too. I must have been clenching them really hard. I stood back and watched Rhonda drop. I walked over to her. Boy, I was trembly. I'd had enough. You got two jumps but one was enough. I didn't need to do that ever again! "Hey, Rhonda!" I shouted. "Ready to go again!?!" I punched an imaginary punching bag. What was I doing? What was I saying? "That was great, eh! I loved it!" I jumped up and down on the spot. Was I nuts or something?

"Um. Sure." Rhonda was getting off of the ground where she'd fallen. A man was helping her too. "You really want to?" Rhonda looked a little weak-kneed too.

"Of course I really want to!" I scoffed. I most definitely did *not* want to.

Rhonda and I were heading back to our camp building. It was suppertime. We walked over the sidewalk chalk drawings. Some of them were fantastic. Much better than mine. Too bad it hadn't rained.

"I knew we'd get away with it," I said.

"But you remember that we are going to have to do it again with the others, right?" That had never crossed my mind. I was going to have to go through that whole thing again. Climbing. Falling. People had nightmares about that.

"That's great, because two jumps would not have been enough for me!" I was such a big fat liar. "That means we will get to jump four times. Too bad we have to go through the training, though. That'll be boring. And we don't need it. We're good."

"What would you have done if the parachute ripped or got caught up in the strings? They just haul the same parachute you used back up to the tower without even checking it." Rhonda kicked a stone off someone's picture.

That hadn't crossed my mind, either.

"I'm not sure but I think they would have taught us what to do if we'd gone to the lessons." Rhonda was going towards the ramp to the balcony that led to the dorm.

"It's suppertime, Rhon. We better just go to the meal hall." I started towards the dinner hall, which was on the main floor.

Little Karl ran past me. "You two are in the biggest shit ever! Nya, nya!"

"Big shit?" Rhonda stopped on the ramp and we stared at each other with big eyes. She didn't need to say "told you so."

"How?" I said. Karl was gone. Rhonda shrugged. "How'd they find out?" I was utterly shocked.

"No one at the pit knew who we were." Rhonda gripped the cement rail. It had little pebbles in it. I had been picking them off up at the top, across from the glass door the boy walked through. I had cleared a whole little section of pebbles out of the concrete.

"Let's just go to dinner like nothing is different." I didn't want to walk into the dinner hall alone. I wanted Rhonda with me.

"I have to pee." She jiggled her hips.

"Hold it. Let's not get separated and let's not be late." I stood my ground.

"Okay." Rhonda followed me. "Okay. Just talk and act normal."

"Let's sing," I said. That was normal. We did that all the time. I started off with the chorus of "Afternoon Delight." It was on the radio all the time. It was my favourite Starland Vocal Band song.

"I don't think we should sing anything about sky or flight or …." Rhonda had a point.

"Okay." I started to sing Elton John's "Daniel." "I'm joking." Well, I was, sort of, but everything that was popping into my head had something to do with flying.

"'Delta Dawn.'" I knew the words to the tune Rhonda had chosen very well. It was Helen Reddy's big hit from four years ago. We sang it at school in music class.

"Stop!" I shouted when Rhonda got to the part. Rhonda laughed.

"Skyyyyy." We both sang together. Everyone at our table was gazing at us. They looked stunned. I didn't see Adrian anywhere, which was good.

"You guys should start running now!" Dee Dee warned.

"Did you really do it?" Oksana asked.

"What was it like?" Iggy was grinning from ear to ear.

"They might kick you out of camp, right back on that plane home," Jay said.

"Are we that dead?" Rhonda sat down. I couldn't. I was more scared now than I had been jumping and that had terrified me.

Alexi took a big breath. "I think it's bad, you two. Adrian was talking about how there could have been an international crisis. That if anything had happened to either of you—"

"You might have started a war, you know." Little Karl jabbed at us.

"Oh, shut up, Darwin!" Rhonda snapped.

"The Soviets are furious," Big Karl said. There was still no sign of Adrian or Chip over at their table.

"How did you do it without the lessons?" Oksana asked.

253

"No problemo." I tried to be cool but I wasn't.

"You two are nuts!" Dee Dee had not cracked a smile yet.

"I hope they don't make you go back to Canada," Oksana said.

"It would serve them right," Little Karl snorted.

"I'm inclined to agree." Big Karl swallowed. "I don't think you realize how serious this could have been."

"Well, nothing happened and everything is fine!" Rhonda stood back up. "You're just jealous that we went parachuting before you did! You're just jealous that we even thought of it and that we had the guts to do it!"

I saw Oksana and Dee Dee looking behind me, then Iggy and Sam. He was there. Adrian. I knew it. I could see it in their faces.

"This way, you two."

Rhonda and I followed him out.

"What were you thinking?" Adrian was pacing. Rhonda and I were sitting on our beds in our room. Chip was standing at the foot of my bed. I was glad she was there. Nadia was over by the windows, leaning on the sill. "And don't deny it. We know there is a photograph of you parachuting on YOUR camera, Kirsten."

"I couldn't wait," I owned up. "I wanted to go parachuting more than anything."

"But Kirsten, you were all supposed to go for lessons and, besides, you are too little. You probably weren't going to be allowed to do it anyway because there isn't small enough equipment!" Chip had that look that was called distraught. You could see the muscles in her neck and there were indents of concern on her forehead.

"I ... oh ... what?" I was shocked. They had been keeping it from me that I wasn't going to be allowed to parachute. That sucked. I was too little to do anything in the Soviet Union.

"Kirsten, you are too little." Nadia was translating English to English.

"They won't be doing the lessons now!" Adrian shouted.

"They have done their jumping! You will not be permitted to jump off the tower when the others go! That is your punishment!" Big deal. They'd just said I couldn't have gone for the parachute jump even if I'd had the lessons. Big deal.

"If something had happened to either of you two, it would have been very serious." Chip's eyes were stressed. "You had no idea what you were doing."

"You are very bad girls!" Adrian was still pacing. I wished he'd stop.

Nadia looked at her watch. "They are going to miss dinner."

"Go," Adrian said to us. And that was that.

The others still weren't talking to us after dinner, at the dance. Rhonda was right, they were jealous. Especially now, since we weren't even really being punished. Rhonda and I were doing the bump on the dance floor. The music wasn't right for it but we were doing it anyway.

"*Bonjour, mesdemoiselles.*" A curly-headed French boy started to bump his bum to my hip, making me the sandwich filling in the middle of the bump. The three of us did the bump. It was tough being the middle person in a three-way bump. "*Je m'appelle* Slip." Now we were all doing a low bump with bent knees. Bums banged together. Bums banged together.

"*Je m'appelle* Kirsten," I grunted.

"*Ah! Vous parlez français!*" He got really low now and we were all banging bums, inches off the floor.

"*Comme ci, comme ça.*" I loved saying that. It made you sound better than you were. Better than just saying *un peu*, a little. It got the reaction I wanted. Slip applauded. Then we all fell to the floor.

"*Voilà! Nous sommes arrivés,*" Slip chuckled. We lay there laughing in the middle of the outdoor dance floor. We just decided to stay down. People stared at the three of us.

"*Quel est son nom?*" Slip asked me.

"Rhonda." I answered.

"Rrrron-dah," Slip repeated.

THERE REALLY WERE SHOOTING STARS. THOUSANDS OF THEM. LIKE FIREWORKS.

L iar liar pants on fire. That was what I was. I put my diary down. I didn't want Mom and Dad to know that we weren't supposed to go parachuting but I still wanted them to know that we *did* go parachuting.

"Accccchhhooo!" The nicer of the two German girls was very sick.

"*Gesundheit,*" I muttered.

"*Danke,*" she husked back. She looked surprised.

"I declare this a tan day." Dee Dee rubbed face cream on her thighs.

"Oh no! Not another!" Oksana wailed. Ana got so fried on tan days. Poor redheads. They just didn't tan.

"Let's go look at the Italians, before we go down to the beach." Rhonda licked her lips. The Italian girls had started first thing in the morning, preparing for the Italian holiday of the shooting stars. They were making us dinner.

"Fine. Ready?" Dee Dee put her towel around her shoulders.

"It's weird, you know, but if we had a Canadian holiday of the shooting stars and were asked to make dinner for everyone, well, what would we make that is Canadian?" I picked up Dee Dee's towel, which had slid off her shoulders, and we all headed downstairs.

"I have no idea! What is a Canadian dish?" Dee Dee asked.

"Apple pie, not that I could make it," Oksana said.

"No, that seems more American," Rhonda shook her head.

"Gee, what is Canadian?" Oksana two-foot-hopped down the stairs. I copied.

"I don't know if we have anything." Dee Dee thought for a second. "Stop it, you two." Oksana and I stopped jumping down the stairs.

"French onion soup?" I was pretty sure that was from Quebec.

"French." Dee Dee curled her lip at me like I was dumb.

"Sourdough pancakes," Rhonda stated.

"No. They're Dutch." I had had them at the Dutch pavilion during Caravan. That was a festival that took place every year in Toronto. You visited all the different countries' pavilions and tried their food and saw shows. It was great. You even got a pass-port stamped. The Dutch pancakes were served with sprinkled icing sugar instead of maple syrup and they were made on this huge griddle. The griddle was like a waffle iron that didn't fold in half and it had silver-dollar-size holes in it for the cakes. They poured the batter on the surface and then scraped it into the holes.

"Hamburgers?" Oksana sounded doubtful.

"They're called that because they were invented in Hamburg, Germany." Dee Dee told us. "I don't think we have a national dish.

"Popcorn!" I yelled. "The Indians invented it!"

"I don't know if we can count that." Dee Dee opened the kitchen door.

"Why?" Two of my best friends were Canadian Indians. Bobby and Betty Lil' Canoe, my friend from school who pre-tended to get her period every week. They were twins. They were Ojibwa. Their dad played the drums. Fiona was friends with their little brother Tippy. Fiona and Tippy went to pre-school together. And my mom was great friends with their mom Shawna, Mrs. Lil' Canoe. Mrs. Lil' Canoe sold Avon makeup.

"Wow." Rhonda held the kitchen door open for Oksana and me. Two Italian girls were standing on stepladders on either side of a giant caldron. They were stirring with spoons bigger than canoe paddles.

"*Ciao!*" The Italian girl with the haircut like a boy waved to us. "You like spaghetti?" she called to us.

"When it has a sauce," Dee Dee laughed.

"We make sauce." The girl smacked her lips. "In the big pot. Sauce."

"How do they know how to do that?" I mumbled.

"All Italians cook." Dee Dee thought she was such an expert on things because she was from downtown.

Nighttime at the beach. Rhonda and I lay on our backs in the sand, staring at the sky.

"There's one," I gasped. This was incredible. It was called "night of the shooting stars" for a reason. There really were shooting stars. Thousands of them. Like fireworks.

"Did you make a wish?" Rhonda asked.

"I forgot."

"Bozo."

"Do you think that German girl liked the flowers we gave her?" I asked. Rhonda made one of those sighs like you heard crowds do at firework displays. "Where? I don't see it."

"It's gone. No, she didn't like them."

"What about the candies? Do you think she liked them?"

"No." Rhonda sat up. The sand slid off her body.

"You wrecked it!" I stayed in my sand tomb. Just my face was showing. "If I get up to re-bury you, then who will bury me?"

"Ow. Ow. Ow. Ow." Oksana hobbled over to us. She was absolutely scarlet. She couldn't even walk, she was so burnt.

"*Où est le lapin?*" Slip was back. *Le lapin*, that's what he called me, because, he said, my braids were like rabbit ears.

"*Dans* her hole," Rhonda pointed at me.

"Ohhhhh, *moi aussi, moi aussi.*" Slip lay down beside me and indicated to Rhonda and Oksana to bury him too. They did.

"*Pas mon visage ni ma bouche.*" Slip spat out a mouthful of sand. I could hear him but not see him. Another shooting star blazed overhead.

"My parents have a meteorite. My mom found it in some foothills in England. It's cool. You can see how it went splat when it hit the earth because it was still molten hot." It was hard to talk when you couldn't move your hands. Then the dinner bell rang. I was moving now. Bolt upright. Spaghetti. Spaghetti! We ran down the beach. All of us. Even Oksana.

"Ow, ow, ow, ow, ow." Poor Oksana.

"It tastes like ketchup!" Iggy was walking towards us with a full plate of spaghetti and sauce. He was eating like he'd never seen food before. The pasta had been boiled in a massive pot over a bonfire on the beach.

"As long as it's Heinz." Rhonda was in front of me. She was handed a plate. Sauce spilled over the side and onto her hand. She licked it. "It does taste like ketchup!"

"Ssssshhhh." Chip put her fingers to her lips. "Don't be rude." I noticed Chip didn't have a plate.

I got mine. It had some ash on it. I dove my fork in anyway. The sauce ran off the noodles. I shoved them in my mouth. I felt sad. The stars were beautiful.

We were lying in our beds in the room. It was after midnight. The big people were still at the beach but we kids had to go back to the dorms at eleven for bed. I wanted to have a midnight swim. I had done that before in our pool at home. The water felt so nice and warm on your body at night. Completely different from swimming in the day, when you could barely get in our pool, it was so cold.

"Hey!" Rhonda sat up. "How come Slip isn't camping with the other French and German kids?" It was nice having our room back.

"He says they aren't nice to him." There was sand in my bed. Sand was worse than cookie crumbs.

"I don't think that is enough for them to allow him to stay

behind. You'd have to be sick like that German girl." Oksana couldn't even put her sheet on her body, her skin hurt so much.

"Do you think the German girl has something catching?" Dee Dee asked. "I'd hate to have to go to that crappy hospital. I can't believe that Mary chose to go."

"It might cure Mary's snoring. Is she having the same treatments as Kirsten?" Oksana asked.

I felt sorry for the German girl. When we got back she was being taken to the san. I knew what she was in for. Dee Dee had said "good." Dee Dee was scared of germs. I couldn't fathom Mary wanting to go there, either.

"Yeah, for sure they're radiating Mary. The Soviets love it. But I thought she was going for her acne." Dee Dee said.

"No, because if the treatment doesn't work she said they might cauterise her adenoids," Rhonda yawned.

"Shit! I know my tooth is chipped from that damn spaghetti. There was sand in it." Dee Dee got out of bed. She was probably looking for her mirror to look at her teeth again.

"I hate sand in my food." Oksana was lying on her back, spread-eagle.

"Sometimes it's in escargot. Wait a sec … escargot? Are they Canadian?" Rhonda sounded excited.

"No, French," I said. "My mom says they are just a medium for garlic butter. Maybe that's what we Canadians do! We take food from other countries and make it taste even better. My Gram always says that the Chinese food in Chinatown, in Toronto, tastes better than the Chinese food she had in China.

"Your Gram went to China?" Rhonda sounded surprised.

"Yup. And Bali, she brought back a chess set from there but my sister flushed one of the pieces down the toilet. And Japan and Singapore. She brought me back some Japanese candies. They were ghastly."

"Ghastly, were they?" Dee Dee was making fun of me again. It was probably the word *ghastly*. But the candies were. They were horrid. Made from seaweed and shit. Well, not real shit but gross stuff.

TONIGHT WE MIGHT
PLAY A TRICK...

Another gorgeous, sunny day at camp. We had just got back from sunbathing again at the beach. We'd be leaving soon to go back to Moscow to see things like Lenin's dead body and then home and we wanted to have the darkest tans in the world.

"Ohhhh. Gross, what the hell is that?" Rhonda was looking at something on the floor. I went over.

"Some of Oksana's skin, I think." I looked at the shard of waxy film on the floor. "Yup. It's skin, all right."

"That is the grossest thing I have ever seen." Rhonda picked up the sheet of skin on the end of my red felt-tip marker.

"Can you see her freckles?" Maybe if all her skin peeled off she wouldn't have those ginger freckles any more.

"Freckles don't peel off, silly." Rhonda came towards me with the skin.

"Don't!" I yelled. I didn't want it on me. Oksana entered the room.

"What's that?" she asked. She didn't come to the beach today. She'd got permission to go do something else.

"Some of your skin." Rhonda held it up. Dee Dee came into the room.

"It is not!" Oksana was blushing. You could see her blush even through her burnt cheeks.

"Yes, it is. I bet we can find the place on your back where it came from even." Rhonda walked over to Ana, holding up the specimen.

"I HATE YOU!!!" Oksana ran out of the room. What was happening to the group?

"Get rid of that." Dee Dee looked like she could barf.

Rhonda and I stood at the perimeter of the parachute pit. We were only to "watch" the others. I had to act like it didn't bother me. I didn't want to parachute again but I didn't want to be seen just standing at the bottom, watching. Big Karl and Jay were talking about their balls for the benefit of the younger boys.

"Watch when the chute catches after the free fall. It really jerks and your balls could get broken." Jay was tugging the harness at his crotch. I didn't know balls could be broken. I was sure he was exaggerating. Big Karl hadn't done his first jump yet. Jay had done his and was acting like such a pro.

"At least your harness fits you. Mine was so loose it hung past my knees. I could have fallen out," I told them.

"That is better than too tight like these ones," Jay said. It was not. He didn't know what he was talking about. "It's really painful. It could be dangerous, you know. They said they didn't have any parachute harnesses to fit a man over six foot." Jay headed over to the tower ladder for his second jump. I was puzzled by his last comment.

We were back up in the room again. Dee Dee and Oksana and Mary couldn't stop talking about their jumps. Rhonda and I kept rolling our eyes at one another.

"Ba ba ba *da*. Ba ba ba *da*." Chip blew her imaginary bugle as she entered into the room. "Important announcement to make! The lost luggage has arrived from the airport!" With that Chip swept her arm to the side and a couple of Soviet boys brought in Dee Dee's first missing suitcase.

"Excuse me?" Dee Dee said. "Now!? We leave here in two days!"

"But isn't it great that it wasn't completely lost?" Chip asked.

"Where was it?" I asked. Dee Dee dragged her big bag over to her bed.

"Was everyone's found?" Oksana asked.

"Yes, everyone's. Check out the tags on your bag." Chip went over. "The luggage has been all over the place."

"What's this stand for?" Rhonda asked.

"Frankfurt." Chip lifted up another tag on the handle. "And look at this. Morocco!"

"Berlin too." Dee Dee opened the suitcase. "I hope everything is here. My toothbrush! Oh, here is my blouse I was telling you about." She pulled out a fabulous white lace blouse.

"There're your runners." Rhonda pointed to a shoe sticking out of a grocery bag.

"My runners!" Dee Dee kicked off her sandals. "It would have been way easier to parachute in these. Who parachutes in sandals? God, the things I have done in these sandals!" She tossed her sandals into the wastebasket. "*Adios! Bon voyage!*"

"You can say that again." I think Rhonda was making a comment about the smell that was coming off Dee Dee's sandals. They were rotting. Probably from the sea water.

"Well, I'll leave you then." Chip started for the door. "Oh, the movie tonight is supposed to be a really good one." She left.

"Underwear!" Dee Dee was lucky to get nice, clean, new clothes now. I wasn't just sick of looking at my clothes. They were starting to make me sick; dirty, stiff, and not smelling so good, anymore. Which gave me an idea. Outside the window to our room was a series of clotheslines. Clean clothes were always flapping in the breeze on those lines. Our clothes never flapped in the breeze on those lines.

I did not have a clue what was happening in the movie. Chip was wrong about this one. It wasn't good at all. It was a beautiful night, though. Our second-last night at camp.

"Rhon?" I whispered.

"What?"

"I think we should do something tonight. They aren't going to kick us back home now if we get caught."

"What type of thing?"

"A trick." I raised my eyebrows up and down.

Rhonda tapped Dee Dee. Dee Dee was wearing this great pantsuit. "Kirsten thinks we should play a trick tonight."

"Good idea."

"Trick?" Oksana moved to the empty bench in front of us so she could hear.

"Sssshhh." Some guy behind us was actually watching the stupid film.

"*Prasteetee,*" I said. That meant *sorry* in Russian.

"What kind of trick?" Oksana whispered.

"Tttcchh." The guy made an exasperated noise.

"*Kakoy?*" I wanted to say "what's your problem" but all I knew was "what."

He babbled at us, shaking his hands in the air. If he was missing the movie, it was more his fault now than ours.

"*Ooydee!*" I made a face at him.

Now he looked really mad. He got up and left, pissing people off behind him and pissing the people off down the entire row who had to get up to let him past.

"What did you say?" Dee Dee was giggling.

"Go away," I answered

"He can sit on it." Oksana had her back to the movie screen and was facing us. These benches were awful to sit on for two hours to watch a movie since they had no backs but they were great for chatting like this.

"So what should we do?" Dee Dee was sitting with her legs crossed. She looked so refined. Like a model.

"I was thinking maybe something like ... wet the clothes on the clothesline." There was a silence after I said this. Brother. They didn't like my idea.

"You know, that is kind of funny," Dee Dee nodded.

"Really soak them!" Rhonda agreed.

"All the Soviets' marching uniforms for tomorrow's competition were hung out there this evening." Oksana covered her mouth with her hand. "Ooooooo. That's excellent. The clothes will be wetter tomorrow morning than when they hung them out this evening."

"Exactly." I did the thing with my eyebrows again.

"Stop doing that. You look like Groucho Marx." Rhonda started to snicker.

"Maybe, for a change, people won't be laughing at us during roll call." Dee Dee rubbed her palms together.

Yelling outside our window woke us up. It was before morning reveille. The French and German girls were back in our room. They had got back last night from camping, while we were at the movie. They were so tired that they hadn't even heard us get up in the night.

"Oh my God!" Oksana had her head out the window and was looking down. She started to laugh.

"Let me see." I was over there in a flash. I crammed my head out the window beside Oksana. Russian women were flapping around the laundry, shouting.

"They think it was one of the washerwomen's fault," I relayed to Rhonda.

"What are you talking about?" Mary got up.

"Nothing. I'm not sure. Something seems to be wrong with the Soviets' laundry on the line." This was not the sort of thing you could let Mary in on.

We had all cracked up, even our leaders, when Canada came in third in the marching competition. We laughed harder at that than at the Soviets in their wet uniforms, which actually didn't seem as funny as it did the night before. We were standing around the outside of an open-air dance floor. It was a big cement circle with a roof. Mary was going to be in a ballroom dancing competition. I didn't know she had been taking dance lessons at camp. I didn't know that you *could* take dance lessons at camp.

"Mary is going to be doing the tango." Chip put her hand on her heart. "I love the tango! It's so romantic, so sexy!"

"I didn't know you could take dancing here, Chip." I would have loved to have learned how to ballroom dance.

"Well, you couldn't have, Kirsten. It wasn't offered to the young children. There are tons of things to take at Orlyonok, though." Chip looked at me like I was from Jupiter. I didn't know there were things we could have learned to do. I just hung around with Rhonda all summer. "Mary really took full advantage of the activities!" Chip said proudly. How did Mary know about all these things? My parents would have wanted me to do everything. That's what happened when you missed the start of something. Stupid hospital. It was just like a movie, you missed the start and you didn't know what was going on.

Slip put his hands over my eyes. I knew it was him. I pretended not to, though. "Ummm, Oksana?"

"Sh sh sh sh." Slip was probably saying that to Oksana.

"Rhonda?" I heard him giggling.

"Ohhhh, *attendez! Je sais, je sais—*"

"How you know?" Slip poked me. He held my braids up straight in the air. "*Regardez! Le lapin.*" Why this was so amusing to him, well, who could know. I had an idea that Slip had a crush on Rhonda. Actually, I was sure of it. I was just his little buddy but he wanted to *go* with Rhonda.

"The compulsory waltzes are over!" Chip applauded.

I leaned on the rail that ran around the dance circle. "Will Mary be dancing with the same guy in the tango?"

"Yes, that's her partner. Aren't they great together?" Gross, I thought. Chip was holding hands with Adrian too. Adrian was the only one who'd gained weight here; every pound we'd lost was around his middle.

"Did Mary get to choose her partner?" I asked.

"I'm not sure how they picked partners." Chip was swaying

to the music. Adrian didn't look as inspired. I doubted he was much of a dancer. Not the type.

"What kind of music is this?" We had tangos in skating but this wasn't one. I knew that.

"Foxtrot," Chip said.

"Two-step," Adrian corrected. Well well well.

"It's almost Mary's turn." Chip checked that we were all watching. Jay didn't give a shit. You could tell. Sam and Iggy were sitting on the ground, watching through the iron rungs. They were pretending they were in prison or something. Rhonda and Dee Dee were leaning with their elbows on the top rail. Dee Dee really hated Mary. She was probably thinking "flub it" in her head. I did that sometimes. It worked when you thought it hard enough. Oksana was talking to Alexi. Little Karl and Big Karl had on their mirrored sunglasses. They could have been standing there with their eyes closed but I thought they were watching. I turned my head to the dance floor. Mary had on a dress. It went below her knees and my mom said that was a very unflattering length. But that was probably because Mom had great legs. Dad called them "pegs" and sometimes "yams." Though if someone told me I had a great set of sweet potatoes, I'd probably punch them in the head. Mom liked it when fashions were short, and when they were not, you could bet she'd find a skirt with a slit in it. The tango started. It was very dramatic. Mary was pretty good; she didn't just dance it, she acted the part. No, they were more than good, they had flair.

"They're good!" I said to Chip.

"Why do you sound so surprised?" she asked. It was a rhetorical question. So I didn't have to answer, which was good, because I was mad that Mary got to dance.

After the dance competition we were surprised with our hydrofoil ride. The Soviets were doing everything to make our last day at camp a real blowout. There were even going to be firecrackers later to say farewell. We were sitting inside a cabin on the hydrofoil. The seats were like coach seats on a fancy bus. I looked at

Mary. I hadn't congratulated her yet for winning the dance competition and she deserved congratulations. She was wearing her medal. I really should say something to her. Maybe later.

At dinner it had been decided that we would fool around all night long, as it was our last night at camp. After the fireworks we headed back to the rooms.

"Let's go up to the movie theatre," I said.

"Why?" Dee Dee asked.

"Because we are supposed to go to bed now."

"Okay," Dee Dee agreed. So when the path divided, we took the right instead of the left. The moon was out. It gave us really long shadows.

"Slip, I hope you don't get in trouble." One of the nice things about Oksana was how she thought of other people. Alexi was considerate too.

"Yeah, Slip. It isn't *your* last night at camp." Rhonda was walking beside Slip. He'd like that.

"*Non.*" Slip looked sad. "It is *your* last night. Me, I do not mind trouble."

"Slip, why do you hang around with us and not the French kids?" Dee Dee asked.

"He won't understand you," I said to Dee Dee.

She tried again. "Slip. *Pourquoi est-ce que tu va avec nous,* um instead, um, *mais pas les autres Français?*" She made a face that said she knew it was bad but it was good enough this time that Slip could understand her.

"*Parce que je* ... how you say?" Slip puckered his lips. "You Canada no mind. You no mind me." And he touched his hair. What was he going on about? "How you say? *Ma famille est Africaine? Nous avons le sang des nègres. Tu comprends?* Negro?" That had never occurred to me before. Slip was just Slip. Now that he mentioned it, I noticed he was a little darker and his hair sure was frizzy. Did the French kids really not like him because of that? That seemed crazy. We all loved Slip. He was so funny. The Soviets were concerned about appearance too, but in another way. Dee Dee's second missing case had turned up, the one that was taken at the start of camp. We decided the Soviets had lied, it wasn't lost, they kept it because her fabulous clothes and jewellery would have made her the envy of the camp. When I thought back to the start of the trip, I realized that her clothes had made me feel poor. I was guilty too, though. I thought a boy from the Middle East had gross acne when he had scars from a bomb. I had to stop thinking less of people because of red hair or pimples. I'd done it to Mary, too, and she'd accomplished more here than any of us.

"We should do things tonight like put people's hands in hot water when they are sleeping," Oksana giggled.

"Why would you do that?" It sounded a strange thing to do to me.

"It makes them go pee, ya dummy." Dee Dee said that too often, "you dummy."

"Or put toothpaste on them!" I said.

"What's that do?" Oksana asked.

"Nothing. There's just toothpaste on them," I replied. Dee Dee was looking at me with the "you dummy" look now.

We arrived at the amphitheatre and sat on the empty benches and looked at the empty screen.

"Hey!" a man shouted. So we got up and left.

MAYBE IT WAS ME WHO
WAS WEIRD, NOT THEM.

We were leaving. Standing outside a line of three coaches. Lots of groups were leaving. Us, the Italians, the Middle Easterners, tons of Soviet kids. Lots were staying, though, too. People were crying. We had all been given roses and the camp record, which had the song "Orlyonok" on it plus more. Lots of people were crying. It made me feel weird. Slip came up to me. Tears were streaming down his face. He clutched me. I couldn't understand a word he said. This was just bizarre. I didn't feel like crying. I didn't feel anything. A little tired maybe from the late night.

"*Où est* Rhonda?" Slip blubbered.

"*Là*," I pointed. He staggered towards her. "Good grief," as Charlie Brown said. Then I saw Jay crying. He was hugging some Soviet chick and bawling his eyes out. When did he get a girlfriend? I hoped he didn't have one when I was putting my head on his shoulder on the bus. Shit, what if his girlfriend was on the bus when I did that? Jay's girlfriend surfaced from their embrace. Oh my God, it was the girl from the bus, the girl who put my head on her lap and cooed. I looked around. Chip was crying. Even Dee Dee was crying. Mary was crying and holding hands with a boy, not her dance partner. What was wrong with everyone? There wasn't a person with dry eyes in the group. Then I realized there was a person with dry eyes. Me. This wasn't affecting me. Was there something wrong with me? Maybe it was me who was weird, not them.

"Nadia!" I called out. I felt too odd standing by myself. "Nadia!" I looked around. Alexi was making out with a Soviet chick. Who were these girls? I'd never noticed them before. I guessed the big kids had made girlfriends and boyfriends. I didn't think Dee Dee had, but she'd made friends with some Russian girls. I hadn't even done that. "Nadia!" I hollered.

A Soviet woman babbled something at me. She knew where Nadia was, apparently. She ran off. The next thing she was back tugging another girl. "Nadia," she said.

Jay's girlfriend patted my head and cooed. The humiliation was too much. All of a sudden, I started to cry. But I wasn't crying for the same reasons as everyone else. I was crying because I was embarrassed and because I felt nothing about leaving and that made me feel bad. "Thursday's child has far to go," that's what my grandma always said to me. It meant I was a goer. I would go places. I'd go to many places. Far places. I just went. Jay's Nadia dried my tears. She smiled at me. She went back to Jay. I stopped crying.

"Other Nadia," I called. "Other Nadia!"

Little Italian Gina came up to me. She wanted my address. She was shorter than me. I'd never met anyone my age that was shorter than me. Getting addresses was a good idea. I was just going to leave without doing that. I reached into my bag and handed her my travel diary. At the back was an address book. We wrote our addresses in each other's books. I'd get Slip's too.

Moyseen's Nadia was here now. That wasn't the Nadia I wanted, either. I wanted our translator Nadia. Someone to hang out with until this was all over. I handed Moyseen's Nadia my address book. She wrote her and Moyseen's address in it. Cool. I had Moyseen's address. She left. I turned around and there was Olga from the hospital.

"Goodbye, Olga." I wasn't going to ask for her address.

"Goodbye, Kirstyanushka." She hugged me. I was kind of glad

we weren't really huggy or touchy in Canada. The English weren't, either.

"Time to go!!!" Adrian yelled. I couldn't believe it when I saw his face. His eyes were swollen and red. His moustache had snot in it. If even Adrian was crying, there really had to be something wrong with me for feeling nothing. I wanted to get on the bus. I pushed through the crowds. "Get on the bus!" Adrian yelled. Now why did he have to go and do that? I wanted to board the bus but now that he had ordered it, I couldn't do it. I stopped in my tracks. Didn't want to look like some obey-the-boss kind of kid. The kind who sat in the front row. The crying was still going on. It was unbelievable! I got on the bus.

"You won't be able to leave after all because you will flood the bus with all your tears!" someone shouted. I'd never seen that someone before. I tried to cry. No more tears came out. I tried again. I thought of a sad thing. I thought of my parents catching on fire. It didn't work. I guessed because it hadn't really happened and I couldn't fool myself. I was sure if it had happened I'd cry really hard!

We were on the bus but we still weren't underway. Jay and Alexi were wearing red Pioneer scarves. Their girlfriends had given them as parting gifts. Another person I didn't know made the same joke about flooding the bus with our tears and not being able to leave. I knew they weren't looking at me before they said it. I was already tired of my roses. I wondered how long I'd have to hang onto them. At home the flower stores usually removed the thorns.

"We should probably just go," Adrian sobbed to Sonya. "It's not going to get any easier. I wish, I wish we could just stay here forever! It has been so wonderful!"

Sonya nodded. I didn't think he should have said that to Sonya. She probably wanted to go back to Moscow. She pushed her way past the Soviet girlfriends and Slip to get to the bus driver. Slip was pushing his way towards me.

"*Le lapin!*" He handed me his address book. I quickly wrote my address. Then gave him mine. "*Ecrit!*" he said to me.

"I will," I said back. "You too, huh?"

"*Moi aussi.*"

"Everyone who is not going to the airport, please get off the bus." I didn't know why Sonya said that in English as everyone who spoke English had to stay on the bus.

Slip grabbed my braids one last time and held them straight up in the air. I was excited about going on another prop plane. "*Au revoir.*" He pecked me on both cheeks. He was still crying. Silly goof.

"*Allez*, Slip!" I said. "*Désolée! Il n'y a pas de place pour toi dans mes bagages.*" We always joked about that at home before one of us went on a trip without one of the others. We'd always say "is there room for me in your suitcase?"

WAS SHE ACTUALLY
CAUGHT IN THE ACT?

Back in Moscow, it was really cold compared to camp. It was cold for anywhere for August. Only fifteen degrees Celsius. It was also grey and dark. We were going to go to a monastery today and then shopping.

"Does this food ever seem good now!" Iggy was gorging on breakfast. He was a slim boy now. His clothes hung off him like they were never meant for him.

"You're right." Sam shovelled a mouthful of breakfast into his face. "When we first got here the hotel food seemed like shit, but now, compared to camp, it's gourmet."

Adrian made a noise of disapproval. I was not sure if it was because Sam was speaking with his mouth full or if it was because he called the food shit.

"I can't wait to go shopping." Dee Dee was dressed in another sensational outfit. She was acting different now she had her clothes back, her stuff made her happy.

"Shopping's after lunch," Adrian said gruffly.

"What's at the monastery?" Oksana asked.

"Monks?" Iggy winked.

"No, there are no monks any more. Art." Adrian was in a bad mood. And it sounded like a boring day to me.

"Guess what?" Rhonda sat down at the table.

"What?"

"I ran into those Americans from before. You remember the same ones who were here when we were, the ones who went to the other camp?"

"Yes, Rhonda, we know! What!?" Dee Dee asked.

"The ... girl um ...." Rhonda looked at Adrian. He wasn't paying attention. "You remember the one with ..." she held her top out in points to mime "big boobs" and mouthed "the Sex Maniac." "Well, she was sent back to the States after their first week at camp. In disgrace."

"Why?" Jay looked disappointed. So much for his Soviet "love of his life." Perv!

Rhonda looked at Adrian again. "Later," she said, shaking her head. This had to be good. I couldn't wait for later.

We were strolling through the aisles of a store. The shelves held all sorts of Russian, whoops, Soviet, crafts. I didn't know what to buy. I didn't have much money left after buying lemon wafers at camp. I would have starved to death if it hadn't been for lemon wafers but now I hoped I'd never see another lemon wafer as long as I lived. I picked up one of those colourful wooden dolls that you could open in half and then would find another painted doll inside and if you opened it again there was another and so on and so on.

"Are you getting it?" Rhonda was holding an armful of souvenirs.

"I don't think so. My mom already has one of these. Hers is better. The smallest one is the size of a pinhead." I put the doll back.

"Now, finally ..." Rhonda watched Chip leave the aisle. "Big Boobs was caught having sex! That's why she was kicked out of the Soviet Union!"

"No way!" Oksana was holding the wooden doll that I had put back.

"Do you mean sex like all the way?" Dee Dee asked.

"You betcha. With a Soviet guy. But get this. He wasn't the first one. Apparently the Sex Maniac did half the guys at the camp." Rhonda picked up a lacquered egg cup.

"Was their camp as big as Orlyonok?" I asked.

"Bigger!" Rhonda held up the egg cup. Dee Dee shook her head. Rhonda put it back.

"Was she actually caught in the act?" Oksana looked as though she was going to get the wooden doll. Maybe I should have.

"They had to be ripped apart!" Now Rhonda was holding up a Soviet teacup. Soviet teacups were beautiful. I definitely had to get one. The Soviets drank tea out of cut-crystal glasses. The glass sat in a fancy holder, sometimes silver, sometimes painted metal, which had a handle. Dee Dee nodded this time. That meant it was good. Rhonda kept it.

"Like when you have to spray dogs with a hose?" That was what people did to try to separate dogs but it wasn't true that dogs got stuck together by accident, that was part of how they did it. If you separated them, there wouldn't be puppies. I put the china dog I was holding back on the shelf because Dee Dee made a face like she was in pain. I wanted the dog, though. Dogs were the best things in the whole world.

"She wasn't old enough to have sex," Oksana said. "How old was the boy she was caught with? Was he kicked out of camp too?"

"He's probably in a Soviet jail by now." Rhonda was taking us to the next aisle.

"Alexi had some Soviet chicks come on pretty hot and heavy with him. Girls he didn't even know made out with him in the bushes," Dee Dee whispered.

"Wow. Wow, check those out." Rhonda was standing in front of a display of balalaikas. "Are they real or just ornaments?"

Dee Dee picked one up. She was the only one of us with empty hands. She strummed it. "Real." She flipped it over.

"How much is it?" Rhonda asked.

"Ummmm. It would work out to about two hundred and fifty dollars in Canadian." Dee Dee did the math in her head. I'd have had to use my fingers.

"Oh." Rhonda looked sad. "My dad would have loved that but then I couldn't get everyone else something."

"I'm getting one." Dee Dee strummed a different instrument. This was out of my league. The whole aisle was.

"I'm just going back over there." I wanted to get that china dog. I hoped it was a Soviet kind of dog. The others weren't watching me. I'd get the teacup too.

We were on a Moscow bus. They were honour system. You took and paid for your own ticket. None of us were sure how to do it, not even Adrian or Chip, so we were dishonourable. We were loaded down with our shopping. Well, I wasn't really loaded. I'd bought some Russian chocolate bars, the silver teacup holder with glass, a funny little fat stuffed Soviet dancer I had named Boris but wouldn't tell anyone, and the china dog I wouldn't show anyone and had named Ralph.

"Could you take my balalaika for a sec?" Dee Dee asked Jay.

"I can't, Dee Dee. If I put down my vodka bottles they might crash and break." Jay had bought vodka! But he was only sixteen!

"Can you?" Dee Dee looked at Iggy.

"I don't want to break my dad's vodka, either." Iggy had bought vodka too.

"Shit." Dee Dee had so much stuff.

"I can take something, Dee Dee." I only had one bag. The bus stopped and I stumbled.

"No, forget it. You'll break it." Dee Dee headed to a seat that a man got out of as it was his stop. She sat down. "There."

"Wait! This is us too!" Chip called.

"Brother!" Dee Dee bundled her stuff up and we got off the bus.

Most of us were hanging out in our room. The sleeping arrangements were the same as last time. Little Karl was snoring on Chip's bed.

"I think maybe we should go to bed. We have to get up early to line up for Lenin's mausoleum." Chip probably wanted Karl to get off her bed so she could get in it. Sometimes you could tell what people really meant even when they said something else.

I had been handing my address book around all night, getting the group's home addresses. I flipped through the pages to see what people wrote. Jay had written *the mean one* after his name. That was from my diary. He'd read it again!!! I felt my forehead crease. Rhonda, grrrrrrrr. "Hey! Mary didn't write her address. She just wrote her name."

"She did that on purpose." Rhonda blew out air in a puff. "She said she isn't giving any of us her address as she doesn't want to hear from any of us and none of us can expect to hear from her ... EVER!"

"That's sad." My forehead creased deeper. I smoothed it out with my fingers, so it wouldn't stay that way. "She really never wants to hear from any of us ever again, as long as she lives, never ever?"

"Nope. She hates us." Rhonda got up and headed for the loo. "These toilets seem great now, eh?" She closed the bathroom door. The showers were great too and a bathroom with a door. And the bottles of pop and mineral water in the rooms. And the beds themselves. Heaven.

"It *is* sad." Chip wouldn't talk about Mary behind her back so I wasn't sure what she really felt about the whole situation. It was weird to have someone disown the whole group of us, like Mary had. It also seemed weird that Mary had written her name at all. Just a name in red marker, on an address & phone number page. Chip stood beside her bed. "Come on, Darwin. Uppty-up. Time to go off to your own bed." Little Karl sat up and then flopped back down again. Chip shook him gently. "You'll be happier in your own bed."

"Yeah. I'm tired too." Sam got up off the floor. "Come on, Iggy, let's go."

"'Night." Iggy crawled after Sam. Sam couldn't even spell "Alberta," where he lived. He wrote "Albrela."

"'Night, guys," I said after them. I flipped to the next page. Oksana had written "*your friend til United States drinks Canada Dry.*" I laughed. Canada Dry. Ha.

I BANGED THE EMPTY GLASS ON THE TABLE.

We had been in the lineup for hours. We were on Red Square now at least. We'd even been let in ahead for some reason. That didn't make sense to me because everyone in the Soviet Union was supposed to be equal and letting us in wasn't equal. I was glad, though; who would want to be equal if it meant always starting at the back of lines? Though if someone had been let in in front of me and I'd been lining up since three in the morning, wow, I'd have gone mental. We were not far from the mausoleum.

"Rhonda, you know what I did last night? I got lost in the room."

"What are you talking about?"

"I had to get up to use the can, only I forgot where I was. I think I thought I was at camp still. I bumped into everything and ended up over at the windows. That was when I remembered where I was. Have you ever had that happen before?"

"No."

"Are you scared to look at a dead body?"

"Move up." Sam pushed me.

"Don't push, you little wiener!" I yelled at him. I was playing with fire.

"Fuck off."

"Sam!" Adrian rumbled.

"Maybe a little scared. I've never seen a dead body before," Rhonda answered. "It's gross, though, don't you think, that they've kept him around all this time for people to stare at?"

"I love the mummies at the ROM in Toronto. I wouldn't mind being kept around for people to look at." I was pretty excited, actually. Right up there with amusement park excitement; like before going on a scary ride or in the house of horrors.

"Why would you want people to stare at you when you are dead?" Rhonda was eating one of the chocolate bars she had bought as a souvenir.

"To be famous." I looked at Rhonda's chocolate. "Chip, will we get to go shopping again?"

"I think so," Chip nodded.

Adrian nodded too. "We will."

"Good." I went into my purse and pulled out one of the chocolate bars I was taking home for my dad.

"I think you have to be famous first before people want to come stare at your dead body." Rhonda put a whole row of chocolate in her mouth.

"Oh, I guess maybe I thought I could get famous *that way*, by being on display. That sucks. I thought I could be pickled or mummified and then people would want to come look at me." We moved up some more. "Is Lenin pickled?"

Chip was laughing at me. "He's been preserved! Not pickled. Adrian ...Ad ..." She was laughing at me and was going to tell Adrian. What was the difference, pickle—preserve? Mom's pickles said "preserves" on the jars.

He was in a glass case. Everyone was very quiet inside the mausoleum. He looked like a waxwork at Madame Tussaud's.

"Lenin looks like he's made of wax." I could see the makeup on his skin. His pores looked clogged. My mom's friend, Mrs.

Lil' Canoe, the Avon lady, she always went on about makeup that didn't clog your pores. Now I knew what she was talking about. Lenin had big pores. So did Mrs. Lil' Canoe.

"Sssshhh," Big Karl scowled at me. "He looks like he is sleeping peacefully. This is truly wonderful." It was? Karl was crazy. I wished you were allowed to take photos. It would have been really cool if they had put one of those breathing motors in Lenin's chest. They had a breathing motor in one of the waxworks in London and the woman's chest heaved up and down. The only problem was you could hear the motor.

"If Lenin wasn't in a vacuum-sealed case, would his body rot instantly?" I pictured him crumbling and turning to dust.

"Kirsten." Chip sounded stern. I wanted to know more. How'd they keep him for so long? How often did they have to do his makeup? What would happen to him if you took a photo with a flash? Did they take out his organs like the mummies'? Where were his organs kept, if they did? Did they still have to trim his nails and hair? Did they have to do everything in a vacuum? Wouldn't it have been easier to have kept him in a freezer? Did they dip him in wax, because he sure looked like a waxwork? Why did you have to whisper? He was dead. We shuffled through the tomb. I couldn't take my eyes off him.

It was after dinner. Adrian and Chip were going out to some special event for foreign group leaders. We'd been given a "behave" lecture. We were all in Jay's, Big Karl's and Alexi's room. Well, all except Mary. Who knew where she was?

"Okay, let's party!" Jay had been watching out the door for Chip and Adrian to get on the elevator. Big Karl pulled out a bottle of vodka and started to pour.

"I don't think I can drink this straight, what proof is it?" Alexi sniffed his glass. "Phew!"

"Just chug it back. That's what the Russians do," Iggy said. "Then bang your glass on the table when you are done. I'll show you." Little Iggy was handed a full glass of a million-proof vodka.

"*Prost!*" He lifted the glass in the air and then downed it. He slammed the glass on the table and went "ah" after.

"Sheesh. Being taught to drink vodka by an eleven-year-old," Jay snorted. "Well, Karl?" They raised their glasses. They both maybe got two gulps in them before they choked.

"Shit, that's strong!" Big Karl spluttered.

"How the hell did you do that, Iggy?" Jay's face was beet red.

"Like this." Iggy had another full glass. He downed it. "Good stuff!"

"I think I want some pop in mine." Dee Dee got a bottle of pop from the iceless ice bucket. "Anyone else?"

Alexi held his glass out for pop.

"With a name like Alexi, and you can't drink your vodka like water?" Jay jeered. He wasn't doing so well himself, so I don't know why he was bragging.

"More." Iggy held out his glass, so did Little Karl.

"I don't think I like vodka," Rhonda whispered in my ear.

I stood up. "Hit me," I said to Big Karl. He laughed at me as he poured a splash of vodka in my glass. "No, come on! Full!" I'd done this with gin. I could do it with vodka. I held up the full glass. "*Lechayim!*" I gulped, chugged, ignored my gag reflex, swallowed, swallowed . . . empty. I banged the empty glass on the table.

"Shit! Holy mackerel! Get a load of that!" The boys stared at me.

The girls all cheered and jumped around the room. I had a talent!

Iggy was lying on the top bunk in his underwear. Singing. We had moved the party first to the room of some boys from Uzbekistan then somehow back to Rhonda's and my room. I couldn't remember why or how or when precisely.

"They're back!!!" Alexi stuck his head in our room.

"Quick. Hide the booze!" Dee Dee grabbed the bottle of vodka that had been circling the room. She capped it and dashed to the loo.

"Whatcha doing, Dee?" I couldn't have moved that fast.

"Putting it in the toilet tank."

"Good sh-place." Rhonda had to be exaggerating. She hadn't had that much.

"Put a lid on it, Iggy. Pretend to be sleeping." My vision wasn't very good. I rubbed my eyes. Iggy was singing some song in Polish. Or maybe it was English.

"HI CHIP!" Dee Dee said, coming out of the bathroom. "HOW WAS YOUR NIGHT OUT?" Dee Dee was being too loud. She looked incredibly guilty too. Chip stopped in her tracks. She stared at Dee Dee. Iggy was still singing. Where were his clothes? We were done for.

"Very nice." Chip walked straight over to the bunk beds, where Iggy was yodelling.

"Babushka, sh-abushka, bushka ya ya." It sounded almost like a Nana Mouskouri tune. My dad had it. Iggy was loaded.

"This is terrible!" Chip's face. We had never seen her angry.

"I'm gonna be s-thick." Iggy struggled off the mattress. He must have forgotten it was the top bunk. He fell to the ground.

"He's drunk!" Chip was shocked, angry, sad, and I didn't know what else, all at the same time. She dragged Iggy across the floor towards the can. Iggy hurled. "Get Adrian!" Chip demanded.

Rhonda started for the door but she wasn't exactly walking in a straight line.

"My God," Chip said. "You're all drunk!" She managed to get Iggy to the toilet for his next bout. He sure had a lot of liquid in him.

"Um, Chip?" Rhonda hadn't made it out yet.

"What!?!" Chip shouted. Wow, Chip shouted.

"Are you mad at us?"

"Why won't this toilet flush?" I could hear Chip trying the handle over and over. Then Iggy threw up again.

"Chip?" Adrian had arrived.

"I can't get this toilet to flush and Iggy's been sick every-where. Damnit, Adrian, they're pissed! They're all absolutely rip-roaring drunk!"

Iggy puked again.

"How much did he have?" Adrian asked. There was just me left in the room. Where had everyone gone?

"I'm not sure." I tried to look sober.

"How much have you had?" Adrian wasn't shouting. He seemed really calm.

"Not as much as Iggy. He had the most." And to prove my point, Iggy chucked again.

"Let's get him back to his room." Adrian started looking around our room. "Where are his clothes?"

"I really don't know. He was wearing them earlier. I don't know." I looked around, tried to be helpful.

"Adrian, Iggy is in a bad way." Chip sounded like she was going to cry.

"Forget his clothes. Let's just get him back to his own room." Adrian and Chip each took a side and I opened the door for them.

I cleaned up Iggy's barf. Rhonda couldn't. I normally couldn't have, either, but being drunk seemed to make me not care so much. Chip had been gone for ages.

"We should move the vodka bottle so the toilet can flush," Rhonda said.

Just then the door opened. It was Adrian. "Is there any alcohol left?"

"No." Rhonda stopped in her tracks.

Adrian was holding a couple of bottles; one was Big Karl's and the other belonged to Iggy. Adrian emptied them down the sink. "Iggy drank over half a bottle." Adrian shook his head. "I don't know if you realize it but it can be dangerous if you drink too much. People die sometimes." Adrian was fully relaxed. He wasn't freaked.

"Will Iggy die?" I asked. I didn't know you could die from drinking.

"Iggy is very sick. Chip is with him to make sure he gets through the night. One of the most dangerous things is that people sometimes vomit in their sleep and asphyxiate. Then there is actual alcohol poisoning." Adrian leaned on the counter, looking at Rhonda and me. "You put Chip and me in a very bad position tonight. We're responsible for you all. Your parents have trusted us with your safety." He paused. "We thought we could trust you. Well, I have to get back." He dropped the empty bottles in the wastebasket. They clanked. "Go to bed."

Chip and Adrian were mad at us all day. Though Dee Dee said they were hurt more than mad. We went to the Kremlin again and to the Beriozka, or something like that, shops again. Iggy couldn't come. He was sick in bed, with a headache and the dry heaves. That was something else I had learned about drinking, something called a hangover which you got the next day if you had too much. I'd learned a lot in the Soviet Union. I wandered around the hotel, eating chocolate. The Americans were sad because they heard on Radio America today that Elvis Presley had died.

KIRSTEN, DID YOU
LOSE YOUR MONEY?

Our third-last day in the Soviet Union. Some of us had spent the day at the Economic Achievements place. That had been plain boring. Adrian was really into it. That was why we were there so long. Then on the bus Little Karl and I got in a huge argument about the Moscow Radio tower, which he said was the tallest building in the world, but everyone knew it was the CN tower at home. I knew a girl whose dad died when they were building the CN tower. He was blown off. I'll never forget the horrible day she was hauled out of our classroom. It was just like Sonya, on the bus. We also saw the space monument. The space monument was a shiny glass tower, a sculptural thing with a rocket on the top. It was really huge. We were now sitting in the Moscow Circus. It was a permanent circus and had its own building. It was the best circus in the world! I was mad, though, because I thought it was going to be another human circus and there were animals here. I was hoping the tigers would break loose and start eating the audience before they were whipped and made to jump through burning hoops. The lights went out. The trapeze artists performed in the pitch black. You could see them because their

costumes had phosphorescent stripes. Not only that, the trapezes
revolved. I realized I was holding my breath. I had never seen
anything like it in my life. You'd hear about kids saying they were
going to run away and join the circus. I didn't really understand
what that meant until now. This was my first circus for real. Mom
had always refused to take me to the circus. Rhonda was clutching my leg. This was death-defying! This was fantastic. Now I
wanted to stay in the Soviet Union and be in their circus, if only
they'd get rid of the tigers and bears and elephants. They could
keep the poodles. Dogs didn't mind doing tricks. And the horses.
The horses probably were okay too. I'd stay in the Soviet Union
and study astronomy, be in the space program and perform in
the circus at night. Too bad about the food. The trapeze artists
finished. Wow! We cheered.

"This is great, eh?" Rhonda was watching the ring. "Get a
load of this! Kirsten, look!" The whole floor of the circus was
disappearing below us. Going down like an elevator. The entire
circus ring.

"It's hydraulic. The floor." Adrian had leaned over our shoulders to tell us that. He was behind us with Jay, Big Karl and
Alexi.

"Rhonda?" I asked.

"What?" She was leaning forward on her elbows.

"What is the cold war?" The floor was coming up. Clown car.
Brother. I hated clowns. Especially Bimbo the "Happy Birthday
Clown" on *The Uncle Bobby Show*. I hated Uncle Bobby too.
Clowns were nasty creatures. And I didn't know why they made
people laugh. They upset me.

"I think it's a war in basically everything except using weapons.
But you still threaten to use weapons sometimes." Rhonda slapped
my leg. "Look!" Big deal. So twenty clowns came out of one car.
My baseball team did that with Mom's Mini.

"I still don't understand."

"There is lots of spying. Lots of fear. And I think it is mostly
about politics. Don't you love clowns?" Rhonda asked.

"Yeah. They're great." It was time for the hydraulic floor to
drop like a stone.

The second-last day in the Soviet Union. Tomorrow we would be leaving first thing for the airport. We were getting to do the end of our shopping today, though I had done the end of my shopping on our *first* day of shopping. Most of us had finished and were just waiting outside for the others to cash through.

"We need to get our money organized, people," Adrian said as Dee Dee and Oksana and Alexi came out of the store. They were the last. "You either have to have spent it all, or leave it behind. I remind you that not one kopek can be taken out of the country." Surely one kopek and one ruble wouldn't hurt. Well, it had better not because I for sure wanted some Soviet money for a souvenir. It had Lenin's head on it. I had put a little aside for taking home, ten rubles.

"Wait. Can I go back in the store?" Iggy had found more money in his pocket. "I'll just grab some chocolate bars. I'll be fast."

"Hurry." Adrian was going around collecting everyone's lists of gifts purchased and their value and how much money they changed and traveller's cheques left. It was very confusing. It was for customs. He and Chip would handle all the group's stuff together. "Kirsten." He was looking at me.

"Yes?" He was looking at the original list he had made that said how much we had brought in. Oh yeah. Shit. Farts. I couldn't remember how much I had said I had brought in.

"I don't understand why we can't go back to the bank and change our Soviet money back to Canadian funds," Dee Dee whined. She'd changed too much money over from traveller's cheques to rubles. She'd bought tons of stuff just because she had to spend it. I noticed she even had that egg cup she had sneered at before.

"Because we can't." Adrian sounded like my dad with that answer. That was a lazy, grown-up answer. "Kirsten, this doesn't make sense. What did you buy?"

"She bought a stupid czarist capitalist borzoi china dog!" Little Karl laughed at me. No way he liked me.

Chip was looking over Adrian's shoulder. "Let's see the traveller's cheques you have left."

"I don't have any left." How much money did I say I brought

in? I was usually better at lying than this. I usually remembered my lies. I usually remembered them better than the truth. "I ate a lot of lemon wafers at camp." My face was starting to colour. Damn.

"Kirsten, did you lose your money?" Chip looked really concerned.

"No."

"Then how is it possible that you have only spent twenty dollars on goods that you are bringing back to Canada?" Adrian was drilling me with his eyes.

"I ate a real lot of lemon wafers. Tons. Lived on them, eh?" Everyone was staring at me. Waiting for the scoop. I was so embarrassed.

"You spent one hundred and eighty dollars on lemon wafers?" Adrian was getting impatient.

"No." If I didn't come out with it, it would be worse. I felt it. "I only had fifty bucks to begin with."

"But you declared two hundred!" Adrian didn't understand.

"You only brought fifty dollars to the Soviet Union for an entire summer!?!" Little Karl laughed at me. "No wonder you bought such stupid shit."

"DARWIN!!!" Adrian screamed at him. "How dare you make fun of someone about money! Did you learn nothing here?"

Dee Dee sneered at me. Little Karl had disappeared behind his brother. I was utterly humiliated. Rhonda looked like she felt sorry for me. My face felt redder than my rain poncho and I was shaking. Oksana stared at the ground. She couldn't even look at me and Alexi's eyes were sad.

"Look at all my chocolate!" Iggy came running out of the store with an entire bag of chocolate. He wouldn't be a skinny boy for long.

"Okay, everyone, let's just move along," Adrian said. He whistled to get the group's attention off of Dee Dee's and Big Karl's zithers. Between the two of them they had an entire Russian band. "Back to the hotel. Let's go."

COMMIE!

We were finally on the airplane. The plane had been four hours late! They didn't say why. Rhonda let me sit in the window seat this time. Mary was on the aisle. Mary's face was puffy from crying. It was really sad saying goodbye to our translators, especially Nadia. Mary kept breaking down in tears every ten or fifteen minutes. She'd kept her uniform from camp. No one else had even thought to do that.

"Remember when we were just coming?" I said to Rhonda.

"We are going to make short stop in Kiev. Please fasten seatbelts," a stewardess told us over the loudspeaker.

"Ahhhh no," Rhonda moaned. "Why?"

"Do you think there is something wrong with the plane?" It was the first thing Mary had said to us. I'd have rather she had just stayed quiet.

"Yeah, why are we suddenly having to land?" Rhonda looked around. "How do the engines look?" she asked me.

I looked out the window. "Like engines," I shrugged. I looked again. Was that smoke I had seen? Maybe it was mist or clouds or steam. I stared hard.

"What?" Rhonda squeezed my wrist.

"Nothing." I looked dead ahead at the seat in front of me. I was sure now that it was smoke. The left engine was smoking. I looked out again but we were in cloud. I couldn't see the wing except in glimpses and glances.

"Why we going down so fast?" Rhonda asked.

"There was hardly any warning at all, just 'we are landing in Kiev.'" Mary was looking at the ceiling, her head pressed against the seat back.

"Nothing is wrong." I tried to sound calm. "If there was, they'd be doing that whole spiel about 'put your head between your knees.'"

"Seat back up." The stewardess tapped Rhonda's chair.

"Oh my God!" Rhonda wailed.

"That's normal." I waved my hand as if to say "that's nothing" and nonchalantly looked out the window to see if I could see the engine.

We were asked to get off the plane and then we were shuffled to this waiting area. It wasn't in the main part of the airport. It was a round outbuilding with a hard concrete floor and light blue plastic seats, like the ones from the zebra room. It was freezing.

"I think one of my dad's parents is from Kiev," I told Rhonda and Oksana. They're both from the Soviet Union somewhere. Maybe Ukraine, Belarus or Lithuania. When Zaidi Koza came to Canada he was a model for Tip Top Tailors.

"No kidding. This is a drag." Dee Dee sat down beside Oksana.

"I'm so cold." Oksana tucked her legs up inside her sweater.

"This place isn't heated or anything. Watch." Rhonda blew. You could see her breath in the air.

How long were we going to have to wait here? There wasn't even a pop machine. There was nothing to do. It was cold, like sitting in the bleachers in an arena in the dead of winter.

"Do you think someone will call our parents to say we are going to be late?" Dee Dee shouted across to Adrian.

"Dee Dee, you know as much as I." Adrian closed his eyes.

It was four hours and ten minutes later. Jay, Big Karl, Little Karl and Alexi were fast asleep on the floor. They were using their carry-on luggage as pillows.

"This is crazy!" Dee Dee stood up. "I can't even feel my feet any more.

"How long will the stopover in Paris be?" I asked Chip.

"Aw, sweetie, I don't know." She looked miserable. "Maybe you should try to get some sleep."

My bum ached from the seats. I was colder than I'd ever been in my life and I was so bored I could cry.

We were headed back onto the plane with no explanation and no apologies. I'd heard a woman grumble about that when we were boarding. I slumped into my seat at the window. It was the same plane. I recognized the decor. There was one unmatching orange seat among the powder blue. I put my head against the window. I'd sleep now.

Montreal finally. We were in Canada, "our home and native land."

"And only eight and three quarter hours late!" Dee Dee stood on one leg.

"I hope all the luggage is here this time." Alexi pulled Oksana's bag off the carousel. I was watching Chip and Adrian at the same time as keeping an eye on the luggage spitting off the conveyor belt. They were having a conference.

"I'm so tired." Rhonda yawned. "What time is it?"

"Almost eleven." Dee Dee had both her suitcases.

"Listen up, everyone!" Adrian approached. "We are going to go through customs fast. We have missed most of our connecting flights, obviously. There's still one flight left to Toronto but it leaves from Dorval."

"What's that?" I asked.

"Another airport. If you, Dee Dee and the Karls hurry, you will make it. You have to catch a bus, so hurry. Chip and I will stay here with the rest of the group."

"Where's here?" I asked.

"Mirabel," Chip answered.

"Stop interrupting," Adrian said to me. I saw my bag and pushed through to the carousel.

"Now we are cutting it close. Everyone got your bags?" Adrian marched around checking us all over.

Rhonda was looking at me through the crowd. She didn't have her suitcase yet. I started towards the carousel. This part of the trip had never occurred to me before. Rhonda lived in British Columbia, that was far away.

"We are really going to have to move fast, no time for good-byes." Adrian pushed me towards the exit. Rhonda was crying, she mouthed something. It looked like she said, "I never took your diary."

Dee Dee and I had lost sight of Big Karl and Little Karl. We were done customs and were running down the length of Mirabel.

"You know what, Dee Dee? We didn't find out what hotel everyone was going to be at, you know, in case we don't make it," I panted. My arm was falling off.

"Shit, stop. I'm wiped." Dee Dee rearranged her bags. She looked up. "Do we even know if we are going the right way?"

"Just follow the crowd. It is the best way when at an airport. Dee Dee, I didn't say good bye to Rhonda." Silent tears streamed down my cheeks.

The bus was the right one because it took us to Dorval Airport.

Dee Dee looked at her watch. "We have fifteen minutes until the plane departs. We aren't going to make it."

"We have to make it, Dee Dee. We don't have a choice." This

was scary! I wished the people would move faster down the bus aisle.

"Come on, come on!" Dee Dee tapped the back of a seat.

"We should have sat at the front with the Karls."

We were off, grabbed our suitcases from the sidewalk, ran into the terminal and ..."Dee Dee, which way now? The crowd isn't moving the same way any more." I couldn't believe Chip and Adrian had made us go off on our own like this.

"This way if you are going my way," a businessman said to us. He had on a long trench coat like my dad's.

"Is your way Toronto?" I asked.

"Come on, you are going to miss the plane." The businessman grabbed one of my bags and another man grabbed two of Dee Dee's souvenir bags.

"Thank you," I said.

"No time for thank you's," the man said briskly.

I woke up as we taxied to the terminal in Toronto. I saw my family at the bottom of the escalator, Mom, Dad holding Fiona, Grandma and whoops, the Camerons, Chip's parents.

"She's so thin!" I heard my mom say.

"Look at her tan!" Grandma said. "Kirsten, Kirsten." Gram was waving like a maniac.

Hugs from everywhere and everyone. I was squeezed to death.

"I broke my foot," Fiona said. Someone needed to teach her to kiss with her mouth closed.

"How did you do that?" I looked at her funny, tired little face.

"Roger dropped a brick on it." Fiona reached for me. "Kiss?" I blew her one. She was too high up, anyway, being in Dad's arms.

"I cried," Fiona said.

"I bet you did."

"It hurt. I broke six bones." Fiona offered me her licorice. Normally I would have been grossed out by eating her slobbery licorice but I took it. "And I had a cast."

"Shall we?" Dad had my luggage. I was so tired. I was glad to be going.

I looked at the Karls with their parents. They were busy. Dee Dee's dad was going back over to Dee Dee at the carousel with a buggy for her bags. I decided it would be easier just to leave.

I had been home from the Soviet Union for a few weeks and was sitting at the kitchen table. I closed my diary. I had to write a speech about our trip, to deliver at the Soviet Friendship Centre. Dee Dee was going to show slides.

"Muzik, get off!" I pushed my cat off my photos for the hundredth time.

"So?" Mom said as she came back into the kitchen. I looked at my blank paper. I couldn't talk about the parachuting, or the drinking, or the missed treatments, or the secret toilet and the secret room. I didn't want to get in trouble. Also, I was not supposed to say anything not nice about the Soviet Union. "Can I go outside?" I asked.

Mom looked at me with her homework face. "Fine, but you are doing this."

I bolted out the door before she could change her mind. I grabbed my bike from the front of the house. Coolit, my dog, watched me. I pedalled down the driveway. It was still warm and sunny. We came in third in the baseball championship last weekend. Betty Lil' Canoe pitched. I was going steady with Betty's brother Bobby now.

"Commie!" Clancy Murphy was at the end of the driveway. "You're a communist!" He stuck out his tongue. Man, some things never changed.

"I am not!" I yelled back.

"Well, my dad says you are a Commie!" Clancy threw an apple at me.

"You don't even know what it means!" I shouted back.

PAKA

ACKNOWLEDGEMENTS

Big thanks to the following: to my mom for being the enforcer of record keeping, to my dad for deciding a whole summer of Kirsten in the Soviet Union was well worth four hundred plus fifty dollars, and also thanks to Dad and Kim Peters for pointing out how terrible my French is. Thanks to Ann Mollon for aiding me with Russian and tripping down memory lane with me along with Dale Roberts, Yuri Jmaeff, Tamara Johnson and Jo-Ann Baran. My computer guy, Alex Gallacher, wow, we all need one of these guys. Mary Shoman and her amazingly informative thyroid website led me to finding the great doctors Alvin Pettle and David Derry who solved the nuclear fallout I was left with after suffering (what my friend Hamish MacDonald dubs) Cold War medicine in the USSR. Cheers to Malcolm for reminding me to leave the computer and go work out and Rigel for requesting Quake tournaments. Ta to Julie Suzanne Pollock for the Aeroflot letter. Peter Sibbald provided me with my author's photo—my head is keeping great company, www.petersibbald.com.

Huge gratitude to the terrific team at Turnstone Press and especially to Todd Besant for paying me the most massive compliment of my life!